Last Man Standing

THE HISTORY OF LLANDUDNO CRICKET CLUB

J.L. Nicholls

With Best Wishes
J. L. Nicholls
12/7/2015

First published in Great Britain as a softback original in 2015

Copyright © J.L. Nicholls

The moral right of this author has been asserted.

All rights reserved.

No part of this publication may be reproduced, stored in a retrieval system, or transmitted, in any form or by any means, without the prior permission in writing of the publisher, nor be otherwise circulated in any form of binding or cover other than that in which it is published and without a similar condition including this condition being imposed on the subsequent purchaser.

Typeset in Iowan Old Style

Editing, design and publishing by UK Book Publishing

UK Book Publishing is a trading name of Consilience Media

www.ukbookpublishing.com

ISBN: 978-1-910223-39-0

Cover photo: Jordan Kane in action

The author wishes to acknowledge the following books

The Cricket Pocket Bible

Greg Vaughan - PB Pocket Bibles

www.pocketbibles.co.uk

NO-BALLS and GOOGLES

Geoff Tibbal's – A Cricket Companion

Michael O'Mara Books Limited

9, Lion Yard, Tremadoc Road, London SW4 7NQ

www.mombooks.com

My Spin On Cricket

Richie Benaud

Hodder and Straughton Limited

A division of Hodder Headline

338, Euston Road

London NW1 3BH

Acknowledgements

Thanks are extended to Susan Ellis and her staff at the Llandudno Archives in Lloyd Street, Llandudno who have been of great assistance to me during my many months of research there. Nothing was any trouble for them. They were extremely helpful and efficient members of a dedicated team of a first-class Aberconwy Borough Council Library Archives Department.

It has to be said that without the marvellous newspaper match reports especially in the Llandudno Advertiser, the Pioneer, the Daily Post and the North Wales Weekly News, this book would have been extremely difficult to produce. Over the many years cricket has been played in Llandudno I would like to give a massive thanks to all the dedicated volunteer reporters (especially from the 1950s onwards) who were and are fully paid-up members of the Llandudno CC. The rise and fall and rise again of the club on and off the field of play, has been described in words by means of the fullest attention to detail through the pages of the four well-distributed and well-read local newspapers. Upon reading their reports such feelings of joy, and in some instances disappointments, were captured by the power of the pen. I do hope that the joys and mixed emotions are suitably captured and ably re-written amongst the pages of this book for your acknowledgement and enjoyment once again. They are the late Huw Tudno Williams and Ron Beswick, Selwyn Jenkins, Mark Hughes, Graham Boase and Joe Lambe.

I would also like to thank Brian Baister, Colin Abbott, Clive Stock, Allan Hughes, John Rimmington, Graham Gibbons and Rene Clayton for their contribution. To Adrian Hughes, Custodian of the Home Front War Museum, Llandudno, for his assistance in researching details regarding the two World Wars and the involvement of some members of the cricket club who were volunteers and who gave their lives during those terrible years.

A special mention is extended to Mrs Iris Tudno Williams who kindly donated photographs to the club and with the club's permission are shown in this book.

I would also like to thank the UK Book Publishing Company.

To Stephen, Jenny, Jessica and Sam

Contents

Foreword by Anthony Neville (President)

This publication has been compiled by former club member J.L.Nicholls and includes written records and a collection of team photographs stretching back over 100 years.

J.L.Nicholls and I were in John Bright Grammar School in the 1950s and both played under the wing of Mr H.Hughes (Woody Mallet!) who spent many evenings after school coaching us all.

This book is the result of countless hours of careful research. It represents not just a celebration of our first 150 years or so but also the platform on which we can record our future efforts.

It also records what happened during the two World Wars and details of many of our players' greatest cricketing achievements.

Introduction

(by John Rimmington, Chairman)

Jeff asked me, as the current Chairman of Llandudno Cricket Club, to give a view from the Chair by way of introduction to his wide-ranging history of the Club.

It is a great honour to enter my 15th season as Chairman of the Club and a rare treat to be able to look back through Jeff's researches to the events in the history of our great club.

The early days of Llandudno Cricket Club give us much to think about as we take for granted the location of the Club at the Oval. The Club has always been however a collection of like-minded people getting together to play the game of cricket and still remains that today.

The structure of cricket in North Wales has never been stronger. The North Wales Cricket League provides a League Structure in which we play, stretching from Chirk in the Marches to Pwllheli and Dolgellau in the west. The Cricket Wales administered Welsh Cup gives the chance to play further afield in the later stages, right up to Sophia Gardens (or the SWALEC if you prefer) in Cardiff. The travelling to South Wales on a Sunday requires commitment and determination to give our best, over 200 miles and four and a half hours away – we could get to Lords quicker!

Junior cricket is the lifeblood and the priority of the Club. A policy that I have always favoured and has seen many talented young players progress and proudly represent Wales at age group levels. From soft ball primary school cricket through Under 9's, 11's 13's and under 15's our juniors play in Eryri Leagues and the Welsh Cup with success and enjoyment. All this is possible through the determination and unpaid commitment of our ECB qualified coaches and the support of parents, Monday evening Junior Nets and the game nights are a joy to behold.

As an ECB Club Marque Club and Premier League Club we strive to meet the ever more complicated requirements. Sound Child Protection policies are key to keep our young people safe. Running a facility like the Oval in the centre of town is a task where we are helped greatly by the generosity of sponsors and Conwy County Borough Council and Llandudno Town Council. That is not new as you can see from Jeff's narrative, nor is the support of volunteers and local tradesmen.

Jeff has worked diligently to bring items from the archives and records about our Club, this is a labour of love and an act of generosity on his part and to my view is a marvellously interesting and readable drawing together of our past. At the Club we would be delighted to receive other contributions from members or friends old and new as we document our past. History is written by those who write and the weakest pencil survive the strongest memory of the pages of Jeff's book testifies.

Meanwhile; back to the future, a new season beckons and the miracle that is a cricket club bursts into life with the spring...

"The Winds and Rains of the winter are done,

And Lo! In the sky the beneficent sun.

The pitch is close shaven and firm for our tread

There's a thrush on the bough and a lark overhead

So cricketers all,

Hark, hark to the call! –

And on with your flannels and into the field,

The leather to grasp and the willow to wield."

E.V.Lewis (1868-1938)

Lord Llewelyn Nevill Vaughan Lloyd Mostyn (3rd Baron)

1856-1929

Lord Mostyn (3rd Baron) greatly aided the development of Llandudno as a town and its sport, especially cricket in the area. He succeeded his grandfather Edward Mostyn Lloyd Mostyn (2nd Baron) to his titles in 1884.

He was President of the Llandudno Cricket Club from 1890-1929.

He was a founder member of the North Wales Cricket Association in 1922 and President 1922-1924.

He was President of Llandudno Town Commissioners for 37 years from its inception and was also Chairman of the Llandudno Urban District Council from 1902-1903.

His father Hon Thomas Edward Mostyn Lloyd Mostyn had predeceased the second baron in 1861 at the age of 31. He was a Member of Parliament for Flintshire in 1854. He was also a first-class cricketer who played for Oxford University and the MCC. Born in 1830, he played a few games for the Conwy Cricket Club at the age of 19. There is a report later in this book of a match which he took part in between the Gentlemen of Conwy Cricket Club and the Gentlemen of Liverpool Cricket Club held on 21st July 1849. Present at this game was Lord Mostyn's mother, Lady Henrietta Augusta Nevill Lloyd Mostyn and his sister-in-law, Lady Pamela Georgina Lloyd-Mostyn (the wife of the Hon Henry Richard Howell Lloyd Mostyn).

Lord Mostyn's brother, the Hon Henry Richard Howell Lloyd Mostyn was made Llandudno Cricket Club Captain in 1890. He played regularly for the club. He was Vice-President in 1898. He was a guest player for the MCC against a Llandudno XI in August 1893. He died in 1938.

Lord Edward Llewellyn Roger Lloyd-Mostyn (4th Baron) took over the Presidency of the Llandudno Cricket Club on the death of Lord Llewelyn Nevill Vaughan Lloyd Mostyn (3rd Baron) in 1929. He died in 1965.

1839-1889

The Early Years

There is no exact record as to when cricket was first played but there is reference to the Prince of Wales playing 'creag' (the Saxon name for a crooked stick), an early form of cricket, which appears in the Royal Household Accounts of King Edward 1 of England in 1301. It's quite possible that this is the first reference to cricket. There is a fairly definite testimony that the game was played at Guildford in 1550. On 24th June 1848 it was reported that among articles removed from the Royal Pavilion at Brighton, was a cricket bat which belonged to George IV (1762-1830) when he was Prince of Wales, and which was inscribed with his name in the prince's own handwriting.

As regards the origin of the game, there appears to be as many opinions as there are antiquarians but at one time the most generally received idea was that the game of 'tip-cat', which children played in the streets of English towns in the 1700s, was the true origin of cricket. So little was the game understood in the year 1743, that there was an article in the 'Gentleman's Magazine' abusing the game as it was then, on the grounds of taking men of low degree out of their regular calling to mix with people of quality, and making a business of the sport. It was drawing crowds together of people who could not afford the time and denouncing the game as a notorious breach of the laws, as it openly encouraged gambling. The real supporters of the game were shocked that the great players of the period, who were being paid a wager by grandeur gentlemen match-fixers, were being encouraged amongst themselves to fix results and to benefit by means of gambling. Something had to be done to stop this practice of encouraging gambling which was being seen to lead to the fall of cricket unless these matches were stopped.

Tip-cat (also called cat, cat and dog, one-a-cat or piggy) is a pastime which consists of tapping a short billet of wood (usually no more than 3-6 inches) with a larger stick (similar to a baseball bat or broom handle); the shorter piece is tapered or sharpened on both ends so that it can be 'tipped up' into the air when struck by the larger stick, at which point the player attempts to swing or hit it a distance with the larger stick while it is still in the air (similar to swinging at a pitch in baseball or cricket, etc) and drive it as far as possible while fielders try to recover it.

It's somewhat strange that a sport which was based on gambling should have acquired its present growth, on being divested of the gambling element and so strong does the 'anti-gambling feeling' now prevail, that the real supporters of the game of the present day look on with horror and dismay.

In 1700 the newspapers began to advertise matches and report on them and in 1744 James Love wrote his celebrated poem – 'Cricket – An Heroic Poem'

> *Hail Cricket! Glorious, manly, British game!*
> *First of all Sports! Be first alike in Fame!*
> *To my fir'd Soul thy busy Transports bring,*
> *That I may feel thy Raptures, while I sing!*
> *And thou, kind Patron of the mirthful Fray,*
> *Sandwich, thy Country's Friend, accept the Lay!*
> *Tho' mean my verse, my Subject yet approve,*
> *And look propitious on the Game you love!*

The first eleven-a-side match for which there is documentary evidence took place in Sussex in 1697. It was in rural Hampshire in the small village of Hambledon that the origin of a cricket club had certainly been founded by 1768.

Hambledon's stature grew till by the late 1770s it was the foremost cricket club in England. Adjoining the ground at Broad Halfpenny Down is the now famous 'Bat and Ball' Inn. It is renowned and quite unique in that it is the birthplace of cricket where the rules were formulated, and there are now lots of cricketing memorabilia inside.

In 1774, cricket as we know it made a great start. Sir Horace Mann, who had promoted cricket in Kent, and the Duke of Dorset and Lord Tankerville, who seem to have been the leaders of the Surrey and Hants eleven, and other noblemen and gentlemen, formed a committee under the presidency of Sir William Draper. They met at the Star and Garter pub in Pall Mall (in the city of Westminster, London), and laid down the first rules of cricket. The old skeleton hurdle was abolished, and wickets (two in number, twenty-two inches high and six inches wide) were substituted. The weight of the ball was determined to be five ounces and a half to five ounces and three-quarters. In the following year, 1775, a middle stump was added.

The next great step in cricket was the establishment of the White Conduit Club, and amongst its members, in addition to the before-named patrons of the game, included the names of Lord Winchilsea, Lord Strathavon and Sir Peter Burrell. Their place of meeting was still the Star and Garter pub, and their ground was in White Conduit Fields in Islington. After a few years White Conduit Fields was abandoned. One of the members and employee of this Club was a cricketer and groundsman, Thomas Lord, who is known to have begun playing about 1780 but his first recorded game was on his 'own ground' now referred to as Lord's Old Ground, on the site which is now Dorset Square. As well as playing cricket he had a successful wine business. In 1787 he was persuaded to purchase the ground. Under the patronage of the old White Conduit Club, a new Club called the Marylebone Club was formed at the Old Lord's ground. Thomas Lord relocated in

1811 to Lord's Middle Ground, a site at Lisson Grove in the vicinity of Regent's Park. He lost that venue after only three years because the land was requisitioned for a canal cutting. In 1814, he opened the present Lord's Cricket Ground, formerly a duck pond in St John's Wood. It would be superfluous to say anything about the Marylebone Club, as the fact is notorious that the rules of the Marylebone Club are the only rules recognised as authentic throughout the world, wherever cricket is being played today.

There are some North Wales clubs that can boast they have been in existence for over 160 years. Some will argue that Llanrwst is the oldest when it was said the 'wild boar roamed over parts of Lancashire' and when one local newspaper stated it confidently as early as 1839. However, Dolgellau boast that their cricket club was founded in 1826 and claim they are the oldest cricket club in North Wales and the second oldest in Wales. Denbigh Cricket Club was established in 1844; Bangor Cricket Club in 1856; and Northop Cricket Club in 1864. There is evidence that Llandudno had a cricket club before the 1850s. In those early years of the 1850s and 1860s the development of the game was very slow in North Wales with the addition of Wrexham, Conwy, Caernarvon, Porthmadog, Beaumaris and Holyhead being the only other mentioned teams to play in competition.

The report of a cricket match between a Llandudno club and a Conwy club on the top of a mountain appeared in the Caernarfon and Denbigh Herald on 9th June 1849.

On Whit Monday, a cricket match was played at the top of the Great Orme, or Llandudno Mountain as it was also known then, worthy of its splendid and beautiful scenery. The weather was delightfully fine, and a place calculated for the sport of the day could not have been better selected. The match was between 11 of the Conwy club and 11 of the Llandudno club. A contest of this description was quite a novelty in the locality, and it was not a surprise that the fair daughters of the men, in considerable numbers, graced the occasion with their presence. Mr and Mrs Jones, of the Telegraph Station, won "golden opinions" by their kindness and attention to the visitors at their elevated residence. The cricketers appear to have been pretty equally matched, but the Llandudno gentlemen came off victorious, having scored 46, whilst their opponents only marked 42.

In 1826 the summit of the Great Orme was chosen as the location for one of the 11 Telegraph Stations that would form an unbroken 80 mile (130 km) chain from Liverpool to Holyhead. The original Telegraph Station consisted of a small building with living accommodation. In March 1855 the Great Orme Telegraph Station was converted to electric telegraph. At first the new equipment was installed in the original Telegraph Station on the summit until it was moved down to the Great Orme lighthouse in 1859. By the late 1860s, Llandudno's blossoming tourist trade saw many Victorians visit the old semaphore station at the summit to enjoy the panorama. This led to the development of the summit complex. An 18-hole golf course was laid out nearby. A building was erected in 1909 as a club house for the Great Orme Golf Club. Later the building became the nine-bedroom Telegraph Hotel for golfers. The course closed in 1939 and is now a sheep farm. During the Second World War, the RAF built a radar station at the summit. In 1952 the site was taken into private ownership until it was acquired by Llandudno Urban Town Council in 1961. Conwy County Borough Council continues to manage the summit. Among the summit complex attractions today are a tourist shop, cafeteria, and visitors' centre, a play area for young children and a cable car terminal and funicular railway/tram terminal.

After the outdoor sports of the day had concluded, the players descended from the mountain, and paid their respects to 'The King', whose good cheer they continued to enjoy till a late hour. No doubt they were all in excellent spirits and anxiously looking forward to the next cricket match at the top of the Great Orme.

A return game between the two teams was played five weeks later and again on the Great Orme on 7th July 1849. The two-innings match occupied the hours between 11am and 4pm. On that occasion Conwy won easily by seven wickets.

At that time in 1849 one particular game rates highly as a historical document concerning the Llandudno Cricket Club and its relationship with the Mostyn family. It was Lord Mostyn's father who played in this match and it was his grandfather, Lord Edward Lloyd Mostyn (2nd Baron), who attended this game as a spectator.

Tuesday 24th July 1849 – North Wales Chronicle

A Grand Cricket Match was played between the Gentlemen of the Liverpool Cricket Club and the Gentlemen of the Conwy Cricket Club.

The match was played on the Conwy ground on Saturday 21st July 1849 when the Conwy club came off victorious winning by six wickets. The match commenced at 11 o'clock, with the Liverpool eleven going in first to the bowling of the Hon Lloyd Mostyn and Mr Conwy. The Hon Lloyd Mostyn took the first over and after playing the third ball one of the Liverpool men was beautifully caught by Mr Evans, the Conwy wicket-keeper. Another man then appeared at the wicket but he was speedily disposed of by a terrific 'shooter' from the Hon Lloyd Mostyn. Mr C.Langton then went in and after playing in a very excellent and steady manner was bowled by the Hon Lloyd Mostyn. He was their top scorer with 18 runs. The remaining seven wickets were soon down, the Hon Lloyd Mostyn taking three wickets and Mr Conwy taking three and catching one. The Conwy eleven now went in but were not very successful in consequence of the steady bowling of Messrs Langton and Reynolds and three of their batsmen being run out. Their score amounted to 39 runs. The first innings over, the players retired to a tent on the ground where a cold dinner was prepared. After dinner Mr Osborne Morgan proposed the health of the Liverpool Cricket Club to which Mr Langton returned thanks. The same gentleman proposed the health of Mr Gaskell of Bodlondeb who had kindly supplied the tent etc. Immediately after the dinner the contest was renewed. The Liverpool gentlemen, the favourites at 3 to 1 was being freely offered and taken in their favour. During the second innings the Liverpool eleven batted very steadily but the bowling of Messrs the Hon Lloyd Mostyn, Conwy and Hilton and the beautiful fielding of the whole Conwy eleven proved too strong for them as they again scored only 43 runs thus leaving the Conwy men 48 to win. The Conwy eleven now went in and batted far better than they had done in the previous innings. Sir Thomas Erskine and Mr Hilton went in first but the latter being soon bowled by Mr Langton. Mr Penrhyn took his place. Sir Thomas Erskine batted steadily until he was run out. Mr Leigh then joined Mr Penrhyn when the state of the game soon changed with the excellent batting of these two gentlemen and in a short time the score was increased to 33 runs when Mr Leigh was caught by Mr Hornby fielding at point. Mr Steavens followed Mr Leigh but Mr Langton soon compelled him to resign his bat to the Hon Lloyd Mostyn who had, with Mr Penrhyn, quickly run the score up to 48 – the number required. Both these gentlemen carried their bats off the field amidst generous applause. Mr Penrhyn had scored 20 runs. The weather throughout the day was beautiful and the match created great excitement. At the ground was noticed Lord Edward Mostyn Lloyd Mostyn(2nd Baron), the Hon Edward Pryce Lloyd and Lady Janet Erskine, Archdeacon Jones, Archdeacon Barney and most of the principal gentry in the neighbourhood.

Conwy team:

J.S.John Blunt, W.H.Conwy, Sir Thomas Erskine, T.C.Evans, T.Hilton, C.A.Leigh, G.O.Morgan, J.E.Morgan, the Hon Lloyd Mostyn, O.I.Penrhyn, Mr Steavens.

Very little is known during the next few years of what progress had been made regarding cricket in Llandudno. The next reported match involving a Llandudno club does not appear in any local newspapers until 1858. Between 1858 and 1889 there were some very good years where matches had been arranged and played occupying most of the summer months. However, not many were reported in the media and it would seem that when you read closely into the reports they do refer more than once to "the new club" and wonder what was happening. Before 1890 the cricketers seemed to be struggling to find a suitable permanent home ground. In those early days they played in fields on the Great Orme; near Neville Crescent in the Llandudno town (now occupied by the coach park off The Broadway); the Conwy Marshes or Morfa; or the area on the West Shore known then as 'The Warren'. The following reports during that era do give some indication of the determination and commitment of certain members who worked hard and played hard to keep cricket available locally in the town for the benefit of the lovers of the game.

Sat 31st July 1858 – North Wales Chronicle

Llandudno v Beaumaris

On Tuesday 21st July 1858 a return match was played between Llandudno and Beaumaris clubs on the ground of the former at Conwy. The Beaumaris eleven went in first to the bowling of Messrs Davies and Walford and all their wickets were disposed of for 22 runs. The Llandudno gentlemen then took the bat and strange to say their score only amounted to exactly the same number of runs. After the usual interval of a quarter of an hour the Beaumaris gentlemen again went to the wickets of which they were not deprived till they had scored 61 runs to which Mr J.W.Hughes contributed 20 by some very good batting. The Llandudno gentlemen then went in with 62 runs to get of which, in spite of some very beautiful play on the part of Mr Davies Snr and Mr Palmer, they were unable to obtain more than 55, thus leaving their opponents victorious by seven runs. The ground was in as good condition as anyone could wish for, and the day beautiful. The fielding on both sides was very good.

It will be remembered that this was the second match of the season which Beaumaris had won against Llandudno and it was hoped that their success which was highly creditable to a young club will urge them on and still further improve in the skills of the game.

We subjoin the score:

Beaumaris				
Batsman	**1st Innings**		**2nd Innings**	
Jennings	c. and b. Davies	5	b. Davies	10
Phillips	run out	6	b. Davies	2
Jones	b. Walford	0	b. Walford	0
Siggs	b. Davies	0	c. Dawson, b. Davies	5
Williams	b. Davies	1	b. Davies	1
T.Bulkeley	run out	1	b. Davies	5
J.Hughes	b. Walford	0	b. Palmer	20
Pritchard	c. Carter, b. Davies	0	b. Davies	0
Dawson	b. Davies	0	b. Davies	2
C.Bulkeley	b. Walford	0	not out	0
Emerson	not out	0	b. Palmer	1
	Byes 1, leg byes 1, wides 7	9	Byes 3, wides 12	15
	1st innings total	22	*2nd innings total*	61

Total Innings 83

	Llandudno				
Batsman	**1st Innings**		**2nd Innings**		
Walford	c. C.Bulkeley, b. Jones	4	c. and b. Jones		3
Jones	c. and b. Emerson	1	c. and b. Emerson		5
Davies Snr.	b. Jones	2	c. Emerson, b. Siggs		11
Davies Jnr.	b. Jones	3	run out		1
Palmer	b. Jones	0	lbw Jones		19
Johnson	c. T.Bulkeley, b. Emerson	1	b. Siggs		1
Calvert	b. Jones	2	b. Williams		0
Bates	c. Jennings, b. Emerson	2	run out		0
Carter	run out	3	c. Siggs, b. Emerson		10
Fisher	not out	1	b. Emerson		1
Dawson	b. Emerson	3	not out		0
	Extras 0	0	Byes 4		4
	1st innings total	22	*2nd innings total*		55

Total Innings 77

Sat 4th September 1858 North Wales Chronicle

Holywell v Llandudno

On Monday 30th August 1858 a friendly match between Holywell and Llandudno came off on a ground of the former at Holywell. The weather unfortunately was very unfavourable but both parties evinced a determination to compete for the mastership despite the contending elements. The Llandudno gentlemen nearly all are visitors now sojourning at that watering place, represented most of the principal cricket counties in England, and evidently were no novices in the art. But notwithstanding suffered a defeat from the Holywell gentlemen in whose play throughout the game showed a marked improvement of late, was manifested. The Llandudno gentlemen went in first whose wickets were taken for a score of 44. Mr Josephson Senior and Mr Murray were the only two who were fortunate enough to make a stand. In their second innings their score was

14 short of the first. Mr Bond was the only gentleman with double figures. The Holywell eleven in their first innings made 62 runs and a few runs only being required to make up the total score of the Llandudnoites. The second innings was but partially played. The Holywell gentlemen won with seven wickets to spare.

Llandudno				
Batsman	**1st Innings**		**2nd Innings**	
Davies	b. Bowen	3	run out	3
Carter	run out	0	b. J.V.Harrison	1
Fisher	b. Whitehouse	2	b. J.V.Harrison	0
Barker	c. E.J.Davies, b. Bowen	0	b. J.V.Harrison	8
Gindere	c. A.Jones, b. Bowen	1	b. J.Whitehouse	0
Bond	b. J.Whitehouse	1	c. J.Whitehouse, b. J.V.Harrison	12
Josephson Snr	not out	11	b. J.V.Harrison	5
Josephson Jnr	run out	0	b. J.Whitehouse	1
Murray	b. Croft	15	c. Croft, b. J.Whitehouse	0
Pritchard	b. J.Whitehouse	0	b. J.Whitehouse	0
McIntosh	run out	2	not out	0
	Byes 4, leg byes 1, wides 1	6	extras	0
	1st innings total	41	*2nd innings total*	30

Total Innings 71

Holywell				
Batsman	**1st Innings**		**2nd Innings**	
E.J.Davies	b. Davies	4		
F.E.Turner	c. and b. Gindere	9	not out	6
Croft	run out	12	b. Davies	0
F.Turton	b. Barker	15	not out	2
A.Jones	not out	7	c. and b. Davies	0
J.Whitehouse	b. Davies	1		
C.W.Marsdon	run out	0		
J.Bowen	b. Barker	0		
J.V.Harrison	c. and b. Josephson Snr	0		
K.M.Lloyd	run out	0		
	Byes 1, leg byes 2, wides 11	14	Wides 3	3
	1st innings total	62	*2nd innings total*	11

Total Innings 73

After the 1st innings the players sat down to a very excellent cold collation served in the tent by Mr J.Thomas of the Bear's Head Inn. Both parties apparently enjoyed the game and the utmost harmony prevailed throughout. The return match comes off Monday week at Conwy when an equally pleasing contest is anticipated.

Sat 3rd June 1865 – North Wales Chronicle

It gives us great pleasure to hear that the cricket club organised in the town is likely to be in good working order immediately and that it is proposed to inaugurate its first meeting early next week. A spacious tent has been ordered, a good lunch to be provided, and if the day proves anything like fine, we boast to hear that a goodly number of both ladies and gentlemen will do both the club and the lunch full justice. A quoiting ground is to be laid out for the lovers of that game and strangers fond of the manly amusement of either cricket or quoits are to be fully admitted. The only stipulation being that they should send in their cards a day previously to the Secretary. This is a movement in the right direction and deserves the hearty support of all well-wishers to Llandudno.

Extract from the North Wales Chronicle dated 10th June 1865:

It's about a month since a few of the young men of Llandudno made an effort to establish a cricket club in the town. The ground was carefully selected (probably the ground near Neville Crescent), subscriptions asked for, a committee formed and the result was shown yesterday by the throwing open of the new cricket ground to the public. The weather was fortunately propitious, and at one time during the afternoon there was a considerable number of spectators in the ground among whom appeared a fair sprinkling of ladies. Wallace's band was in attendance giving valuable aid towards the gaiety of the afternoon. A tent had been purchased for the use of the club but unfortunately did not arrive on time to be utilised. A small wooden hut which stands on one side of the field was however used as a substitute and the refreshments provided in a most liberal manner by Mr Samuel Lilly of the Alexandra Hotel who had done ample justice to the absence of the tent. The tent was certainly a loss but the interior of the wooden building was very tastefully arranged and we congratulate Mr Lilly on the success of this his first effort in the service of the public. About 22 gentlemen took part in the noble game, and it is rumoured that a challenge has already been sent to the newly formed club to meet their brethren of Rhyl at an early day. Everything passed off well. The play was fully contested as could be expected. The refreshments provided were of first-rate quality and the soda water and bottled porter was vigorously consumed. The wickets were pitched at two o'clock. The game being kept in a most spiritual manner until nine o'clock when the light began to fail and the whole party assembled around the door of the hut. It was a pleasant sight as the declining day light streamed over the pleasant looking faces of the cricketers grouped round their president, Mr Felton who made a most appropriate speech of the occasion. Then under the canopy of the heavenly sky there followed the loyal song "God save the Queen". Hats were taken off, a vote of thanks passed in favour of the president, and another offered to the secretary, Mr Roden, whose efforts in favour of the club have been enthusiastic and unfailing. The evening's amusement concluded with three lusty cheers in honour of the day's success.

Sat 17th June 1865 – North Wales Chronicle

Last week we were able to announce the opening of the Llandudno Cricket Club and to chronicle a very pleasant day passed, not only by the members of the club, but by the visitors who so numerously attended the opening game. Since then the infant club has expanded into proportions worthy of so growing a place as Llandudno. We are happy to be able to tell our readers that a challenge has been sent from the Holywell Cricket Club which has been accepted by the Llandudno players. The game is to be played on the ground, lately rented by the latter club. The day is fixed for Thursday next and a most animated contest is expected. It certainly appears to be a most spirited proposition for so young a body to meet a club well practised in the whole game. We wish the Llandudno players every success and we hope many of the ladies of the town and neighbourhood will grace their presence on the first battlefield of the new club. Wickets will be pitched about twelve o'clock and the new tent lately purchased be used for the purpose of lunch.

24th June 1865 – North Wales Chronicle

The cricket match to which we referred last week was played out on Thursday last. It will be remembered that a challenge was sent by the Holywell Cricket Club and accepted by the Llandudno gentlemen. This appeared rather a hazardous experiment for so young a body, organised so late, and never having had time to get either themselves or their ground into working order. Accepted however it was, and everyone was determined to do their best. The day dawned brightly; Mr Felton was in waiting at the railway station to receive the gentlemen from Holywell and drove them to the ground where they were most hospitably received by their spirited opponents. A handsome marquee graced the ground gaily decorated with flags. The wickets were soon pitched and the Holywell club took first innings.

Our space will not allow us to give a minute detail of the game. Suffice to say that the bowling of Mr Samuel Williams and Mr Boden were really first-rate, contributing very successfully to the success of the day. In fact, no wickets could stand before Mr Samuel Williams's splendid bowling, and when the Llandudno team is properly organised in thorough working order, we predict a glorious career for this young club – who last Thursday went through what the Emperor of the French would call 'The Ordeal of Fire'.

The following is the result of the scoring.

Holywell				
Batsman	**1st Innings**		**2nd Innings**	
D.Edwards	run out	0	c. and b. Boden	0
T.Echus	b. Boden	2	b. Owens	4
Wrightson	c. Owen, b. Boden	0	c. and b. Davies	2
Harrison	b. Boden	2	c. and b. Boden	0
Capt. Wrench	b. S.O.Williams	1	c. and b. Boden	0
Crockford	c. and b. Ward	1	b. Boden	9
R.Lloyd	b. Boden	5	b. S.O. Williams	0
Foulkes	c.Williams, b. Boden	0	not out	2
R.Jones	c. Ward, b. Boden	0	c. Hewson, b. Boden	12
T.Perkins	not out	0	c. Davies, b. Boden	2
E.J.Davies	c. Williams, b. Boden	1	b. S.O.Williams	1
	byes 8, wides 2	10	byes 2, leg byes 1	3
	1st innings total	22	*2nd innings total*	35

Total Innings 57

Llandudno		
Batsman	**1st Innings**	
A.Hewson	c. and b. Davies	9
B.Hewson	c.Davies	0
Jones	run out	0
S.O.Williams	st. Wrench, b. Davies	4
Boden	lbw Davies	41
O.Owen	c. and b. R.Jones	1
Franklin	c. Wrightson, b. R.Jones	1
Ward	not out	12
Blythman	run out	8
E.H.Williams	lbw R.Jones	4
W.Owen	c. and b. Wrench	2
	Byes 5, leg byes 2, wides 8, no balls 1	16

Total Innings 98

The splendid batting of Mr Boden thus scored a number of runs of itself superior to that of the whole first innings of the Holywell eleven. The total number scored by them in both innings meant that Llandudno with the one innings of 98 were the winners by 41 runs.

Everything passed off pleasantly. A gold collation (a light informal meal) elegantly laid out in the marquee and supplied by Mr Lilly of the Alexandra Hotel had done full justice to the strains of Wallace's Band enlivened the company and the ladies who kindly responded to the request made to them by the club. They seemed to take a lively interest in the game and contributed a little by their bright eyes and kind looks to stir up that spirit of emulation which gave the victory to the townsmen. A return match was arranged to come off in about a fortnight's time on the Holywell ground. Three cheers were given to the visitors. At half past six "God Save The Queen" was given by Wallace's Band. The teams were thoroughly pleased with each other with the day's play.

1st July 1865 – North Wales Chronicle.

Tuesday last was the opening day of the junior cricket club at Llandudno. The playing began in earnest shortly after three o'clock on the ground near Neville Crescent when a considerable number of ladies and gentlemen attended. There was some very good playing which was greatly admired. Wallace's band played some lively airs on the occasion. The tent belonged to the Llandudno club which was kindly lent and pitched in the field. Refreshments were supplied by Mr Reeves. Everything went off with éclat, and the game kept up till the youngsters, towards dusk, were well and truly all 'stumped up!'.

23rd September 1865 – North Wales Chronicle

Not satisfied with the fetes on land and on water, on the Parade and on the Great Orme, the good people of Llandudno are about to turn their cricket ground into a racecourse.

On Monday and Tuesday, 25th and 26th September 1865, it is proposed to give a series of races. The cricket club has lent the ground and all details have been planned. The programme of these sports will be found among our advertisements and they appear to have been got up by men well-versed in the intricacies of racing matters. The first race on the list is confined to horses plying habitually for hire in the town of Llandudno. This is how it should be, and if these races be continued from year to year the event will go far, to be of great benefit to their riders. Other races to follow will be for pony and donkeys. The eighth and last race will be a novelty feature.

A grandstand is to be erected. An additional body of police have been applied for. Carriages will be admitted on the course but horsemen excluded, in deference of the cricket club whose ground would be ruined by the riders.

A tremendous boost was given to the game in the area when the United All-England XI played a 3-day match on the Conwy Morfa in August 1866 against a 22 Welsh Squad comprising Conwy, Bangor and Llandudno players.

Amongst the All-England team was a Mr T.Hayward, possibly the father of the great Surrey and England batsman.

30th July 1867 – North Wales Chronicle

Cricket match – On Tuesday 11th July 1867 a cricket match was played between the St Tudno Cricket Club and the Bangor Club. The St Tudno club won in the easiest style imaginable, as they had only two wickets down in their second innings. The play on the part of the Llandudnoites was steady and good. Although not a very large score was made, the Llandudno bowling was too strong for the Bangorians to make any effective good against it.

The following are the returns. Bangor going in first to the wickets:

Bangor				
Batsman	**1st Innings**		**2nd Innings**	
Mr Gomez	b. S.O.Williams	1	c. Pickard, b. Huxham	1
Whalley	b. S.O.Williams	4	b. S.O.Williams	2
Felton	c. Smith, b. Carden	9	c. Isherwood, b. Huxham	3
C.J.Roberts	b. Carden	7	c. Pickard, b. Huxham	0
C.H.Griffith	b. S.O.Williams	7	c. and b. S.O.Williams	0
C.A.Jones	b. Carden	1	c. Smith, b. S.O.Williams	16
Rev. H.Thomas	b. S.O.Williams	0	run out	2
C.Thomas	run out	0	c. S.O.Williams, b. Huxham	0
W.Savage	b. S.O.Williams	0	b. Huxham	0
W.Dew	b. Carden	0	not out	0
W.B.Roberts	not out	5	c. Huxham, b. S.O.Williams	0
	Byes 4, wides 9	13	Byes 7, leg byes 1, wides 4	12
	1st innings total	47	*2nd innings total*	45

Total Innings 92

St Tudno				
Batsmen	**1st Innings**		**2nd Innings**	
Capt Carden	c. and b. W.B.Roberts	1		
Smith	c. and b. Griffiths	8	b. W.B.Roberts	8
S.O.Williams	b. W.B.Roberts	9	b. W.B.Roberts	0
Mellor	run out	12		
H.Rickard	c. and b. Whalley	2		
W.Jones	b. Griffith	2		
Major Huxham	b. W.B.Roberts	14		
D.Watkins	b. W.B.Roberts	4		
Isherwood	b. W.B.Roberts	4		
Dr R.Lewis	b. W.B.Roberts	3		
M.T. Hughes	not out	0	not out	7
	Byes 5, wides 10	15	Byes 3, wides 2	5
	1st innings total	74	*2nd innings total*	20

Total Innings 94

Cricketing Terms

The word 'wicket' comes to us from the small hurdle which formed the diminutive gate to a sheep pen. This had two uprights or 'stumps' and a moveable bar across the top called 'the bail'. This gate was termed a 'wicket'.

It was not until 1777 did the wicket change from two to three stumps. If a ball went through the two stumps and did not remove the bails the batsman was not out.

The lbw rule came into operation in 1744. Wides were not counted in the score until 1827 and it was 1836 when the bowler was credited with wickets taken by catches or stumpings off his bowling. The 1744 Laws state: "Ye wicket is still pitched directly opposite at 22 yards distance from ye other wicket." The author says: "Thank goodness no one has messed about with that law!"

In the early days of cricket the ball was delivered at speed along the ground. In other words it was 'bowled'. Although underarm deliveries are no longer part of the game the overarm variety is still called 'bowling'.

The actual meaning of the word 'umpire' is 'an odd man' and in the early days he was indeed called the 'odd man'. He was called to settle any point which the contestants were at variance.

Sat 30th November 1867 – North Wales Chronicle

The Annual Dinner of the St Tudno Cricket Club was held at the Alexandra Hotel, Llandudno on Tuesday 26th November 1867 when the following gentlemen were present: Capt. Carden, James Meller Esq., John Williams Esq., Bodafon, George Felton, Esq., Chin, Esq., O.Owens, Esq., Llanrwst, Messrs. W.G.Roberts, Robert Hughes, J.H.Lloyd, Robert Price, William Brookes, Edward Owen, John Owen, W.Griffith, Thomas Owen, Charles Fisher, H.Parr, Thomas Hughes, Thomas Williams, B.R.Daivies, H.H.Ward, J.L.l.Hughes, E.R.Hughes, John Williams, Morris Griffith, William Jones, H.Hughes, Thomas Parry, R.D.Owen, S.L.Woodley.

The dinner which was provided by Mrs Parry gave general satisfaction. The catering was excellent and great credit was due to the hostess not only for the getting up of the dinner but also for the perfect arrangements which had been made for serving up the good things provided.

The Chairman, proposing a toast to the success of the St Tudno Cricket Club, said that it must be gratifying to them all to see the club in a state of such thorough efficiency and shows a good omen of future success to see so many friends support them by their attendance that evening. He believed that they were all contributors and he trusted their presence that evening indicated their determination to continue their support in the future.

The Secretary, Mr E.R.Hughes, responded and thanked him on behalf of the members for his kind manner which he had deliberated. They had fortunately succeeded during the past year in every respect and he trusted that the next year would be as prosperous a one for them as the last had been.

Mr Meller stood up and quoted the old saying "that the proof of the pudding was in the eating" and when he informed them that they had won ten challenge games out of eleven he thought that would be sufficient proof that they had not been idle. Credit was due to all the members but particularly to Mr W.Jones who had devoted much time in making all the arrangements.

Mr Felton next proposed the health of the Chairman Capt. Carden who was the chief organiser of the St Tudno club and the thanks of the town at large were due to him for the successful manner in which he organised the club and brought it to its present efficient state. He had proved not a man of many words but a man of action who had not shrunk from his duty at any time. Mr Mellor was thanked as a prominent working member of the ground committee for his commitment in conducting the field arrangements.

Sat 18th July 1868 – North Wales Chronicle

Llandudno v Bangor

The match was played on the Llandudno ground on Tuesday 14th July 1868 when the game ended in a draw. The stumps, as had been arranged, were drawn at 7pm precisely, when the Bangorians had to make 5 runs to win, and 6 men to go in. Neither side scored very high, in fact, from the state of the ground it was playing cricket in difficulties. For the Llandudno side, Mr Strong and Mr Beard scored well in the first innings but in the second innings not one double figure was made. On the Bangor side, E.Hall 46; W.E.Clarke 17 and C.H.Griffith for a somewhat smaller score played very well. Hall's batting being very much admired. We think that credit is due to the Bangor eleven for sustaining the honour of Bangor for the fourth time this year by their prowess in the field of play.

Llandudno 104, **43** total **147**, **Bangor 48**, **95** total **143**.

Llanrwst Grammar School v Llandudno XI. This was a 2-innings match played at Llanrwst on the 25th August 1875 on the school ground, and resulted in an easy victory for the school. Several of the Llandudno XI missed the train, and this, of course, much weakened their team. Llanrwst scored 41 in their 1st innings and 33 in their 2nd innings. The Llandudno XI scored 22 and 23. The home team won by 29 runs.

Sat 24th August 1878 – North Wales Chronicle

Penmaenmawr v Llandudno

This cricket match was played on the Conwy Marsh on Monday 21st August 1878 and Penmaenmawr commenced batting having won the toss. Messrs Downton and Blanchard were the first representatives of Penmaenmawr. The latter was soon bowled by Mr Arrowsmith. Mr Gunnell then came in and commenced batting in good style, while Mr Downton exercised great patience and bothered the bowlers by his steady play. Not until the score reached 60 was the latter bowled for a steady put together 11. Mr Gunnell was soon after caught at cover point for a well hit 51, comprising 4 threes and 10 twos. Mr G.Forshaw was caught for 3. Mr Ralli scored 8 and Mr Hanson made 5 not out. The innings closing for the total of 100, this was very fair considering the state of the ground. Messrs Roberts secured 3 wickets and Moore 4 wickets were most successful with the ball. After a short interval Llandudno went to the wickets. The brothers Moore were the only two who made any stand whatever against the Penmaenmawr bowling making 14 and 6 respectively. The wickets fell in quick succession and the innings closed for the small total of 37. Mr Gunnell took 5 wickets and Mr Forshaw 4. Llandudno then went to the wickets for the second time. They managed to score 46 for the loss of 2 wickets thus leaving Penmaenmawr victorious by 17 runs.

Penmaenmawr			Llandudno		
C.Downton	b. Pettifer	11	E.A.Cross	b. Gunnell	3
Blanchard	b. Arrowsmith	2	J.Moore	c. Sub, b. Forshaw	14
H.Gunnell	c. Cross, b. Moore	51	W.Moore	b. Gunnell	6
G.Forshaw	b. Roberts	6	S.B.Carnley	not out	4
A.C.Bennett	b. Moore	1	J.W.Pettifer	b. Gunnell	0
Milnes	b. Roberts	0	E.Arrowsmith	b. Forshaw	0
H.Forshaw	c. Cross, b. Moore	3	J.M.Roberts	b. Forshaw	0
G.Ralli	b. Roberts	8	W.Sutton	b. Gunnell	3
Pearson	c. Carnley, b. Moore	8	H.M.Sutton	b. Gunnell	0
A.Hanson	not out	5	F.Hind	not out	2
Byes 2, wides 3		5	Byes 6		6
Total		100	Total		37

In the second innings for Llandudno: S.B.Carnley not out 24; E.Arrowsmith
b. Blanchard 2; J.Moore b. Gunnell 4; W.Moore not out 4; Byes 5; wides 5;
no balls 2; - Total 46.

Sat 14th February 1880 – North Wales Chronicle

A letter sent to the editor.

"*Dear Sir,*

*May we hope to have a cricket club at Llandudno this year? And we may
further hope to have a properly laid ground. There can be no proper cricket if
it is intended not to lay the ground. There should be an immediate movement.*

A Resident

Llandudno

9th February, 1880"

Llandudno Cricket Club v Visitors

A very enjoyable match was played on Monday 17th May 1880 between the Llandudno Cricket Club and some visitors from Liverpool reinforced by members of the Llandudno club. By the kind permission of Mr Edward Owen the match was played on the new cricket ground at 'The Warren'.

The following is the score:

Visitors			Llandudno		
F.Peckworth	lbw Brookes	41	W.R.Churchill	run out	16
J.Hodgson	b. Clark	35	G.H.Pugh	b. R.A. Woods	5
R.Hayley	c. Pugh b. Brookes	29	Clark	b. Peckworth	18
R.A. Woods	lbw Brookes	1	Carrol	b. Peckworth	5
E.H.Ridge	c. Pugh, b. Clark	1	J.R.L.Hazeldine	c. Hartley, b.R.A.Woods	4
H.Thorp	c. Danks, b. Brookes	0	Greene	st.Hodgson, b. R.A.Woods	1
R.Wood	c. Hazeldine, b. Brooks	0	Nickolson	b. Peckworth	0
F.Chantrey	run out	4	Pritchard	run out	2
W.Williams	b. Hazeldine	4	W.A.Hughes	not out	22
Taylor	b. Hazeldine	0	J.H.Danks	c. Chantrey, b. Hodgson	11
H.J.Edge	not out	6	O.Brookes	b. Woods	8
Extras		9	Extras		3
Total		130	Total		95

During these early times Llandudno cricketers played on a ground near to the Church of Our Saviour, just off Bryniau Road, which was part of 'The Warren'. In 1883 the population of Llandudno was 6,000. The piece of land called 'The Warren' is now known as the

West Shore. There were no houses in this area at the time except 'The Ddol', Penmorfa House and the Penmorfa cottages.

Alice Liddell's parents, the dean of Christ Church, Oxford and his wife, after honeymooning in Llandudno, decided to build 'Penmorfa' as a permanent holiday home on the West Shore. The house was subsequently the Gogarth Abbey Hotel which was demolished in November 2008. Though there is no evidence that Lewis Carroll ever visited Llandudno, Alice Liddell, who was the inspiration for 'Alice in Wonderland', spent many childhood holidays there.

There was no Gloddaeth Avenue as such but the thoroughfare to the West Shore was then called the Green Lane. On either side of the lane were green fields for pastoral purposes. At the town end the Green Lane started just past the Palladium Theatre (now Wetherspoons). On one side was the Rotarian Hewitt's Works of Arts building and on the other side was the Welsh Calvinistic Chapel and house. Not in existence then was King's Road, Alexandra Road, Winllan Avenue, Morfa Road, Dale Street and Maelgwyn Road. St. Mary's Road, St. Seiriol's Road, St. Andrew's Place, Claremont Road, Gt. Ormes Road, Bryniau Road, Dyffryn Road, and other small thoroughfares. All this area was known as 'The Warren'.

The North Wales Golf Club, situated on 'The Warren' was established in 1894 as a 9-hole course. By August of that year the course had developed into 18 holes because it had attracted more members than expected. Four years earlier the Llandudno Cricket Club had been formed by a few gentlemen of the town for their benefit only and was well established on the new Recreation Ground (now known as the Oval). In those days youngsters who were keen to play with bat and ball were not given much encouragement to join the new club and had nowhere else to play except on the old Warren ground. It was a Mr Cummins in 1894 who took up the offer of the lease to extend the golf course to 18-holes. The story goes that one afternoon Mr Cummins and a friend set off from the golf clubhouse to look over their extended course in the direction of the Church of Our Saviour area and were amazed to find a juvenile cricket match taking place with the wickets pitched on the fairway leading to the new second hole. The lads had to be driven off "by rather more than tact".

25th December 1880 – North Wales Chronicle

Llandudno Cricket Club

The Annual Meeting of the members was held on Thursday 23rd December 1880. Capt. Carden was in the chair. The report of the committee was passed from which it appeared that out of 16 matches played last season, 7 were won, 8 lost and one a draw. This was very satisfactory for a young club and gave good promise of future success. The question of the ground was then discussed and it was ultimately decided to lay a new ground and a committee was appointed for this purpose. It was to be hoped that the club would be heartily supported by the inhabitants of the town who would probably not forget the great interest taken in the game by the visitors during the season. Mr Pugh was elected Captain, Capt. Carden Secretary and Mr Davies Treasurer.

Llandudno played Conwy on the 29th May 1881 at the Marsh, Conwy, in splendid weather, and resulted in a decisive victory for the home team (Conwy) by an innings and sixteen runs. Conwy won the toss and batted first. They scored 55 runs. In reply, Llandudno in their 1st innings were all out for 26. They were put in to bat again and were all out for 13.

Sat 25th June 1881 – North Wales Chronicle

The Works and Sanitary Committee met on 26th May 1881. The committee recommended that proceedings be taken in the County Court for the recovery of one guinea for the use of a field by the cricket club last season. The club having hitherto taken no notice of the several applications made for the payment of the amount.

George IV

Cricket For Kids

Junior Cricket

Lord Llewellyn Nevil Lloyd Mostyn (3rd Baron)

Thomas Edward Lloyd Mostyn

Lady Henrietta Augusta Nevil

Convalescing at Mostyn Hall

Lord Mostyn's Car

The Summit, Great Orme, Llandudno 1856

David Roberts

HMS Cornwallis (1901) sinking 9 January 1917

West Indies 1928

South Africa 1924

Llandudno Bowling Club

Archie Abbott

Sat May 17th 1884 – North Wales Chronicle

A Cricket Club formed.

We are glad to learn that a new cricket club has been started in the town. Mr Percy Green of the Adelphi Hotel convened a meeting on Wednesday evening, 14th May 1884 which was well attended by lovers of the fine old English game. Mr Geo.H.Pugh, Solicitor, occupied the chair and a resolution was passed forming a club. Mr Pugh was asked to be captain but said he would rather some other member held that office. A good captain was elected in the person of Mr Percy Green who also undertook to discharge the office of Treasurer. Mr Evans of the Collegiate College was elected Secretary and Deputy Captain. It was agreed to ask Mr J.R.L.Hazeldine, JP to be President and Capt. Carden and Mr Morris Pugh Vice-Presidents. Arrangements were made for collecting subscriptions and it was resolved to make an offer to the Lawn Tennis Club for the use of the Conwy Morfa to play on. A committee was elected. It was agreed to play an opening match at an early date and to arrange a series of matches during the season. Gentlemen wishing to join should communicate with Mr Green or Mr Evans.

On 5th June 1889 a formal meeting in connection with the formation of a Llandudno Cricket Club was held at the Gogarth Abbey where it was reported a good attendance. The following officials were appointed. Captain: D.R.Lewis (Gogarth Abbey Hotel), Vice-Captain: Capt. F.W.Jones (Castleton Hotel), Captain 'A' team: John Evans (Ruabon House), Joint Secretaries: D.R.Lewis and J.R.Humphreys, Treasurer: Mr Johnson (National Provincial Bank).

On Saturday 25th June 1889 a Llandudno team played members of the Pier Pavilion Orchestra. Four days later Llandudno entertained the Members of the Riviere's Band. On Saturday 20th July they played Conwy and on the following Saturday they drew with Colwyn Bay in a very low scoring game which was not unusual because of the poor state of the unprepared pitches in those days. This was a two-innings match. Colwyn Bay managed 37 and 19, and Llandudno 28 and 39.

An item in the Caernarvon and Denbigh Herald on 28th July 1889 recorded encouraging news regarding cricket at Llandudno. Hitherto there had been difficulty in obtaining a suitable and accessible ground. Mr D.R.Lewis of the Gogarth Abbey Hotel and captain of the local club had communicated with Lord Mostyn on the subject, with the result that his lordship had expressed his readiness to become patron of the club and to encourage cricketing in every way. He had promised to have a meeting on the subject of a cricket ground during his visit next month to Llandudno.

The following is a letter which was published in the North Wales Chronicle on 3rd August 1889. It was in reply to a letter from Mr Lewis advising Lord Mostyn of the setting up of a new Llandudno Cricket Club and, it seemed, requesting his help in finding a new ground. The outcome is no doubt – history!

Carlton Club
3 Portland Place
London W1
8th July 1889

Mr D.R.Lewis
Llandudno Cricket Club
c/o Gogarth Abbey Hotel
Llandudno

Dear Sir,

I am in receipt of your letter of the 15th inst., with regard to the cricket club. I am most anxious to see one started in Llandudno and have some idea of making a ground there myself. It seems to me rather late in the season to start a club now but I shall be very glad to meet any gentlemen who are interested in cricket when I am at Llandudno next month and we could then talk matters over. The difficulty seems to me that at present there is no good ground.

Believe me.

Yours faithfully

Lord Mostyn

An article which appeared in the Caernarvon and Denbigh Herald on 29th November 1889 read:

> The cricket and tennis ground.—The contract for stripping, levelling, and relaying the new cricket and tennis ground, situated in Gloddaeth Street, Llandudno, has been let to Mr. Nash, Birmingham. At present only 10,000 superficial yards will be laid, but the syndicate who have the matter in hand expect that they will be soon able to double the area.

The final matches played at The Warren before the Llandudno club moved to the new recreation ground (The Oval) for the start of the 1890 season were as follows:

1889

Aug 3rd – Llandudno (39) v Visitors (69) – lost

5th – Llandudno (80) v Liverpool Wanderers (27) and (21) – won

6th – Llandudno (66) v Northampton (46) – won

7th – Llandudno (12) and (22) v Manchester (116) – lost

Sep 6th – Llandudno (85) v St Georges Hotel (40) – won

21st – Llandudno (39) v Colwyn Bay (111) – lost

When cricket was first played on rough and uneven common land it was a pretty dangerous pastime with no pads or other protection for the batsman. The first recorded fatality on the cricket pitch was Jasper Vinall, who was hit by a bat while fielding in 1624.

1890-1905

Lord Mostyn's Gift to the Town

On the 10th May, 1890 a new recreation ground (now known as the Oval) situated just off Gloddaeth Avenue had been laid and formally opened by Lord Mostyn. The promoters, on behalf of Mostyn Estates, who carried out the works were Lord Llewelyn Nevill Vaughan Lloyd Mostyn (3rd Baron), The Hon Henry Richard Howell Lloyd Mostyn, Lord Edwin Hill-Trevor (1st Baron), Messrs T.T.Marks, C.E.Thomas, Thomas Williams (Bron Meillion), E.E.Bone (Solicitor), R.S.Chamberlain (Plas Brith), A.T.Marks (Plas Myrddin), G.H.Pugh (Solicitor), D.S.Gillart (Estate Agent) and D.R.Lewis (Gogarth Abbey Hotel).

The ground, approximately 11 acres, was granted by Lord Mostyn for cricket and other sports. There were a number of enclosed asphalted tennis courts including three lawn tennis courts, a football pitch, space for athletics and an asphalted bicycle track. The whole place was eventually bound by a fence, a great part of which had already been erected. Chas.F.Farrington, the club captain in 1922, described the scene so poetically when the recreation ground was enclosed and described as a lush and magnificent site easily thought the best in North Wales.

"One does not associate the wonderful game of cricket with corrugated iron fenced enclosures but with hedged fields where the scented wild rose mingles with tall and sturdy hawthorn and white honeysuckle shedding its fine fragrance, and where the sounds of the hedge birds whistle gaily. It is very pleasing. The corrugated iron fence on the west side of the cricket field was the pleasantest part of the ground with protection from the damp and biting winds one could sit and smoke and lazily watch in comfort the day's play in progress."

The land for cricket was an estimated one hundred square yards. A newly formed cricket club was born and the first officers appointed then were President: Lord Mostyn, Club Captain: Hon Henry Richard Howell Lloyd Mostyn, Deputy Captain: J.J.Marks (son of T.T.Marks), Secretary: G.A.Humphreys. Several other gentlemen were elected to serve on a 'working committee'. Mr Jack Shaw of Nottingham was appointed as the club professional for the coming season and the groundsman, a Mr Jones, formerly gardener at Friars School, Bangor. A pavilion was erected on the ground which had a refreshment room, changing rooms and sleeping accommodation for the professionals and the groundsman.

It had been mentioned that in previous years cricket had been sadly neglected at Llandudno but the advent of enterprising and professional men had brought about a welcome change. The scheme led by Lord Mostyn and the support given to the movement had satisfactorily created a recreation ground of some merit, not only in the interest of the promoters and developers, but also to the whole population of Llandudno. Members joined from Bangor, Beaumaris, Llanrwst, Penmaenmawr, Conwy and Colwyn Bay.

After the formal opening of the ground that afternoon there was a special match between a Llandudno XI and Mr Dockray's XI. Llandudno won by four runs with four wickets in hand. The Hon Henry Richard Howell Lloyd Mostyn was the official umpire.

Mr R.Dockray scored 23, the only double figures in his side. On the winning side, Chas Farrington came to the rescue when Llandudno were three wickets down with only 14 runs on the board. He hit out and scored a quick 21. Jack Shaw (18) was highly praised for his steady play, which went a long way towards winning the match.

Score:

Mr Dockray's XI.

F.Foulds b Savage **1**, Hughes c Blackwall b Savage **6**, A.Halstead c G.H.Pugh b Shaw **2**, R.Dockray b Blackwall **23**, A.A.Edwards run out I, Williams lbw Savage **1**, W.Norton run out **8**, W.A.Thomas b Blackwall **5**, E.Nicholls run out **2**, E.Bennett b Blackwall **0**, H.Marshall not out **2**, Extras **11**, Total **62**

Llandudno XI

J.J.Marks b Thomas **2**, J.Blackwall c Nicholls b Thomas **4**, G.H.Pugh b Foulds **4**, T.B.Farrington c and b Foulds **21**, A.G.Pugh b Thomas **0**, Shaw not out **18**, L.I.A.Savage lbw Foulds **1**, W.Wood not out **2**, Extras **15** Total **67** G.A.Humphreys, J.Jones, D.R.Lewis did not bat.

The first recorded match on the recreation ground was before the formal opening when the Jules Riviere's Orchestra played against a Llandudno XI.

In 1887, many of the town's visitors would certainly have made their way to the Pier Pavilion in the evenings to hear a concert given by Jules Riviere's Orchestra of 42 players. One of the largest resort orchestras, it could not be fitted into the pier-head open air bandstand so evening concerts were always held in the Pier Pavilion (destroyed by fire in 1994). Jules Riviere (1819-1900) was appreciated in the town and was honoured by a banquet in 1899 at which Lord Mostyn made a presentation.

A difference of opinion between Riviere and the pier company resulted in a move for the orchestra. A hall named Riviere's Concert Hall was built in the town and concerts continued there until 1900, when the Riviere's Orchestra finally left for Colwyn Bay to play on the town's new Victoria Pier.

A few months later after the formal opening of the ground a letter appeared in

'The Advertiser' addressed 'to the editor' as follows:

> *"Sir – Some months ago I saw a paragraph in your paper stating that a fine pavilion was being erected upon the cricket ground so on Saturday afternoon I went down to the ground to see it. I was delighted with the pavilion. It is a beautiful erection made of the finest pine so spacious and lofty.*
>
> *Regards – 'Old' Parr"*

It was decided that a small charge would be made to enter the cricket field to watch a game but this would not apply to members of the club, nor would it to ladies who were admitted free.

Hugh Jones was chauffeur for Lord Mostyn in the 1890s. He also drove for Prime Minister David Lloyd George. He was Colin Abbott's grandfather. Colin was a playing member of the Llandudno CC. He was chosen to play for the Caernarvonshire Schools XI against Anglesey on June 4th 1960. His father, Mr Archie Abbott, was made a Life Member of the club on 4th March 1961 in recognition of many years' service. Colin and his father emigrated to Australia in the 1960s. Both are well and in good health at the time of writing. Mr Archie Abbott, 95 years of age, is no doubt the oldest Life-Member of the Llandudno CC.

First established in 1787, Lord's Cricket Ground in St John's Wood is owned by the Marylebone Cricket Club (MCC). The current ground is its third location. Members of the club are permitted to watch matches from the Long Room, a paintings gallery with a view of the notoriously sloping pitch.

The pavilion with its famous Long Room was built in 1889-90. Much of the ground was re-built in the late 20th century. In 1987 the Mound Stand was opened followed by the Grand Stand in 1994. In 1998-9 the Media Centre was added and won The Royal Institute for British Architects Stirling Prize.

Lord's is home to the oldest sporting museum in the world with a collection of the world's most celebrated cricket memorabilia including The Ashes (an urn, satirically signifying the death of British cricket after their defeat by Australia in 1882).

One of the most distinctive features is that the ground itself has a significant slope across the field. The north-east side of the pitch is eight feet (about 2.4 metres) higher than the south-east side.

Lord's holds Test Matches, One-Day Internationals, Middlesex home matches, Marylebone Cricket Club matches and twenty20 games (a shorter than normal match designed to help cricket appeal to new fans).

The first Test Match was played at Lord's in 1884 when England defeated Australia by an innings and five runs. Since then there has been over a hundred Test Matches played at Lord's. Lord's typically hosts two Tests every summer. This includes the first Test of the summer as well as two one-day internationals.

The following is the very first notice in 'The Advertiser' on 5th July 1890 of a cricket match to be played on the Recreation Ground (The Oval).

Llandudno Cricket Ground

Saturday July 12th 1890

Llandudno v Plas Newydd (The Marquis of Anglesey XI)

Wickets pitched at 2.15pm

Admission (from Gloddaeth Street only) – 6p

Children under 14 years – 3p. Ladies and members of the club free

The committee met again on 19th February 1891 and after the reports and discussions at the progress and expenses incurred during the 1890 season matters proceeded to make arrangements for the ensuing season. It was hoped to include some first class matches at the Oval and in particular the MCC of which Lord Mostyn was a member. It was also hoped a game between North and South Wales would take place.

A meeting of the syndicate of gentlemen representing the cricketers and Mostyn Estate officials who initially promoted the ground met at the Mostyn Estate offices on Wednesday 4th March 1891. Present was Lord Mostyn in the Chair, Messrs Pickering, Chamberlain, J.J.Marks, E.E.Bone, W.Laycock, C.A.Hartley, Rev. Tudor Owen, G.H.Pugh, Gillart and G.A.Humphreys. It was recommended that the ground be let at £5 for the first year with the option of taking a lease for an additional four years at an increased rent. This was agreed.

It was mentioned that the work carried out on the cricket ground and the tennis courts was in excellent order and a confident belief was expressed that the undertaking would soon not only be a great boost to the town but a source of profit to the promoters. The meeting concluded with a vote of thanks to Lord Mostyn.

In March 1891 definite arrangements had been made for an encounter with the MCC to be played over two days in August followed in the same week a two-day match against a Lord Mostyn XI. It was hoped to integrate into the club fixtures a 'cricket week' which had been a success in Scarborough and Hastings and other places. Already arrangements had been made to commence a 'cricket week' on the 24th August when a strong Lancashire team known as the Normans would play a Llandudno XI. Other matches would include a team selected and captained by Lord Mostyn and also a match against the MCC. On the Thursday of that week special efforts would be made to make the ground and surroundings attractive for a 'Ladies Day'. During the week the ground would be decorated and space would be made available to anyone who wanted to put up a stall or tent free of charge.

A club professional had been appointed for the season, a Mr Wall who was formerly employed by the East Lancashire cricket club.

Fixtures arranged for the 1891 season included games against Friars School, Bangor, Crewe Athletic, Plas Newydd, Bangor, W.H.Parsons XI, Riviere's Orchestra, F.W.Stubbs XI, Otterspool CC, Porthmadog, Birkenhead Gymnasium, The Normans, Lord Mostyn XI, MCC and Caernarvon.

A summer fete was held on 31st July 1891 — under the auspices of Mr and Mrs Jules Riviere, a most successful fete took place on the cricket ground, and attracted a large audience. The proceeds from this event went towards the cricket club funds. Music was provided by the Conway Brass Band, a choir of 60 voices from the Clio training ship with their drum and fife band, the Merliton Club Band, Mr Underwood's Promenade Band, and Jules Riviere's orchestra, a team of which played a match with the Llandudno Cricket Club during the afternoon.

The Clio was an Industrial Training Ship which served 'North Wales, Chester and the Border Counties' during the period 1877-1920. During this time it was moored in the Menai Straits, near Bangor. The ship had a dual purpose, namely to take care of and train boys under the age of 14 who were regarded as being in need of special educational or custodial care; and secondly, to provide a regular supply of seamen for the Royal Navy and Mercantile Service. Although boys who had been convicted of crimes were not permitted to enter industrial training ships, the Clio was regarded by many people as a 'reformatory' ship.

On 6th/7th August the Original English Lady Cricketers came to Llandudno and gave an exhibition on the Oval of how their game was played, no doubt to the satisfaction of the most critical. It was said that many male (and maybe a few female) supporters entered the ground in confused anticipation but most remained to the end to give loud applause.

Unfortunately, the 'cricket week' was spoilt by the persistent rain. In the first two matches play was only possible during the first day of each game while in the most important game of all against the MCC the ground was so soft the wicket had to be changed on the second day.

However, the rain did not completely spoil it for everyone. On the first day the match against the Gentlemen of Cheshire did attract a large and fashionable gathering to the ground. Amongst the crowd and gracing the ground were Lady Henrietta Augusta Nevill Lloyd Mostyn and Lady Mary Florence Edith Clements Lloyd-Mostyn. The Hon Henry Richard Howell Lloyd Mostyn batted on the first day and scored a tidy 21 runs. Unfortunately, that was not enough as the Gentlemen of Cheshire won by 93 runs. On the 17/18 August there was a large company present for the Llandudno v MCC match including Lord Mostyn, Lady Henrietta Augusta Nevill Lloyd Mostyn, and Lady Pamela Georgina Lloyd-Mostyn. There were several tents erected around the ground. A formal lunch was provided on each day sent out from the Clarence Hotel for players and officials with Lord Mostyn presiding.

The season ended on the 19th September with a match against members of the Riviere's Orchestra of which the club professional, Mr Wall, took his Benefit.

On Wednesday 25th November 1891 a musical entertainment evening was held in the Pier Pavilion in aid of the Llandudno Cricket Club funds. The event was under the management of Madame Riviere, and under the patronage of Lady Augusta Mostyn. The vocalists were Miss Mabel Berry, Miss C.V.Cox, Misses Jones and Hobson, Messrs J.R.Jones and Thomas solo harp, Mr Ffrench Davies; the Claxton family (string quartet); pianoforte accompanist, Mr Llewelyn Jones, ACO. An interesting feature was a series of tableaux vivants, 'The Smuggler's Cave', being sustained by the following: The mother, Miss Lizzie Williams; the victim, Mrs G.H.Pugh; the villain, Dr E.Luke Freer; the innocent, Mr G.H.Pugh; the pedlar, Mr D.Gillart; the governor of the prison, Mr T.T.Marks; the gaoler, Mr Ernest Winter;

the coastguardsman, Mr T.T.Marks. The second tableaux was 'The Toto Family', represented as follows: Mamma Toto, Madame Riviere Papa; Toto, M.Riviere; Young Toto, Master J.Claxton; Sylvia, a young laundress, Miss Mabel Berry and a waiter, Mr Wheeldon.

At the start of the 1892 season in April the new club professional Mr A.Simpson from Nottingham arrived to commence his duties. A full season of fixtures had been arranged and the prospects of a busy and successful season on the ground which was stated to be in splendid condition and with a little rain was expected to be 'as level as a billiard table'. A new approach to the ground was being made from the Lloyd Street end and the final work to include a dining area in the pavilion had been completed.

The following is a list of vice-presidents in 1892 of which Lord Mostyn was president: The Hon H.Lloyd Mostyn, JP, Messrs J.Broome, High Sheriff of Caernarfonshire; George Barker; Thomas Barker, JP, E.E.Bone, R.S.Chamberlain, G.Downing, E.Luke Freer, C.A.Hartley, T.T.Marks, CE, Rev E.Tudor Owen, Mr O.I.Pilkington, Mons Jules Riviere, Messrs John Walker, Thomas Williams, A.Firth, H.Keeling, W.Magrath, J.Platt (Abbey-road), Richard Conway, CC, Dr James Nicol, JP, Dr Bold Williams, JP, Dr T.Dalton, JP. Mr Walter Wood is the hon secretary, Mr G.H.Pugh captain of the club, and Mr J.J.Marks deputy captain.

A great start to the season on 7th May was beating Colwyn Bay. After the home team made 224 for 4 dec they scuttled the visitors out for 45. It was just a few weeks later when they travelled to Llanfairfechan to play Sydney Platt's Bryn y Neaudd side that they suffered their first defeat under some controversy over bad umpiring, the visitors claimed.

On 17th December a Fair in aid of club funds was held in the pavilion which included the appearance of the local dramatic society performing a popular comedy at the time called 'The Obstinate Family'. A few days before there was a concert held at the Pier Pavilion. Again organised by club members in aid of club funds it included musical and dramatic entertainment and it was reported a fairly large audience was present. The first part of the programme consisted of a piano forte by Mrs Crockett and Miss Bessie Brookes as the opening act. A well-played cello solo by W.J.Claxton followed. There was an excerpt from 'The Pirates of Penzance' by Miss Elsie May Edge which well deserved the efforts it obtained it was said. An excruciating funny sketch described Mr Vincent Walker and his banjo which ended the show. The Riviere's Orchestra provided the music and the receipts helped to lessen the deficit on the club accounts. There is no doubt that the members were making tremendous efforts to clear their debts and were anxious to keep on the right side in the future.

During this time there was proof of the growing interest of cricket in the neighbourhood. The number of members had risen to 45 and interest in the game nationally, especially in Wales, appeared to be rapidly increasing.

"Botham just couldn't quite get his leg over" – Jonathan Agnew as Ian Botham tries in vain to lift his leg over his stumps when off balance.

The 1893 season got off to a good winning start on the 29th April against a newly formed club at Conwy situated on the Morfa. The Llandudno umpire was a Mr R.Pedler and in those days, because road transport was not available, the team met at the Llandudno Railway Station and travelled on the 1.25pm train to Conwy and then walked a mile to the ground.

During the interval in a match against Greenfield Park at the Oval on 30th July Miss Nellie Edge and Miss Elsie Edge most kindly entertained both teams and members of the club to afternoon tea on the ground.

In a match against Caernarfon on 10th August, Llandudno won easily. The highlight of the match was Mr W.Hart's eight wickets for 13 runs. It was noted at this time that the ground was in splendid order and Mr Clarke (club professional) was complimented on the excellent wickets he had been preparing during the season.

In August the club played the MCC again and in this match the club captain, the Hon Henry Richard Howell Lloyd Mostyn, played for the MCC. The visitors won by 67 runs.

Over 20 matches were played during the 1893 season of which only three were played away from home. New visiting sides to the Oval included Heaton of Bolton, Davenham, Monkton, Smethwick and Hawarden.

In 1893 on the 24th August in a match against the Rugby Ramblers it was reported that Mr Smith kept wicket for Llandudno admirably but it was said he would have been a lot better if he had put on 'leg guards' earlier in the game! It was heard on the day a visitor remarking that the field was in such wonderful condition and that the preparation of the wicket and square was to be highly commended and in his opinion the standard was far ahead of any other cricket club he had seen in North Wales.

There was a county match played on the Oval on 15th September. Anglesey beat Caernarvonshire by 16 runs.

The 1893 AGM was held at the Marine Hotel on 11th December. T.T.Morris presided. Also present were Mr and Mrs Pugh, J.J.Marks, T.Bibby, G.A.Humphreys, G.H.Pugh, Owen Hughes, W.Smith, A.Connolly, J.Simmonds and W.Wood.

The Secretary read the Annual Report which stated that the receipts for the year including unpaid subs amounted to £112.14s.3p whilst the expenses amounted to £141.16s.1p leaving a balance of £38.18s.10p.

During the past season the 1st XI played 24 matches, won 15, lost 5 and 4 drawn.

The meeting thanked the members of the Llandudno Amateur Operatic and Dramatic Society for their performance held in December 1892 and also to the Riviere's Orchestra for the entertainment they gave on the 2nd October in aid of club funds.

The number of playing members was 45 for the 1894 season.

At a meeting of the town council's Local Commissioners' Board in May, the Chief Surveyor reported that the old grey horse was unfit to continue to work 'on the streets' of Llandudno any longer and they had to decide what to do with the 'old boy'. The Secretary of the Llandudno Cricket club had written to the Chief Surveyor asking if the Commissioners would allow the club to try the horse on the cricket ground for a week. If they found him capable of doing the required work (pulling the heavy roller) the club would be glad to make an offer to purchase. It was agreed to lend the horse to the club for a fortnight and that the purchase be settled at the end of that period if the animal was found to be fit and able. Alas, there is no record of any purchase and what happened to the 'old boy' to this day is not known except that there is no doubt he is at peace now!

William Henry Scotton (1856-1893) was a well-known professional cricketer who committed suicide by cutting his throat with a razor at No. 91, St John's Wood Terrace, London, where for ten years it had been his custom to take lodgings during the cricket season. Since obtaining a divorce from his wife his domestic troubles seemed to have induced a nervous and mentally depressed condition. While umpiring at a match at Clifton in 1893 he gave what was said to have been considered a wrong decision, and this increased the mental disorder which is supposed to have impelled him to take his own life. His landlady made the awful discovery on carrying up his breakfast on a Sunday morning and on entering his bedroom found the famous Nottinghamshire cricketer lying in a crouching position on the floor in his nightshirt. On the arrival of Dr Carter it was discovered that he had knelt on the floor beside the bed with his head over a basin and with his left hand had cut the jugular vein, making a wound about three inches long on the left side of the neck. The news was telegraphed to his friends at Nottingham. Though not by any means a brilliant cricketer, Scotton had done an immense amount of service for the county of his birth. He was a left-handed batsman, a fine defensive player with unvarying patience, and a splendid fielder. His last appearance for Notts was in 1890. He played for England against Australia in the years 1884 and 1886.

His finest performance was undoubtedly his innings of 90 for England against Australia at Kennington Oval in August 1884. The match resulted in a draw with Australia scoring 551 and England 346 and 85/2. In England's first innings Scotton went in first, and was the ninth man out, the total when he left being 332. During a stay of five hours and three quarters he played the bowling of Fred Spofforth, Palmer, Boyle, Billy Midwinter, and George Giffen without giving the slightest chance, and but for his impregnable defence it is quite likely that England would have been beaten. Up to a certain time he received very little assistance, but when Walter Read joined him, 151 runs were put on for the ninth wicket.

Against the Australian team of 1886 Scotton played two remarkable innings in company with W.G.Grace, the two batsmen scoring 170 together for the first wicket for England at the Oval. Scotton's score at the Oval was only 34 out of 225 scored. When Scotton was out, Walter Read came in and made 94 in 210 minutes. Scotton's slow scoring, particularly when compared with Grace and Read prompted London magazine Punch to print the following parody on Alfred Lord Tennyson:

Block, block, block
At the foot of thy wicket, O Scotton!
And I would that my tongue would utter
My boredom. You won't put the pot on!
Oh, nice for the bowler, my boy,
That each ball like a barn door you play!

Oh, nice for yourself, I suppose,

That you stick at the wicket all day!

And the clock's slow hands go on,

And you still keep up your sticks;

But oh! For the lift of a smiting hand,

And the sound of a swipe for six!

Block, block, block,

At the foot of thy wicket, ah do!

But one hour of Grace or Walter Read

Were worth a week of you!

In 1894 on Saturday 22ⁿᵈ August against the Visitors Mr J.J.Marks scored the first recorded Llandudno century (100 not out) in a match on the Oval.

Gentlemen v Ladies

An interesting game was played on 8th September between the Gentlemen and the Ladies. The Ladies won the toss and Elsie Edge and May Crockett opened the batting. It was well known that the ladies had been in strict training for three days before the game not having even a bowling acquaintance with a bat previously. Before the game commenced some of the fairer sex protested against a certain member of the gentlemen's team who was known to bowl too straight! Of course the right-handed gentlemen bowled left-handed and the ladies wielded bats cut down to the width of the handle. The ladies decided there was a considerable difference practising in the nets and playing on open ground with eleven men around one – "you know you are positively afraid to slog at your ball for fear you'll hit one of them so what are you to do?". Unfortunately, the two champion lady-sloggers the other ladies were relying on, were bowled before they made a run. "I can never hit the ball for the first two or three times," one remarked, "but after that I'm alright." It was resolved amongst the ladies that six trial balls should be the rule in future. The men reluctantly agreed. Dorothy Knight, however, came boldly to the rescue and though it was her first appearance on the field she became top scorer. Miss O.C.Emmerdale came next and as their youngest member was highly commended for her efforts by the rest of the team. Mrs Jones played a steady game and as for the rest they did their level best and were given some credit taking into account how nervous and excited they must have felt being involved in the novelty of the situation. At about 4pm the ladies were all out for 53 thanks to the generosity of the umpire. The bowlers for the second half were Miss N.Edge and Harriot Hargreaves. The other team members were D.Knight, D.Emmerdale, L.Garland and L.Crockett. Elsie Edge kept wicket in a manner that did equal damage to her head and hands. Again by excellent management and by good sportsmanship on the part of the Gentlemen players, the ladies won the match. The gentlemen took their beating in the greatest contentment and kindness by inviting the ladies afterwards to a convivial tea in the pavilion.

On 13ᵗʰ July 1895 the governing body of cricket based at Lord's Cricket Ground announced 'The National Shilling Testimonial to W.G.Grace'. All cricket clubs within the UK including Llandudno had been asked to co-operate with the Daily Telegraph to further the fund.

Members of the club who duly subscribed and their contributions forwarded to the Daily Telegraph offices were as follows:

	s.	d.
G.H.Pugh (captain)	1	0
G.A.Humphreys (treasurer)	1	0
M.W.Jones (match secretary)	1	0
T.Bibby	1	0
T.T.Marks	1	0
W.Wood	1	0
F.Edge	1	0
A.Knight	1	0
T.B.Farrington	1	0
C.Rylands	1	0
D.G.Pugh	1	0
Simon Williams	1	0

W.G.Grace (1848-1915)

He was an English amateur cricketer who was important in the development of the sport and is widely considered one of its greatest ever players. He played first-class cricket for a record 44 seasons. He played for Gloucestershire, MCC and captained England for many years.

A groundsman at a public school in Gloucester told a friend that W.G.Grace on one occasion scored 318 runs on the ground which was the subject of discussion between the church dignitaries for some time afterwards. One said that it was 316, the other said it was 318 and gave his reason for being so positive that he had made up his mind the following Sunday by giving out at Morning Service the 318th hymn.

Three young men were arrested and charged by the police with gambling for playing a game of 'Chance' on Sunday 10th November 1895. Mr J.J.Marks prosecuted on behalf of the police. Police Constable Jones gave evidence at the Magistrates' Court to the effect that on the day in question he was on duty on the Llandudno Cricket ground when he saw the three defendants, Robert Hughes(Hotel Porter), John Roberts and Hugh Edwards, playing a game of 'Chance' on one of the seats adjoining the cricket pavilion. He concealed himself and watched the defendants play. When he put in an appearance the defendants ran away. Having seized a full pack of cards and 3d in coppers, he chased and caught Robert Hughes who said he had only just come from having his dinner and denied that he had taken part in the game. He produced a pack of cards and coppers which were also seized. According to the statement of Police Superintendent Williams, the defendant Robert Hughes had been before the court before for using obscene language for which he was fined 5s and costs. He had also been previously proceeded against for playing a game of 'Chance' and on that occasion let off with a caution. John Roberts had also been proceeded against for a similar offence.

The magistrates fined Hughes and Roberts 10s and costs. Hugh Edwards was fined 15s and costs.

It was considered that gambling in Llandudno had become a serious problem in the eyes of the church in those days and it was the Free Church Council who felt more should be done about it. The forces of purity and public morality had at last decided to take steps, if at all possible, to check the gambling evil in Llandudno. The church had been conspicuous in its denunciation of gambling, with some effect, but it was deemed not enough. The Rev H.Barrow Williams, one of the worthiest of local ministers and one imbued with the Puritanical spirit, presided over a meeting of the Welsh section of the Free Church Council. The purpose was to evaluate ideas to help in curbing the growing evil of gambling, and the best means they could help in adopting them. After viewing the matter from all aspects, it was decided to make inquiries as to the position of the Council with regard to securing the services of a private detective. The following resolution was adopted:

"That we convey to all the local churches our expression of alarm at the serious increase of the betting evil in our town, and implore them to join us in calling attention to a matter so fraught with danger. We suggest that attention should be called to this subject by the social services, the Sabbath Schools, and in any other way that may appear appropriate. Members of the Welsh Free Church Council, most cordially recognise the effort of the police to put down the evil."

It was seen that all the Christian Free Churches of the town had joined hands to check the evil. It was accepted that to stamp it out completely would be very difficult, especially among the adult classes. But it was thought that to mitigate its increase among the young people of Llandudno would not be so difficult. The suggestion to obtain the services of a private detective was a plausible one but it very soon proved impracticable. What was needed to be considered so far as Llandudno and Caernarvonshire in general were concerned was an amendment of a single bye-law. If the Caernarvonshire police had the same power as those of Flintshire against the persons who were entrapping the young men and leading them into illegal doings, it would not be long before they were brought to justice. It was thought that if pressure were brought on the Caernarvonshire County Council to amend that particular bye-law which would give the police power of arrest, much ground would be gained.

In November 1895 Mostyn Estate gave notice to the club that the field would be taken back unless some satisfactory arrangement was made as for future payment of the rent, of which a large amount had already been written off by Lord Mostyn. It was evident that the club was struggling financially and that something needed to be done to improve the revenue. It was suggested that the Oval become an athletic ground to include not only cricket but other sports. A proposal to add the laying of an athletic track and a bowling green was looked upon favourably as a means to stop such a calamity for the town to lose the ground. It was felt that such a scheme might encourage local people 'to dig deep in their pockets' especially hotel proprietors, tradesmen and others who would benefit from the influx of more visitors to the town. It was agreed that some steps should be taken to form a limited company and with this in mind arrangements would be made to meet Lord Mostyn and lay the resolution before him for his approval.

At a meeting in 1896 the club secretary read a report stating that the finances of the club were in a better state than they had been in past years and that there was every prospect that the cricket club would carry on with renewed vigour and that the feared collapse would be obviated. It was felt that the arrangements that had been put in hand for taking the ground from Lord Mostyn and working the club generally at less expense was well supported. It was well known that Lord Mostyn had an interest in all forms of sport in the town. The generous manner for several years over which he had sponsored the cricket club would continue when he knew what the objectives were so that the future of the club would be placed upon a better footing than it had occupied for some time.

Playing members of the club were not happy with the selection of the teams playing on Saturdays because the practice was that visitors were asked to name the players. It was decided that in future resident members should decide and it was resolved that the general committee appoint a sub-committee of non-playing members to choose a team each week.

On 1st August 1896 Llandudno played Llanychain (Ruthin) and dismissed them for 38 runs. In those days a match would continue even when the team batting second had scored more than the opposing side. Llandudno replied with 447 runs for the loss of only four wickets. This is still the highest score on record that Llandudno have scored in a match. Dr Travis (Llandudno's Medical Officer) scored 105 and J.C.F.Connolly hit a mighty 238.

On 19th September 1896 Thomas Rawlings, taxi driver, appeared at the Llandudno Police Court before the magistrates charged with stealing a small cricket bat from a branch shop of Messrs Richmond and Co. The assistant at the stall reported the bat being missing, which was subsequently found in the defendant's cab. Police Constable Nelson said that when he spoke to the defendant about it he said he did it for a lark, but that another cabman named Edward Williams actually took the bat and put it in the defendant's cab. Mr W.Chamberlain, for the defence, said there was no intention of stealing the bat and that the men were merely larking about. He then called a cabman, by the name of Thomas Davies, who was near at the time. He said the defendant and the other man had gone for a drink, and were larking about with the bat. There were plenty of people about at the time. In reply to the chairman, he said neither the defendant nor Williams were drunk. The Bench ordered the defendant to pay one shilling costs, and bound him over in the sum of £5 if he should come up for judgement again.

On the 3rd April 1897 it was reported that at the Llandudno Magistrates' Court Richard Foulkes, John Brookes, Edward Davies, and John Owen were charged with playing cricket in the street. It was considered playing cricket in Lloyd Street was exposing the public to danger. The mother of Richard Foulkes stated that her boy was not with the crowd that was playing at the time, because he was in the shop. The other defendants, with the exception of John Owen who did not appear, pleaded guilty, and were each fined one shilling and costs. Mr Davies, the father of the boy Edward Davies, observed that the least the police officer could have done was to caution the children first of all before bringing them before the court. He said it was a disgrace to the town that they had no pleasure or recreation ground where children could play.

The Annual General meeting of the club took place at the Arundale Restaurant on the 13th April 1898. Mr J.E.Hornsey presided. The 1st XI played 27 matches in 1897, won 11, lost three, drawn 13. Lord Mostyn was re-elected president. The Hon Henry Richard Howell Lloyd Mostyn was made vice-president. A vote of thanks was given to Mr A.Garth for his generous gift of a bicycle to the club.

It was decided that because not all youths could afford the 10s. 6d subscription to join the club the committee took the matter into consideration and decided to allow schoolboys to become members for 2s. 6p.

An athletics sports meeting was held on the cricket field in aid of funds for the re-seating of St George's Church. Activities included the 100 yards, a two-mile handicap bicycle race, high jump, sack race and a one mile handicap race. The meeting terminated with a tug-of-war which was won by a team from Blaenau Ffestiniog. Prizes were presented by the Hon Mrs Henry Lloyd Mostyn. During the afternoon music was provided by the Ockley Silver Brass Band.

On 11th September 1898 the secretary informed the members by letter that he had met Lord Mostyn to discuss the terms of the lease of the ground. He reported that the terms were most favourable and that all that remained was to find sufficient capital to lay the additional land fenced in and to build the necessary pavilion. The amount required was almost £1,000. As for the amount promised, that was £470; the largest portion of this was subscribed by individuals. He appealed to the townspeople that the scheme would fail unless they made the effort to help, according to their means. At that moment in time there were only three clubs using portions of the land but without any fixed tenure – cricket, hockey and tennis. The present clubs would remain the same but instead of the cricket club just meeting the demands of rent for the field the idea was that each club would be able to rent their proportion from a newly-formed athletic club. The ground would accommodate a cricket pitch, two hockey pitches, and seven more tennis courts. He concluded that if the appeal failed then the idea of an athletic club would be abandoned. A warning was given that renting the ground held only from year to year was insecure, because the Oval could be reduced for building purposes at any time. The negotiations with Lord Mostyn had resulted in a lease for 14 years being promised if the scheme was floated.

At a club meeting at the start of the 1900 season a member proposed a resolution in the following ambiguous terms – "that the wearing of flannels or some sort of trousers at matches be optional". Upon this another caustic and more educated member proposed as an amendment that "the wearing of one or the other be compulsory".

It was a fact that comparisons were being made by some admirers of the game that 20 years previously there was more individual enthusiasm on and off the field. There seemed to be that earnest, anxious business like interest lacking in the game to what there was in the old days. There was no wasting of time as was in 1900 invariably the rule not only locally but elsewhere; no dawdling about with cigarettes or pipe in mouth whilst fielding and taking long 'tea' breaks much to the annoyance of spectators who had come to watch a cricket match. Many felt that this indefensible waste of time was growing worse, year by year, and that clubs should check this attitude so that players would enable themselves to be more proficient in other departments of the game besides batting.

Some refurbishment of the pavilion before the 1900 season had been completed and the hoarding on the south west side of the field had been extended. This was just a few of the many little improvements that Lord Mostyn had brought about in recent years for the furtherance and encouragement of sport on the Oval ground.

It was reported that on 6th July 1900 a strong team of the Llandudno Cricket Club proceeded to Flint to meet the club of that town. On arrival they found that they were not expected. Though the fixture appeared on their card, the date was blank on the card of the Flint club, owing to some unfortunate misunderstanding. The Llandudno players had to wait some hours before they could obtain a return train home.

On 27th July 1900 a correspondent writes:

"Sunday cricket at Llandudno.

We are often told that the Continental Sunday is sweeping over Wales, and that the land of the white gloves, and the great preaching festivals, is being converted into a modern Babylon. As far as Llandudno is concerned, I must admit that there is not a little truth in the statement. Here we have had Sunday golfing for many years, and yet both the churches and the chapels, as well as the religious leaders that make up local Parliament, have been keeping quiet. The most recent innovation is Sunday cricket. To the astonishment of many thousands of visitors, cricket playing could be seen on the Recreation Field on Sunday. It would be interesting to know whether the council, as tenants, or anyone in authority on their behalf, gave permission to the parties who were so anxious to gain such notoriety."

On Thursday 23rd August 1900, Llandudno played a two-day match against Eckersley at the Oval. On the first day's play they were soundly defeated. The visitors totalled 117 in their innings in reply to the home team's dismal 86. Mr Woodhead was the only batsman who came out of the ordeal with any credit scoring 48 out of the total of 86. The next day Llandudno managed to do better scoring 177. Mr

Woodhead scored 62 not out. The game ended in a win for Eckersley by four wickets.

On 26th August 1900 at home against Bangor they won comfortably. Winning the toss they chose to bat and scored 209/1 dec. J.Ashford (104 no) and A.Halstead (95). Bangor was all out for 58.

A sorry state of affairs since 1900, cricket in Llandudno had been conspicuous by its absence. It had often been a matter of conjecture why it should be so, with one of the best cricket grounds in North Wales available for cricketing purposes. In the latter part of 1902 this situation was remedied by the establishment of a club to be known as the 'Llandudno Cricket Club' in readiness for the 1903 season. A meeting was held, and a committee was formed. Lord Mostyn was elected President.

The following is the detail of the report of a meeting held at the end of the 1903 season (it does not include the batting and bowling averages):

Llandudno Cricket Club's first Annual Dinner. The Llandudno Cricket Club, under its new organisation, held its first annual dinner at the Avondale Restaurant (opposite Llandudno Public Library) on Tuesday evening, Mr F.Vincent Walker presiding. There was a large gathering, and the various toasts having been honoured, Mr Plant, chairman of the Committee, presided at the annual meeting.

Mr Chas F.Farrington submitted the report as Hon Secretary and Treasurer. Mr Farrington carried out the dual office since the departure of Mr H.Berkley, who was elected secretary at the commencement of the season. The following was the report presented:

"Gentlemen,—It is with very great pleasure that I make this report to you for the season of 1903. The season has been a most successful one with respect to popularity, enthusiasm, and finance, and although we have not won as many matches as we should like to have done, I think that I am not wrong in stating, we are all agreed that we have derived a certain amount of amusement amongst ourselves which really was the sole aim of the Committee. The formation of the Club we are deeply and entirely indebted to our Captain, F.Vincent Walker who worked hard and gave a lot of time. He was instrumental in getting together an enthusiastic committee consisting of Messrs W.B.Plank, Ernest Jones, M.W.Jones, and myself. The first meeting was held on November 18th, when Mr R.Buckley was appointed secretary, and preliminary arrangements made. A list of gentlemen was drawn up and invited to become supporters of the Club, as vice-presidents and honorary members. It was an uphill fight, the first appeal being most discouraging. One very amusing letter was received from a gentleman, who stated that "Cricket on the North Wales Coast was a 'dead duck'". This was hardly encouraging but I am glad to say that we received later a very substantial subscription from him. At a meeting held on the 16th December it was decided to send a further circular out to those who had not replied, and by the response to this, it was then very soon seen that the financial position of the Club was assured, and for our success, thanks are due to those gentlemen who came forward to assist us in procuring for Llandudno, one of the healthiest and manliest games played. At this meeting Lord Mostyn was elected President, Mr W.B.Plank, chairman of the Committee Mr F.V.Walker, captain: Mr Edward Jones, vice-captain, and myself hon treasurer which formed the committee, with Messrs M.W.Jones and A.C.Carless. Fifteen meetings were held during the months of January, February, March, April, May, June, July and August. When general business was carried on, and of which correct minutes have been kept, we were very sorry to receive a letter from Mr M.W.Jones at one meeting in January, in which he severed his connection with the Club on account of ill-health. A gentleman whom we looked up to in committee for advice with so many years' experience, it was very pleasing to see him turn up again on the field of battle. I am sorry to say that at a meeting on the 3rd February, we found it again necessary to send out a further circular to those who had not replied to the forms. A general meeting was held on the 10th March, there being a fair attendance. The Secretary's report was read and discussed. A selection committee, consisting of the Captain, Vice-Captain, and Mr W.B.Briggs, was appointed, but they resigned on July 12th, and Messrs W.E.Grundy, M.Brookes, and myself, were asked and consented, to act in their stead. A satisfactory fixture card was arranged, and opened with a match on May 2nd, Married v. Single. The muster for this match was most gratifying and encouraging to the Committee and not any of the enthusiasm seemed to be lost during the season. Of matches played, excluding 2nd XI and Married v. Single, five have been won, seven lost, and six cancelled, or abandoned. On the 16th May the 2nd XI beat the 1st XI and in the Married v. Single matches the former won two out of the three. They were a great feature of the season, and looked forward to by all. At the last meeting of the Committee it was decided to hold the annual meeting and dinner on Tuesday, the 6th October, and notices to this effect, with statement of accounts, have been sent to the President, Vice-President and members of the Club. It gives me great pleasure to draw your attention to the statement of accounts, which show a substantial balance of 9s. od of which has only been attained by strict and economical working of the Committee. Only one trial was made at advertising the matches, and that was for the Married v. Single on the 12th September. Six shillings was spent on the posters, and valuable time in circulating them by Messrs F.Vincent Walker, M.Brookes, and me, and the gate only realized a disappointing 2s. 3d. Three or four posters were however kept, and with the date altered, advertised the next match for the Saturday following. The match, however, did not realize anything, being perhaps too late in the season. With a proper system of advertising, it would no doubt improve the gate takings. I am extremely pleased to state that we have a substantial number of playing members, which will qualify us to run a 2nd XI next season. It is very desirable that any committee appointed should pay attention to the fact in making fixtures that it is very difficult to get a team to go anywhere outside a radius of twenty miles, owing to the train service not suiting the majority of the players. The usual benefit was given to the groundsman on Saturday, August 29th, amounting to £ 1 17s. On the 17th March, Mr F.Vincent Walker kindly promised to present a drama stage production at the end of the season in aid of the Cricket Club, which was gratefully accepted by the Committee. Our sincere thanks are due to Mr F.Vincent Walker and Mr Crockett for allowing us the use of their rooms for our meetings. To M.Walker for providing tea on the ground, Mr Jones for assistance, and J.R.Evans for so faithfully carrying out the duties of scorer at home and away and ought, I think, to be placed on record. Thanks are also due to Messrs W.B.Plank and R.Anthony for the assistance they have rendered. The former in presenting a bat to the Club, the latter in procuring an extension of time for this evening's meeting, and to Mr E.P.Morris for auditing the accounts. I am personally indebted to Messrs W.E.Grundy and M.Brookes for compiling the following batting and bowling averages, and to them and Messrs Howel Jones and F.V.Walker for assisting in selling tickets for this dinner. I propose that a vote of condolence be recorded for the family of the late Mr A.C.Carless, who was a very active member of our committee, and who was greatly respected by all who came into contact with him. Since the 13th August I have acted as honorary secretary, owing to our secretary (who did some very good work) leaving the town.—I am, gentlemen, yours faithfully, Chas Farrington."

The election of officers for 1904 followed. Lord Mostyn was again unanimously elected President, and to the list of vice-president power was given to the names of several gentlemen mentioned. The election of Captain was by ballot, and Mr W.E.Grundy was announced by the scrutinisers, Messrs Adonai Evans and A.G.Pugh, elected, Mr Vincent Walker being unanimously appointed vice-captain. Mr Maurice Brooks was voted to the post of secretary, and Mr C.F.Farrington treasurer. Mr W.B.Plank was unanimously elected chairman of the Committee, the Committee being Messrs Howel Jones, R.Anthony and E.Jones. Considerable discussion took place on the question of the team selection committee, which was finally decided should consist of three members, The Captain, Vice-Captain and Mr Halstead. A proposal, by a facetious member, that the annual meeting should be held in future, prior to the dinner, was greeted with loud laughter, but nothing definite was decided. At the termination of the meeting a 'Smoker', under the presidency of Captain W.E.Grundy, followed, at which Messrs Vincent Walker, A.Dunphy, Powell, Hornsby, G.Harding, C.Luckman, and Reginald Taylor, took part. Mr Jack Roberts presided at the pianoforte in his usually able and efficient manner.

In May 1904 a match was played between representatives of the club and the Llandudno Hockey Club. The cricket club led by skipper W.Grundy batted first and scored 161 for 1 dec. (A.Nicholls 87 not out). The hockey club replied with a respectable score of 134.

Bohemians Cricket Club

It was in 1904 a newly formed Llandudno Amateurs Cricket Club (later called the Bohemians Cricket Club) was engaged in their first match on home ground on the Council Field (now the Llandudno Retail Park) on the 17th June. It was against a Colwyn Bay 'A' side.

The Llandudno team was: T.E.Reid, J.R.Evans, J.Rainsford, E.V.Jones, H.P.Temple, J.Evans, E.Hobson, O.R.Hughes, J.Fowler, D.J.Roberts and A.Sidebottom.

This club had been formed by young boys who it was said did not feel comfortable playing alongside gentlemen, did not feel welcomed and that in some instances there was a question of lack of finances. There was no reason for any animosity between the two Llandudno clubs; in fact a match was played on the Council Field on 30th July 1904 between the newcomers and a Llandudno XI. The visitors won by 42 runs.

At the Llandudno cricket club dinner on 26th October 1904, Mr Chamberlain, who was presiding over the meeting, said that he had made enquiries as to why these young members of their club who were now playing on the Council Field where the wicket would be a little rough and the ball would bounce badly, did not want to join the club. The general feeling amongst the lads was that they did not think they could fit in with 'men of honour' and there was also the question of cost. Mr Chamberlain went on to say that this was not as it should be. He said that every member should be made to feel that he was welcome and if it was a question of finances felt sure that the Llandudno Cricket Club would sort out this matter and make it easier for the young men to join the club. They would then have an excellent ground to play on and every opportunity offered to them of developing into really good cricketers.

The MCC and the 'no ball' rules

At a special general meeting of the MCC held at the Lord's ground on 28th October 1899 the proposed alterations to Rule 10 and Rule 45 empowering the umpire at the batsman's end equally with the umpire at the bowler's end to 'no ball' for throwing was unanimously carried. It was agreed that either umpire who does not agree to the fairness of the bowl where the ball is thrown or jerked can call out 'no ball'. The alteration in Rule 10 was first suggested in 1884 when the controversy about throwing was at its height. It was no longer practical for a bowler who might have been 'no balled' at one end to immediately change ends to bowl at the other end where he might be favoured by the biased umpire at that end.

At the same gathering of members on the 26th October held at the Imperial Hotel there followed after the dinner the Annual General Meeting of the club. The secretary, Howell Jones, presented the following report: "We had the most pleasant and successful season. The club is in a flourishing and sound condition both as to the number of members and the finances. The members have shown great keenness and enthusiasm in the game and our supporters have been liberal and prompt in their assistance. I consider that the foundations of a really ideal club have been laid and that with time and care we shall have the finest ground in North Wales which is in excellent condition. Lord Mostyn, our landlord, has further improved it by putting up galvanizing fencing. On the field we have been very successful in the majority of the 18 matches played. We won 10, lost 6, and drew 2."

At this meeting there was a lot said regarding the lamented death of Mr M.W.Jones. The club had lost one of its oldest and best supporters of the time. He worked hard and continuously for many years for the good of the club. His death was a great loss to local cricket circles as his experience was of great service.

Very much 'against the grain' of today's affluent modern society the thinking in those days by some of the Llandudno club members was against following the practice of the old cricket club in engaging the services of a professional when they had a balance in hand. They doubted whether a professional in a town of the character of Llandudno did the club any material good and some were certain a professional would take away any surplus they would otherwise have.

The first International hockey match was played at the Oval on 11th February 1905. This was a match – Wales v Scotland. The cricket club pavilion facilities were made available to the players and officials on the day.

The weather for cricket proved ideal on 15th May 1905, and a fair number of spectators put in an appearance to welcome the Betws-y-Coed Cricket Club, who were to oppose the local eleven on the field. A capital wicket had been prepared, and the fact it wore well was proved by the large score put together by the home team. The visitors won the toss and batted first, but failed to take advantage of an excellent batting wicket. They were dismissed for a meagre 79 runs. The chief factor in the downfall of the Betws-y-Coed batsmen was O.Briggs, who bowled throughout the innings and captured six wickets for just 20 runs, finishing off the innings by accomplishing a hat-trick. The three wickets being clean bowled. Howel Jones took three wickets, with the remaining wicket being credited to A.Halstead. Of the Betws-y-Coed men, Griffiths, Hassall, Watts, and R.O.Edwards reached double figures, the latter being not out at the close. Hassall gave a splendid display and had scored 19 before Briggs bowled him with a beauty. Briggs and Gaythorne opened the home club's innings, but the latter was caught off Hassall for five, with the score at 20. When S.Ell joined Briggs, a prolonged stand was made. The bowling at the start was very good but was gradually worn down by the batsmen with the ball cleverly dispatched to all parts of the ground. The Betws-y-Coed score was passed without a second wicket falling, following which S.Ell made a big drive clean out of the playing portion of the ground. Briggs' total reached 79 before he was bowled by Ironside. It was a capital display, and well merited the applause from the spectators. Briggs was never in difficulties, and placed the ball with great accuracy. S.Ell retired with his score at 51, which included some lively drives to the boundary. Halstead contributed 13, and then another prolonged stand was made between C.N.Jones and Fairless, who defied all attempts to dislodge them until call of time. The innings had ended on 230 for four wickets. The spectators were delighted with the free scoring of the home batsmen, and warmly applauded the home team's victory.

Score Card:

Betws-y-Coed: V.F.Ward c and b Briggs 5, Griffiths c and b Howel Jones 13, A.E.Young b Howel Jones 3, J.R.Horsley b Briggs 4, H.Stone, b Howel Jones 9, R.L.Hassall b Briggs 19, C.Watts b Briggs 1, R.O.Edwards b Halstead 12, P.Ironside b Briggs 0, W.H.Roland b Briggs 0, Extras 3 Total 79.

Llandudno: O.Briggs, b Ironside 79, G.H.Gaythorne c Stone b Hassall 5, S.Ell retired 51, A.Halstead c Roose b Ward 13 C.N.Jones not out 44, O.Fairless b Watts 23. W.E.Dix, E.Jones, A.Nicholls, A.G.Rogers, Howel Jones, did not bat. Extras: 15; Total 230

In June 1905 a letter was read out at a meeting of the Llandudno Works Committee of the Town Council from the secretary of the cricket club requesting permission for a notice board advertising the cricket matches on the Oval. This, it was hoped, would encourage visitors to go down and watch the game, and would be fixed to a permanent position either on the promenade or in Mostyn Street. The request was granted. Where is this Notice Board today?

In the same year Lord Mostyn was present at the Annual Dinner held at the North Western Hotel on Monday 24th October 1905. He agreed to present the Toast to the Llandudno Cricket Club and had much to say regarding the development of the club over the years.

He remembered clearly when the Llandudno Cricket Club started as well as the excitement it created. They all thought then that they were all going to be great cricketers. They laid down a good cricket ground. They didn't think they could be disputed in any way. They spent a large sum of money on it and then invited the MCC down to come and play on it. The members of the MCC team all agreed that it was one of the best grounds they had played on and some of them even remarked that if the club continued to pursue the intended improvements, in two or three years' time Llandudno could have one of the best and nicest grounds in the North. They had a special cricket week to commence with but unfortunately the MCC were good cricketers and too strong for them and they enjoyed a good week of 'leather bashing'. The old club eventually grew to be a very strong one but for some reason or other the club became defunct. So for a number of years afterwards they had no cricket club in Llandudno. Then the present club came into existence and attempted to reinstate cricket in the town and he congratulated all who were involved in the venture and the way it had been conducted. He understood that they had had a most successful season and from the report read to them by the secretary he had concluded that the cricket played had been good. He was very pleased to see the way the club was being supported when the long list of Vice-Presidents was read out. What the club wanted was more encouragement and to see more visitors to the ground to watch matches and the press giving a better coverage in the local newspapers. He was not able to explain why it should be so, but there was no denying that cricket did not seem to appeal to the masses in Wales like football did. Nevertheless cricket was still regarded 'King of Games' and he trusted that as the club progressed it would increase in popularity and in years to come they would have better players. He was very glad to know they had a 2nd XI and hoped the club do all it could to encourage the juniors. They had presented a bat that evening to a junior who had a remarkably good record and Lord Mostyn hoped they would see him playing regularly in the 1st XI next year.

His Lordship then referred to the great need of cricket matches among the North Wales counties and said he remembered that some years ago on the Llandudno ground they played a cricket match that was called a county match. Although they did their best to keep the fixture going on a regular basis they were unable to do so. Lord Mostyn suggested that a certain number of county matches should be played annually and that grounds at Denbigh, Mostyn and Llandudno would be suitable for this. There had been one match during the year between Flintshire and Denbighshire. He saw no reason why other counties could not arrange games and that as many as eight or ten county matches be played during a season.

Dr Lochart Mars, a vice-president, stood up at the meeting and said the club was honoured to have Lord Mostyn to propose the toast and that the honour belonged to him for without his Lordship he did not think there would be a Llandudno Cricket Club. His Lordship had been the moving spirit in the original formation of the club and it was due to his generosity that the wheels rolled on smoothly. He warmly supported the idea of endeavouring to arrange Welsh County matches and felt that the club should go one further and see that a North Wales Association be formed. He felt sure that such an association would do an immense amount of good to the game in the principality and he hoped in time they would be strong enough to meet not only second class but first class English Counties.

In reply Mr O.Briggs said that there were many in the room who had a longer and more integral connection with the club than he had and with the duty that had been entrusted to them. In most towns the cricket club was looked upon as a public institution and its non-success eagerly criticised. He thought their record in 1905 was a credit to the town. Following a good year in 1904 it had been even better in 1905 having played 19 games and only losing four – making it evident that the Llandudno club was as great as any in the district. The batting averages showed that the players were very talented. Eleven players were averaged in double figures. The results were evident that the Llandudno team had been playing some first-class cricket and that the club would be able to hold its own with any amateur club in the country.

Regarding the future, Mr Briggs felt three hours was not sufficient time in which to finish a game and hoped consideration would be given to question this matter for the next season.

Rules of the Game

If a fielder stops the ball with his cap, five runs (as a penalty) are added to the striker's score.

If a dog ran onto the field to chase the ball and carried it over the boundary the rules state four runs to the batsman.

1906-1913

North Wales County Cricket Association

During the winter of 1906, an important one in many respects was the inauguration of the North Wales Cricket Association. There was no doubt that the honours belonged to the Llandudno Cricket Club in the action that had been taken. The fact that Lord Mostyn had been elected as the first President of the Association was to ensure Llandudno would profit in staging some of the county matches on the Oval. However, the main objective of the Association was to foster the game in the Principality and for that reason alone deserved the support of all the clubs in North Wales.

Members of the Bohemians had formally been invited to join the premier club and the way had been made smooth for them to do so. The club received several recruits which enabled the club to field eight 2nd XI matches during the season.

A match against West Derby, a well-known Liverpool side, on 2nd June 1906, was slightly delayed because they had chosen the Irish Sea as the means of transport by steamer ship from the Liverpool Docks which was late arriving at the Llandudno Pier.

A two-day match on 22/23 August 1906 between Caernarvonshire and Flintshire played at the Oval was the first match between counties arranged by the North Wales Cricket Association.

During 1906 there were 25 playing members and only ten had their own bats so the club decided to purchase six new bats.

In June 1906 it was reported that a new cricket club had been formed in Llandudno by members of the Holy Trinity Church situated in Mostyn Street. The Holy Trinity Choir boys and the boys attending Sunday school had been organised jointly into a Cricket Club, of which the Rev. W.E.Jones had been elected captain. All Church boys had been invited to join the club, out of which it was hoped in time, that members of the Church Lads' Brigade would also join. There was a request for assistance from anyone willing to help organise this new venture set up by the Holy Trinity Church officials.

During the season five centuries were scored, which was a record for the Club. C.L.Fairless 100 not out in a practice game; O.Briggs 100 not out against West Derby; G.Field 116 against Rhuddlan; Rev. N.I.E.Alban 108 not out against Mostyn; Dr Mure 118 against Llanrwst.

The first Annual General Meeting of the North Wales Cricket Association was held at the Alexandra Hotel, Rhyl on 2nd February 1907. Lord Mostyn was re-elected President and E.P.Morris (Llandudno) Secretary.

Denbighshire were congratulated on their unbeaten record, Flintshire for its organisation and Caernarvonshire for its praiseworthy efforts in raising teams in spite of the scarcity of players and other disadvantages not mentioned.

At the Annual General Meeting of the club held on 11th November 1907 some concern was shown at the negative comments about cricket in Wales by the club captain, George Field. In his long-winded speech he threw a wet blanket over the proceedings and it required the tact and optimism of the President, Lord Mostyn, to fan the embers into anything like a blaze. He said perhaps Mr Field at heart was not quite so absolutely without hope for the future of cricket in Wales.

He was an Englishman and as such had not considered the matter of all its bearings and it was thought one of the facts may perhaps help to cheer him up. At the time and in the first place cricket was a comparatively recent introduction into Welsh life. In England for generations cricket had been the chief feature in village life. It was the common ground upon which men of every rank met on an 'equal playing field'. Many cricket legends has the village blacksmith as the hero and the Squire as another with the Parson coming in as the third partner in a dead heat. That being the case it was but natural that the youth of every English village took to cricket as ducks take to water. In fact they were born with the love of cricket in their veins. This was not the case in Wales but Lord Mostyn went on to say there was no reason why it should not be so although it was unlikely it would attain such a strong hold because of the popularity of football in Wales. In his opinion, with which many agreed, cricket demands the element of patience and stubborn determination the Welshman of the day lacks but is hoped in time will acquire.

Attempts had been made in Llandudno to encourage cricket among lads who were likely to be residents in the town and expected to join the club. Every private school in the district had a cricket team including John Bright County School which had a headmaster like Mr Thompson, a keen cricketer. The John Bright school team was the champion school team in the district at the time. A trophy for a competition among the schools was offered as an incentive. It was hoped that the authorities could see their way to permit youth matches on a Saturday morning on the Oval.

During the year many improvements had been carried out by Lord Mostyn on the ground at a cost of over £60.

The 1907 season was not a good one due to the fact that many playing members resigned because they had been struck by 'golf fever'. The great difficulty was raising a decent away team because many of the players left were unavailable. Lord Mostyn said that he was very sorry that from a playing point of view the last season had not been as successful as the previous one. He had read with great interest the reference to 'golf fever' and admitted he had also become a victim. He agreed that with fewer than 22 players, and those not being available every week, the time had arrived when it was very necessary to earnestly encourage young boys to join the club otherwise it would not be possible to see two teams playing regularly. He wanted the ground made full use of as in the past. More members were required but none were forthcoming. The conditions in 1907 were a lot different to a few years previously. The spirit that animated young men 15 years ago was no longer evident. The ground was failing to attract. Llandudno had grown into a large town yet it was sadly lacking in attractions. The ground was being underused because of a lack of fixtures at weekends. There were no tennis tournaments or special cricket weeks. However, Lord Mostyn said that it was not all doom and gloom as he was witnessing in other districts a revival interest in the game which he optimistically felt would 'catch on' in Llandudno in time.

Not for many years had the cricket club had such a bad start as in 1908. Against Bangor Normal College batting first they could only score 38 runs and against Llanrwst just 28 runs after Llanrwst had scored 246 for eight declared. There was concern from a player's point of view that the club had not enjoyed a successful season. The main reason for that was the difficulty in raising a decent side for the away matches. In 1908 to win a match was an exceptional occurrence. Not all was doom and gloom though. The season did actually end in great style, when they met and defeated Rhyl Commercials on 13th September. The club had not exactly covered itself with glory during the summer, but two records were set that Saturday which stood for some time. The first was the partnership for the first wicket between Messrs Halstead and A.N.Wills, who scored 178 without being separated, Wills making 104 and Halstead 70. The second was the bowling feat of Bird, who sent down 12 overs for just four runs and capturing two wickets in the process. Eleven of the 12 overs were maidens, ten being in succession. In reply to the home total the Commercials could only score 51, and were therefore well beaten. Halstead took four wickets for three runs, taking the last three wickets in one over.

Visit of HMS Exmouth and HMS Cornwallis of the Atlantic Fleet

On the 28th September 1908 the visit to Llandudno was made by two battleships, HMS Exmouth and HMS Cornwallis of the Atlantic Fleet. A cricket match between a Llandudno eleven and officers of the Atlantic Fleet was held during the day on the Oval which proved to be a very pleasant encounter. There were a large number of spectators at the match including the officials connected with the town's welcoming committee. The game ended in a draw but in favour of the naval men, whose first five batsmen evidently believed in the theory of hitting hard and often, for they laid on the wood in fine style. When they had been dismissed the total was 190, and when 14 more runs were scored for two further wickets the innings was declared. In reply, Llandudno found the target of 204 runs too much and had scored only 80 for four wickets by the end of play.

Llandudno team: Rev. W.E.Jones, A.N.Wills, N.Jones, A.Carter, T.W.Orton, E.Jones, F.Foulds, E.Parry, E.P.Morris, Howell Jones, P.Halstead.

Afternoon tea was provided at the ground. The Admiral Curzon Howe, the Commander of the Atlantic Fleet, commented on how the officers and men had thoroughly appreciated the reception they had received from the town officials and the people of Llandudno. He actually apologised because he was only able to bring two battleships. He said HMS Duncan, which was due to make the journey, was detained owing to some measurement tests being incomplete.

Thousands visited the vessels during the day. The Llandudno Pier Company and the steam boat companies provided boats for people to get close to the battleships. Owing to the crush of passengers and the rough sea there was much physical inconvenience amongst the sightseers who were willing to inspect the vessels at close quarters. Even a heavy rainstorm could not dampen the enthusiasm. A huge bonfire was lit in their honour on the Great Orme in the Happy Valley area. A fireworks display created a good deal of interest as well as the 'search light' display from the ships. Pickpockets and purse snatchers were busy during the fireworks. One lady had her hand-bag cut away and the handle left hanging on her arm. The snatcher got away with a five pound note and some other valuables.

Shortly after 10pm that evening the vessels steamed away to join the rest of the fleet docked just off Blackpool Bay, thus ending a memorable day capturing an historical event for Llandudno and the local cricket club.

HMS Exmouth remained in service until April 1919.

HMS Cornwallis was serving in the Mediterranean waters when on 9th January 1917 she was lost to a torpedo from a German submarine. She remained afloat long enough for most of her crew to abandon ship although 15 men of her complement of 720 died as a result of the explosion of the torpedo.

The need for engaging a professional for the 1909 season was now pressing. Lord Mostyn reduced the rent of the ground as an experiment to see if the engagement of a professional and coach would bring out young players. Mr A.E.Hartley from Lymm was engaged. The record speaks for itself as to the all-round improvement. Played 26, won 16, lost six and drawn four was regarded by the club as a most satisfactory season. Mr Hartley was an acquisition to the club and no doubt a great deal to do with the success. Lord Mostyn felt it had been made obvious that it was practically essential to have a professional and that they had to decide whether they could afford to engage a man for the 1910 season. He said he would reduce the rent again to £15 if the professional cut and rolled the pitch as part of his duties.

The first match of the 1910 season was cancelled owing to the death of King Edward VII on 6th May.

Conwy fielded a side on the Oval one afternoon in July 1910 which included a well-known policeman. Robert was known to be on night duty which was the subject of discussion in the pavilion. "He must be keen on the game to sacrifice his sleep," observed one person. "How tired he must be when he goes on duty at night." "Not a bit," replied another, "that's when he sleeps."

As well as the rent being reduced the junior subscription was reduced to 5s which resulted in some promising recruits.

The following letter appeared in the Welsh Coast Pioneer on 28th July 1910:

"Dear Sir,

The Llandudno Cricket Club is at present doing remarkably well, and each game attracts a good number of spectators. I do not for a moment wish to complain, but if public spirit is to be fostered, and cricket brought up to the standard that all enthusiasts would like to see, I feel sure that a few comfortable seats placed on the ground would be thoroughly appreciated by all. Quite frequently, two or three hundred spectators are present, but the seating accommodation is inadequate. I am aware that this would cost money, and venture to suggest that a bazaar or concert might be arranged in order to raise the necessary funds. - an enthusiast"

The annual dinner of the Llandudno Cricket Club was held on 1st November 1910 at the Clarence Hotel. Lord Mostyn, the president, occupied the chair, and R.S.Chamberlain was the vice-chairman. The President gave the toast of the Llandudno Cricket Club. He said the club was really going strong, but in his opinion he thought the pavilion now standing on the ground was no longer able to provide all the facilities required to meet the needs of its members and guests. He went on to say that if the club would start a movement for providing a better pavilion he would do his best to help it along. The Rev W.E.Jones (captain) responded by suggesting that next year they should arrange a "cricket week". He felt that if they had a really good pavilion they would be able to invite some well-established and well-known cricket clubs from over the border in England which would be a great attraction for the people of the town. Mr J.J.Marks proposed a toast to "The Chairman and the Vice-Chairman". Lord Mostyn in his reply expressed his great interest in cricket and in the Llandudno club and what the future might hold. Mr Chamberlain referred to the early days of cricket in Llandudno, 40 years ago, when enough players always made themselves available for matches played on a rough piece of ground near the West Shore then. Now it had become sometimes difficult to find sufficient players locally and also great difficulty in making use of the players who came to stay in the hotels and boarding houses who were invited to play. He said he would like to see more of the youth of the town brought into the game, and facilities given for admitting them, especially to the practices in the evenings, when, as Mr Marks had suggested, sides of some sort might be arranged and better practice and fielding obtained. Mr Chamberlain pleaded for more financial support from non-cricketers and old cricketers.

The professional A.E.Hartley was re-engaged for the 1911 season.

Railings were placed round the front of the pavilion keeping the space reserved for players and members.

Further seating for spectators was added near the tennis courts.

It was hoped more subscribing members would join the club as more revenue was required. Mr Lloyd George's land taxes collected from recreation grounds, including the Oval, had to be paid. It was calculated there would be an extra tax of £20 a year the club would need to find.

A concert in aid of the cricket club was held in the Town Hall on 26th April 1911. The Rector, The Reverend Llewelyn R.Hughes, presided and in the course of a short speech eulogised cricket as a manly sport. There was a piano forte solo and songs from Gilbert and Sullivan.

Lady Henrietta Augusta Nevil Lloyd Mostyn died on 25th January 1912. Born in 1830 she was the daughter of the 9th Earl of Abergavenny and mother of Lord Mostyn.

A match was played on the Oval against the Great Orme Golf Club. The golfers won by 93 runs.

There had been grievance felt by some of the young members of the Bohemians which was said had been sorted out in 1912. In place of the Bohemians a new club had been formed composed mainly of the Llandudno Amateurs Football Club who played on the Council Field. It was known that members of that club were very keen and practised assiduously every night until it was dark and had fixtures arranged throughout the season from May to September. Back at the Oval concern was expressed at the reduction in receipts from subscriptions and it was felt that the blame was due to the running of another team in the town. However, the other town club did not re-form after 1912 and some of them did become new members. Also the new Shop Hours Act came into force which granted a half-day to shop assistants who could now join the club. Matches were arranged mid-week for their benefit.

The engagement of a professional/groundsman, the former Llanrwst player, Mr Orton, for the 1913 season was announced. As well as his talent on the field with bat and ball his quality as coach at bringing out the latent abilities of the younger players was well known.

The 1913 season turned out to be very successful both on and off the field. The club's finances had improved due to an increase in Vice-Presidents, playing members, gate receipts and also more receipts in tea money. Playing members had increased by one-fifth and gate receipts had doubled.

An attempt had been made by the Llandudno CC to form a North Wales Coast Association by approaching Bangor, Llanrwst, Rhuddlan, Mostyn and Prestatyn on the matter. For various reasons nearly all the clubs could not see their way to fall in with the suggestion. The only exception was Rhuddlan which was as enthusiastic as Llandudno in the matter. The prospect therefore had fallen through.

It was especially interesting that there was a great revival of interest in cricket at a time when golf was still making such great strides. Still more could be done and it had been considered then that some arrangement could be made possible for boys in the County School to be encouraged to attend coaching sessions at the Oval which was thought would make for the future prosperity of the game in Llandudno.

The report of the Recreations Ground Committee of the Urban District Council on the terms of Lord Mostyn for the sale of the cricket ground was as follows: That having regard to the large expenditure involved the committee are unable to recommend to the Council to agree to the purchase of the land, but would recommend that application be made to Lord Mostyn for a long lease of the land at a reasonable rent as possible having regard to the purposes for which the land is required.

A Cricket Story

At a cricket match in Yorkshire in 1904 an appeal was made against the batsman for obstructing the field. The visiting side were not quite sure which umpire should be asked so some asked one and some the other. Umpire No. 1 said, "Out". Umpire No. 2 said, "Not Out". Consequently a dispute ensued. At last Umpire No.1 stalked up to Umpire No.2. "Have you shaken hands with Lord Hawke?" he demanded imperiously. "No," said No.2. "Well I have – Out" came the reply. That settled it and the batsman sheepishly left the field.

1914-1918

First World War – The War Years

Sport, and cricket in particular, was passing through a trying time owing to the war. Unfortunately the war broke out just as the season was at its height but in the year 1914 the club was able to complete all its fixtures. The year 1915 was very different. Owing to the fact that a considerable number of playing members of the club had joined the Forces it was decided no regular fixtures be entertained for the coming season. In fact no fixtures were possible because no club in North Wales or out of Wales had applied to play. However it was agreed for the benefit of the troops who were stationed locally the club should be kept alive to arrange matches for their benefit.

A match did take place on 1st June 1918 at the Maesdu ground (present home of the Llandudno Rugby Club) between Llandudno Post Office staff and the Royal Engineers who were stationed in Llandudno. The match was arranged by Mr Chandler (well-known as the official scorer of the Llandudno Cricket Club). At the request of the Royal Engineers, Mr Tipton (another member of Llandudno CC) was elected captain of the Post Office staff and after winning the toss he decided to send in the Engineers to bat first on a hard wicket. The soldiers scored 77 runs. Mr Tipton bowled well capturing nine wickets for 35 runs. This was considered an excellent performance against men in full training and the fact he had not bowled for two years. However, it was the soldiers who won the day. They proved too strong and went on to win the match by 20 runs. The Royal Engineers provided the tea on the field.

Cricket Gear Wanted

An item appeared in the Advertiser asking readers if they had any cricket gear they could dispense with for the men of the 16th Battalion for the use of the soldiers at the front.

The first cricket match on the Oval since 1914 was played on 22nd July 1916 against The Royal Engineers. A collection was taken on the ground in aid of wounded soldiers in local military hospitals.

There was a large crowd on the Oval in August at the gymkhana event which had been entirely arranged by wounded soldiers domiciled at St Tudno and Plas Tudno hospitals. Spectators numbered close on 5,000 and the object was to raise a fund sufficient for providing and equipping 40 more beds and other necessities at these hospitals. The band of the 3rd Border Regiment provided the music. There was an auction of a box of chocolates which the winner gave to Private Edward Law V.C., D.C.M. who was present on this occasion. All the prizes on the day were distributed by Lady Mostyn who was attended by Lord Mostyn. Lord Mostyn referred to the pleasure it gave to him and Lady Mostyn for an opportunity to meet Private Edward Law and how proud they all were to have his presence at the event as it was believed he had won such a distinguished medal as the Victoria Cross for his bravery on the battle field in the name of 'King and Country'.

It was not until 100 years later in 2014, when historian Adrian Hughes, Custodian of the Home Front War Museum in Llandudno, had done an in-depth research on Private Law that it was realised no person of that name had won a distinguished medal for bravery in the 1st World War. Private Law told the Advertiser that he was in the Gordon Highlanders and was awarded the Victoria Cross on 17th March 1915. Adrian said that he couldn't find any VC winner with that name serving in any regiment let alone the Gordon Highlanders. Private Law also maintained that he was on holiday from America when he enlisted in the army in 1914 and that he gained a medical degree before heading out to America. In America he apparently was a cowboy for seven years in Montana before setting up a fruit and veg business! The conclusion is that Private Law was a fraud and had 'pulled the wool over the eyes' of Lord and Lady Mostyn and everyone else at the event. Adrian commented that it was not uncommon for some men in those days to return from the war and claim they had won distinguished medals, with probably the sole intention to impress and to 'win over the ladies'! Newspapers in those days were hungry for good news stories and with no real way of checking, just went along with Private Law's claim.

The Home Front Museum, situated in New Street, Llandudno, was established in 2000 to give visitors and local residents an insight into life in Britain during the Second World War. Curator Adrian Hughes has also carried out detailed research into the roles played by Llandudno during the war, when it hosted the Inland Revenue (moved from London to escape bombing raids), the Royal Artillery's Coastal Gunnery School, US Army personnel and others. His research activities also cover the effects of the First and Second World Wars on communities across Wales.

Following the gymkhana, on 20th September was a sports meeting in aid of the funds for the Caernarvonshire Volunteer Regiment which again attracted a large crowd. In addition to events for the volunteers there were events for NCOs and men of the Royal Engineers and the 3rd Border Regiment. The highlight was a wrestling competition in the Cumberland style. The Llandudno Town Band conducted by Mr F.L.Traversi added to the pleasure of the afternoon. Col. J.E.Groves, Lord Lieutenant of the County, presided over the meeting. He was accompanied by Col. C.E.Dixon, County Commandant, Col. Lloyd Mostyn O.C. No.1 Battalion, Col. C.H.Derbyshire, Major W.Hesketh-Hughes T.D., O.C of the No.2 Battalion and the Hon W.W.Vivian, O.C. Motor Battalion.

Other events included pillow fighting and threading the needle race for wounded soldiers.

Cricket on the Somme.

'Taffy' Thomas had a story to tell when he returned to his home in Llandudno from the 1st World War. It was of his friend and colleague 'Spider' Webb:

'Spider' Webb was a Cockney – from Stepney, I believe – who was with us on the Somme in 1916. He was a splendid cricketer.

We had had a very stiff time for six or seven hours and were resting during a lull in the firing. Then suddenly Jerry sent over five shells. After a pause another shell came over and burst near to Spider and his two pals.

When the smoke cleared I went across to see what had happened.

Spider's two pals were beyond help. The Cockney was propping himself up with his elbows surveying the scene.

"What's happened, Webb?" I said. "Blimey! What's happened?" was the reply. "One over – two bowled" (and, looking down at his leg) – "and I'm stumped."

Then he fainted.

Airship Stopped Play

In Llandudno Cricket Club's 124 year history at the Oval, there could never have been an incident as strange as the day an airship interrupted play on the last day of June 1918.

Since the autumn of 1915 there had been a Royal Naval Airship Station on Anglesey and it was their duty to escort and protect the merchant ships of the Atlantic convoys from the menace of German submarines.

On that sunny afternoon, while a match progressed on the Oval an airship was experiencing engine trouble overhead. The pilot scribbled a note and dropped it onto the wicket below and while he circled he watched as they first studied the piece of paper and then formed an arrow pointing into the wind. As the airship descended he threw out his trail rope and, like a trained landing party, the cricketers and spectators rushed forward and hauled down the balloon. The engineer diagnosed the problem to be a dirty spark plug, which was soon replaced, and the engine re-started. The pilot thanked his helpers and to great cheers, the airship took to the air and the match resumed.

It was not the first time that mechanical trouble had forced a Royal Naval airship to land at Llandudno. Anyone sat on the promenade on the afternoon of 26th April 1918 would have seen the curious sight of a trawler towing a semi inflated 'blimp' out in the bay. That morning, just before dawn, airship Z35 – with a crew of three – took off from Llangefni, tasked with searching for a German submarine that had been seen near to the Formby Lightship. After several hours the engine seized and the on-board engineer was unable to re-start it. As the craft drifted towards the North Wales coast, its Mayday message was picked up by an armed trawler which came to its aid. The initial plan was to tow the craft to Red Wharf Bay but with the wind strengthening, a heavy swell and patchy fog, it was decided to try for Llandudno as the Great Orme was visible through the gloom. From their billets in the town a platoon of soldiers was summoned to the end of the pier and took over the tow rope from the trawler, walking the stricken airship, high in the air, to the promenade and soon after five, tethered it close to the Hydro Hotel.

A large crowd milled around, excited at seeing the huge silver balloon moored at such close quarters. The police roped off the area and people were warned about the dangers of smoking in the vicinity of the hydrogen filled airship! Meanwhile the pilot, Lieutenant Williams, was invited to take a bath and a meal at the Hydro Hotel but when dressing after his wash found he had no tie to wear for dinner. He was lent one by the hotel manager but recalled that it *"was very gaudy for a Naval Officer and caused considerable amusement"*.

In the meantime mechanics had arrived from Llangefni to fix the engine of the airship and inflate the balloon's envelope and by eight that evening the craft took off "between two lamp standards" for the 40 minute flight back to Anglesey.

The Llandudno Cricket Club, acting, they believed, in the best interest of the county, closed down and except an odd game or two with military elevens, cricket had been a dead duck in Llandudno during the war years. The spirit actuating the decision to close down was because the existence of the nation was at stake and they felt it would not be right to go on playing games as if the deadly conflict in which the nation was involved was of no concern. It was also influenced by the fact that many of the younger players had 'signed up' as volunteers to play their part in the deadly war.

It was reported on 28th September 1918 that 60 American soldiers were due to come to Llandudno to play a game of baseball in aid of military charities. Unfortunately the game had to be cancelled when it was discovered that the cricket field (the Oval) was not large enough for the purpose.

The war took the lives of three regular playing members. They were Captain Phil Hornsby, a good bowler and an excellent bat; Sgt. Ted Jones, one of the best bowlers the club ever had; and Private Bob

Roberts of the Northumberland Fusiliers, noted as a promising young player.

Llandudno Cenotaph

Captain John Philip Skipworth Hornsby

He served with the South Wales Borderers 10th Battalion 'A' Company. He died on 2nd September, 1918, aged 29. He was the son of the Headmaster of the Llandudno Church School. Served on the Western Front in 1914 and sent home in December of that year suffering from frost bite. He was then commissioned as an Officer in the South Wales Borderers, a regiment that did most of its training in Colwyn Bay.

A talented cricketer he once took six wickets for 16 runs for Llandudno in 1914 against a Mostyn XI.

Sergeant William Edward (Ted) Jones

He served with the North Lancashire Regiment, 9th Battalion. He died during active service on 9th July, 1916.

There were some Llandudno men who died for their country in the 1st World War who were not mentioned in the newspapers or even listed on the town's 'Roll of Honour'.

Many John Bright School 'old boys' distinguished themselves during the Great War. Twenty boys made the supreme sacrifice. Their names were inscribed upon a Memorial Tablet of oak and copper which was erected in the school Assembly Hall.

The 24[h] May 1919 had been set aside as a day of gratification and recognition of the services rendered by boys of Llandudno during the Great War. Shortly after the outbreak of the war, at the instigation of the present Prime Minister, Brigadier-General Sir Owen Thomas came to Llandudno and interviewed the Chairman of the Urban District Council (Mr F.J.Sarn) with the object of raising a Welsh Brigade of the Royal Welsh Fusiliers, to be trained at Llandudno. Within a short space of time the fashionable seaside resort was transformed into a garrison town, entertaining over 7,000 soldiers. In a great tragedy such as the First World War, it was inevitable that though many had returned there were others who had been left behind as sacrifices on the altar of patriotic duty. No fewer than 130 Llandudno men made the supreme sacrifice for our sake. It is estimated that no fewer than 2,500 men of Llandudno served their King and country in that war. This was a remarkable proportion of the 12,000 odd inhabitants at that time having regard to the fact that Llandudno was more or less a lodging-house community, and the majority of its inhabitants naturally consisted of women and children. It was just four years before, on Sunday, September 4th, 1915, that the last battalion left Llandudno. It was the 17th Battalion, Royal Welsh Fusiliers, which was commanded by Colonel the Hon. Henry Lloyd Mostyn. The battalion were accorded a civic send-off at the railway station. On that occasion, in addressing the crowd at the railway station, Colonel Mostyn's parting words were:

"I ask that a privilege be granted this battalion, that if we return heroes, may we have the privilege of marching through the streets of the town with fixed bayonets."

Some of them had moved to Winchester for final training in August 1915 where they all met up again and proceeded to France in December 1915. In July 1916 they were in action at Mametz Wood on the Somme, suffering severe casualties. The Division did not return to major action for more than 12 months. In 1917 they were in action in the Third Battles of Ypres, in 1918 they were in action on The Somme, in the Battles of the Hindenburg Line and the Final Advance in Picardy. Demobilisation began in December 1918 and was complete by June 1919.

Although not carrying fixed bayonets, the gallant Colonel Mostyn had his desire more or less gratified by marching through the streets of the town at the head of his men and those of other branches of His Majesty's Forces. The 24th May 1919 was being observed as a general holiday, and all demobilised men had been granted a holiday with a full day's pay. The promenade was gaily decorated with streamers of bunting, and several tradesmen in Mostyn Street had decorated their premises for the occasion. The first event of the day was a procession of demobilised men, which appropriately started from the railway station, the scene of their departure four years before. The procession left the station in the following order: Town Band (conducted by Bandmaster F.L.Traversi); members of the Llandudno Council and the General Committee, including Mr William Thomas, deputy-chairman of the Council; Councillors S.Chaitrev, Hugh Edwards, E.E.Bone, C.E.Sheln, Thomas Smith, Dr Thomas Datton, J.P., Messrs F.J.Sarson, Frank Edge, G.A.Humphreys, and William Arnold. Next came Colonel the Hon H. Lloyd Mostyn, J.P., followed by the following officers: Captain R.Cadwaladr, Lieut. C.Arnold, Lieut. Frank Collins, Lieut. Arthur Williams, and Lieut. Frank Thompson. They were followed by the demobilised men, with motor-cars at the rear carrying the wounded and convalescent. The procession proceeded along Vaughan Street, up Mostyn Street, and along North Parade to the Pier Pavilion. At the Pier Pavilion a united memorial service to Llandudno's fallen heroes was held. Seats were reserved in the body of the hall for the officers and men, and the gallery and the back of the hall was crowded with the general public. This was presided over by the Rev. E.0.Davies, B.Sc., with Mr John Roberts (Arwynfa) as the official presenter. The service opened with the singing of the hymn 'O God, our help in ages past', after which the Rev. J.F.Reese, B.A., vicar of Llanrhos, recited a suitable form of prayer. The Rev. John Raymond conducted an alternative reading of Psalm 103, after which the Welsh hymn 'O Fryniau Caersalem' was sung. A portion of Scripture was read in Welsh by the Rev. Charles Jones. The hymn 'For ever with the Lord' having been sung, the Rev. William Evans, pastor of the English Congregational Church, read another portion of Scripture in English, after which a Welsh prayer was offered by the Rev. Evan Hughes. A deep impression was then created by the singing of the hymn 'Jew, lover of my soul' to the well-known Welsh tune to 'Aberystwyth'. At the conclusion some of the demobilised men were so carried away by the beautiful singing of this hymn that they called out for it to be sung over again in Welsh. The Chairman after having pronounced the Benediction, Corporal George Codman sounded the 'Last Post' and the memorable service came to an end. At the close of the service the Town Clerk (Mr A.Connolly) read a letter from Brigadier-General Sir Owen Thomas (who was indisposed), as follows:

"In the circumstances, I am very sorry it will be impossible for me to attend at Llandudno on the 24th to take part in the public honour to the men of Llandudno who so nobly served the country during the Great War. I have a personal connection with these men, most of whom were my own recruits, and boys of my brigade, therefore every one of them individually, I was privileged at one time to be their chief. I look back upon the period of my Welsh command and also the comradeship that existed between me and all ranks, as the proudest and most cherished of memories. My sympathy is with those who mourn for the brave boys who made the supreme sacrifice. I share their sorrows as one whose own home like theirs is shadowed by a cloud which nothing can remove. Please convey to all ranks my very best wishes and I should like you to tell them that I shall be with them in spirit, but sorely regret having to miss the opportunity of attending in person."

A letter was also read from Major Breese, MP, regretting his inability to attend owing to having to meet the Prime Minister at the opening of the War Memorial Hospital at Porthmadog. Dr Dalton (chairman of the organising Committee) announced that memorial tablets (made in bronze) would be given to the next of kin of every local man who had been killed in action, were missing or had died of wounds. A special design had been prepared by Mr G.A.Humphreys, F.R.I.B.A. at the request of the committee, and approved. A number of servicemen in hospital at Llandudno were entertained to lunch that day, and later to tea at the Town Hall. It was reported that an elaborate programme of athletics and other sports was arranged on the Cricket Field (the Oval) in the afternoon, to which servicemen and their families were admitted free, but a charge of one shilling was made for admission to the general public, which resulted in over

£70 being raised at the gate. The prizes, amounting in value to over £120, were given by the tradesmen of the town and augmented by the Sports Committee, of which Mr C.F.Farrington was the chairman and Councillor W.S.Williams the secretary. Despite the strong wind and driving rain that prevailed throughout the afternoon, it was reported that the events were witnessed by a large crowd.

1919-1923

The Revival of Cricket after the War

At a meeting in April 1919 it was decided that the time was right to revive the club but until the terms of the Mostyn Estate were ascertained for the use of the Oval again, a definite resolution to reform the club could not be made. The cricket ground since 1914 had been used for grazing purposes only and some work was needed to make it fit for cricket again. Arrangements for hockey, tennis and crown green bowls had already been made so there was every reason to believe that satisfactory terms with Mostyn Estate would be reached. Fortunately the terms offered were accepted and the Estate agreed to undertake putting the field in order, which, after a lapse of five years, would be a back-breaking task. The agreement was that the club would then be responsible for keeping the ground in a proper condition afterwards.

In 1922 it was reported that the process of building up the club after the war was proceeding slowly and that the outlook was fairly satisfying. There was a suggestion made from some quarters that Llandudno Cricket Club should join forces with Colwyn Bay Cricket Club. Fortunately this idea was dropped.

The opening match of the season created a lot of interest. A team of colts having got together by Councillor J.Taylor met a Llandudno XI. The Oval was crowded with spectators. The lane leading from Gloddaeth Avenue contained a long row of cars so that it was evident considerable interest was taken by families and friends of the players. The catering had been entrusted to Mr and Mrs Jack Payne of the Esplanade Hotel. A ladies' committee had been formed for the very first time to organise the afternoon teas on the ground.

Mr W.Ward, who had been on the Warwickshire County staff, was the new professional/groundsman for the 1922 season.

On the 24th June 1922 a letter 'to the editor' appeared in the Advertiser:

"Dear Sir – There are a lot of boys in Llandudno who wish to play cricket and other games after school hours but have nowhere to play. We think that it is up to the Town Council to provide us with a green field to play on. At present there is a notice up on part of the Council Field 'Trespassers will be prosecuted' and also on the cricket field. Most of the open spaces on the West Shore have a board up displaying a message that anyone playing cricket or any other games in that area will be prosecuted. A sum of 10s 6d is the fee asked for practising on the cricket field which is beyond our pockets. Where are the boys to play! Can we be sportsmen if we cannot practise or compete with the boys of other towns? – A young sport"

The cricket played by the home team during the 1922 season had its effect on the attendance and at every match all the deckchairs, at a cost of 3d each, had all been in use. The team had many young players who were felt laid the hope for the future. Several new players had joined during the season. The team played 27 matches and had won 14.

Negotiations were ongoing with Mostyn Estate to secure a long lease on the ground which was still on a year-to-year basis.

Some modern day cricketers will be surprised to learn that a proposal in 1922 to establish a cricket league was made and the general opinion being that if a workable scheme could be formulated it would be a great benefit to North Wales.

North Wales Cricket Association (League) 1922

The movement to establish a North Wales Cricket Association had been successful and league fixtures commenced the following year in 1923.

Before then the Association arranged a match at the Oval between a North Wales XI and South Wales (Glamorgan) on 23/24 May during a special cricket week. Sydney Barnes, the great English bowler and Test Player played for North Wales. Included in the side were three Llandudno players – Cyril Rowlands, C.P. Woods and club professional Ingham Pell.

Glamorgan won the match by six wickets. Sydney Barnes for the North Wales side took seven wickets for 57 runs in Glamorgan's first innings.

Amongst the spectators on the second day were Lord Mostyn and Lord Aberconwy.

One of the first matches Llandudno played in the newly formed league was against Colwyn Bay on 16th July 1923. It was on their new ground at Rhos on Sea. The wicket portion was just fairly good but the outfield was decidedly rough and the long grass had wisps of hay which was disconcerting to the fielders. For the record Llandudno trounced Colwyn Bay scoring 133. Colwyn Bay could only score 50. The new Llandudno professional, Ingham Bell, a left handed medium to fast bowler from Yorkshire, took eight wickets for 23 runs.

Twelve months before the league was formed there was no cricket club in Colwyn Bay and no cricket except that played at Rydal School. The new ground was privately purchased and in no time the club grew strong quickly. Lord Colwyn had accepted the office as President. The total cost of their project which included a pavilion was £4,500. Tributes in particular were paid to the new club which had in their first season managed to play 18 matches and though they were heavily defeated at the start they had laid the foundations of what would become one of the strongest teams in North Wales in years to come.

With the last league match played, St Asaph was the outright winner with Denbigh and Llanrwst joint second.

At the Annual General Meeting held at the Town Hall on 18th February 1924 it was agreed there was an urgent need for a new pavilion. The present pavilion was, as one letter said, a disgrace to the ground. The chairman, Chas F.Farrington reminded members present that the club was trying to get a long lease of the ground and that Mostyn Estate had forwarded a draft of a potential lease which, if accepted, meant they could proceed with a scheme to erect a new pavilion. The cricket committee had suggested a few amendments and were on the point of sending it back when unexpectedly Mostyn Estate recalled the draft. The reason given was that they were proceeding with their planning scheme and that improvements to the ground were contemplated in that scheme. Just one month later it was announced that Mostyn Estate had granted a lease for a period of 14 years. Having secured the lease of the ground the next step was a new pavilion.

Sir William Letts KBE (1873-1957) (Pioneer of the British Motor Trade and co-founder of the Automobile Association) was the special guest at that meeting and gave a speech in which he said he was extremely honoured to be invited and be asked to propose the toast by the club. He said he was delighted to be a Vice-President and although he was not able to attend many of the matches it was not because of lack of interest. He remembered that he and a few others in the room knew when the present cricket ground was a barren waste and that a kind of cricket pitch was where the golf house stood. Then with a number of gentlemen together, and with the good will of Lord Mostyn, the present ground was laid out and he did not know of a better one in North Wales. He went on to say the club had not accomplished without a struggle but it had kept going through thick and thin and realistically benefited the town.

The title of world's oldest permanent cricket ground is one that is hotly disputed, with at least three clubs in the south of England laying claim to the honour. They are Mitcham CC in Surrey (which claims to be hosting cricket since 1685), Firle in Sussex (1725) and the Vine Cricket Ground in Kent (1734).

1924-1938

The New Pavilion

The building was described as being of timber and asbestos sheeting with an interior lining on a brick foundation. The length would be 74 feet and the width 21 feet with a veranda along the front of the balcony above. Tiers for seats in front of the balcony forming three rises would further add to the seating accommodation. Inside would be a central club room with seating space for about 200 people and flanked on either side would be dressing rooms.

Monday 8th September 1924 happened to be a memorable day in the history of the club. Lord Mostyn was presented with a Golden Key on the occasion of the official opening of the new pavilion. The pavilion had been erected at a cost, including fittings, of £1,000. Chas F.Farrington presided at the opening ceremony and handed Lord Mostyn the Golden Key for keepsake and in doing so said that the occasion was a very interesting one in local cricket history. The present club was formed, or rather re-started 21 years ago, and had been run with success without a break, except during the war years when no cricket was played in the town. Up to 1924 the club had held the tenancy of the ground from year to year but due to the generosity of Lord Mostyn the club had been given a lease for 14 years at a very low rent of £25 a year. Having secured the lease the club felt justified in embarking upon the erection of a new pavilion, the need for which had been felt for a long time. The 'score box' was on the roof of the building and it was interesting to know then that the box was the body of an ancient stage coach rescued from Gloddaeth Hall which had been used by the Mostyn family. When that vehicle was in use for its purpose it was described as the 'Rolls Royce' of the period and in which royalty had travelled. It was presented to the club by Lord Mostyn and was an interesting link with cricket of the past.

Lord Mostyn offered the old pavilion to the Llandudno Bowling club providing that they removed it to its new site. The offer was accepted and still stands today, more than 120 years old, providing adequate shelter and storage for the bowling club members situated at the Gloddaeth Avenue end of the Oval.

Lord Mostyn, in addressing the audience, said he hardly knew what to say for he had never expected to be presented with a Golden Key to open a cricket pavilion. He appreciated the gift very much and said it would be kept as one of the heirlooms of the family in Gloddaeth Hall. (This was the first house built by the Mostyn Family in 1460 which is now St David's College.) He agreed that the need for a new pavilion was long overdue and he hoped it would help the movement to put cricket in North Wales on a sound foundation. He said that they had made a good start recently when the MCC played a match on the ground in which he had the honour of playing and as one of his friends in the press reminded him he did not make a big score – in fact he was out for a duck. Not to be deterred he commented that the great W.G.Grace had been out for a similar score more than once. He was very pleased to see the keenness for cricket in Llandudno and that the interest was increasing, perhaps not to the extent football was doing. In conclusion he wished every success to the North Wales Cricket Association for the part it was taking in reviving cricket in North Wales and also he hoped before long the Llandudno ground would be completely enclosed.

North Wales Select XI
v South Africa Test XI

The South African Test side's visit to Llandudno, and a match arranged for them at the Oval against a North Wales Select team, coincided with the opening of the new pavilion. They had arrived a few days earlier and made their headquarters at the Imperial Hotel. There was a Civic Reception when the Chairman of the Council, Mr S.Chantrey J.P. formally welcomed the 17-strong party to Llandudno. The following day both teams and invited guests were entertained to a luncheon by the President of the North Wales Cricket Association, Mr C.E.Rowland, at the Imperial Hotel. The North Wales team included the famous England Test player Syd Barnes, Albert Thomas from Ruthin who played for Northants and Wales, and E.Bateson, the Eaton College cricket captain. Also playing for North Wales were four Llandudno club players – A.E.Mallalieu, C.Rowland, J.M.Russell and A.L.Lockwood (12th man).

The match was spoilt by the weather. Scheduled as a two-day match (8th-9th September 1924) there was no play on the second day. The rain which had fallen in torrents the night before had soaked the pitch so badly that play was out of the question until mid-afternoon and even then sawdust had to be used to enable the bowlers to obtain a foothold. Unfortunately, rain fell heavily the next day and saturated the wicket completely which made play quite out of the question. At first the preparation of a new wicket would permit play after lunch but a further heavy downpour at noon dispelled the hope of any play and the match was abandoned.

North Wales first innings

D.Boumphrey c Meintjes b Carter	9
F.Moston b Pegler	0
A.E.Mallalieu c Ward b Pegler	4
S.F.Barnes c Hearne b Blanckenberg	1

C.A.Rowland c and b Blanckenberg	2
A.E.Thomas b Blanckenberg	10
H.E.Edge b Blanckenberg	2
Pell b Blanckenberg	13
W.H.Rowland c Nupen b Blanckenberg	0
Clutton b Pegler	1
D.M. Bateson not out	2
Extras (3 b, 2 lb)	5
Total (all out, 44.3 overs)	**49**

Fall of wickets:

1-7, 2-13, 3-14, 4-15, 5-19, 6-21, 7-40, 8-42, 9-43, 10-49

Blanckenberg 6/12

South Africa first innings

J.M.M.Commaille b Barnes	2
T.A.Ward c W.H.Rowland b Barnes	2
M.J.Susskind c Clutton b Barnes	0
A.W.Nourse c Boumphrey b Barnes	15
R.H.Catterall b Pell	18
G.A.L.Hearne c Edge b Barnes	13
J.M.Blanckenberg not out	27
E.P.Nupen b Edge	5
D.J.Meintjes not out	5
Extras (18 b, 6 lb)	24
Total (7 wickets, 42 overs)	**111**

S.J.Pegler and C.P.Carter did not bat

Fall of wickets:

1-2, 2-4, 3-4, 4-39, 5-51, 6-77, 7-94

North Wales bowling

Barnes 5/32

Result Match drawn

Sydney Francis Barnes (1873-1967)

There is no doubt that Sydney Barnes was very much associated with Llandudno CC. Although there is no record he ever played for the club, in fact it was announced during a match against Bangor at the Oval on 7th May 1927 that the famous England Test cricketer had been engaged to act as coach for Llandudno during May. This was because of the injury to the resident coach Dr Woodhouse which would keep him out of the game for a while. Syd played for Wales during his career from 1927-1930. He played at the Oval for Wales against South Africa and the West Indies. Against the West Indies (which included the world famous cricketer Learie Constantine) he bowled and took 7/51 in the 1st innings and 5/67 in the 2nd innings. There was some controversy over whether Syd Barnes was actually qualified to play for Wales. Mr G.E.Rowland (President of the Welsh Cricket Union) responded to the criticism by saying that Syd had been a resident in Penrhyn Bay for over 20 years and he thought was sufficiently qualified for either country.

Richie Benaud in his book 'My Spin on Cricket' named Sydney Barnes in his All-Time Greatest Cricket XI:-

Team

J.B.Hobbs

S.M.Gavaskar

D.G.Bradman

I.V.A.Richards

S.R.Tendulkar

Gary Sobers

Imran Khan

A.C.Gilchrist

S.K.Warne

D.E.Lillee

S.F.Barnes

12th Man K.E.Miller

Manager: F.M.M.Worrell

Richie Benaud wrote:

> *"Leading the attack is Sydney Francis Barnes, a bowler I met but never played against but one who, from the time I have talked about cricket to older and more experienced people in Australia and England, is said by them to be the finest bowler of all time. I met him in 1953 at Stoke-on-Trent where the Australians were playing the Minor Counties. He bowled the first ball of the match. He had turned 80 years of age a couple of months earlier and the ball he bowled landed on a good length and the batsman played it defensively. Even then he was a tall, straight-backed man with big hands, very long, strong fingers and a firm handshake. Ability to swing the ball with great control and cut it off the pitch made him a formidable proposition. Barnes's record in Test cricket, at a time when the Australians had a splendid team, very strong in batting, and South Africa, the other nation of the time were very good, was quite astonishing.*

He played only 27 matches, a mere ten of which were in England over a period of 13 years up to the start of the First World War. He took 189 wickets. When he went to Australia in 1911-12 he was up against the cream of Australian batting including Trumper, Bardsley, Hill, Armstrong, Kelleway, Ransford and the young Macartney. He took 34 wickets at 22 on short-front pitches. He must have been some bowler!

When Barnes made his debut in a three-day Test at the Sydney Cricket Ground during the 1901-02 tour, he took 5/65 and 1/74. He took 13 wickets in the next Test, which was played at the Melbourne Cricket Ground, but damaged his knee two weeks later in Adelaide and played no more cricket on the tour. Melbourne was a favourite ground for Barnes and ten years after his Test debut he routed the Australians pre-lunch on the first day, taking 5/6 from 11 overs. Those present said he was close to unplayable as could be imagined. England won by eight wickets with Jack Hobbs included in my All-Time Greatest Cricket XI."

Sydney Barnes' final first-class match was for Wales against the MCC at Lord's on 20th August 1930.

A young man of 20 who played cricket in the sun without a cap suffered sunstroke and died from heart failure. His family received £35 from the insurance company under an industrial policy in 1934. Only one guinea had been paid in premiums.

During a cricket match in Yorkshire during the 1934 season a ball was hit into a stream running next to the field and killed a grayling which must have been rising at that moment the ball hit the water. The fish weighed eight ounces and was taken home by the batsman and eaten that night for dinner.

With the temperature at 110 degrees a recent cricket match played in the West Indies was transferred to the beach to continue play. During a last wicket stand a ball was whacked into the sea and swallowed by a shark. The umpire promptly gave the batsman out and was entered in the scorebook as: A.Noone c. fish b. Ullah.

Colwyn Bay members throw a few nasty bouncers!

It was becoming apparent that there was some unrest amongst members of North Wales Cricket Association over how the organisation was being administered. The President, Mr C.E.Rowland, (newly elected) brought this matter to light at the annual meeting of the Association in December 1924. He understood there had been some grievances because all the top first class fixtures last season took place on the Llandudno ground and that all of the top officials of the North Wales Cricket Association were from Llandudno where the entire top matches had been played. It was the Colwyn Bay Cricket Club officials who felt that in spite of the promise that the organisation would be broadened out, it had really narrowed down into one groove in favour of the Llandudno Cricket Club. Mr H.Brown, chairman of the newly formed Colwyn Bay Cricket Club, who was at the meeting, said although the Colwyn Bay ground was not ready to host a first class match, there were other places such as Marchwiel and Denbigh that could.

At a social function a couple of months later Mr Rowland presided, and in his address to the members present, he made the point that despite the fact they had grousers in their midst he was proud of the honour of being president of the North Wales Cricket Association. He was pleased on this occasion to do honour to their Chairman Chas F.Farrington who was the father of North Wales Cricket. He paid tribute to Mr Farrington and a small band of men at the Llandudno club who had kept the flag flying for 30 years; had at one time two professionals; and were able to organise and run a cricket week so successfully. He went on to outline the strides made in the game since the Association was formed. However, he did go on to say that if the one or two grousers would give the Association a fair chance he was sure they could make amends. He said he knew there were one or two grousers in first-class cricket as well as in North Wales and if these men could further the game he would willingly make way to them. He appealed to all clubs on the North Wales coast to sink their differences and play the game in the right spirit.

It would appear this animosity was still apparent two months later up to the time of the annual dinner of the Association which was held in February 1925 at the Central Hotel, Colwyn Bay. Mr Chas F.Farrington presided and others present included representatives from Llandudno, Llanrwst, Rydal School, Denbigh, St Asaph, Shotton and Colwyn Bay clubs. This was an opportunity for the President, Mr C.E.Rowland, during the course of his speech to make a trenchant reply to the criticisms levelled at the Association particularly from Colwyn Bay which was felt to be having a detrimental effect on the game generally. He said that the Association had justified its existence. In 1922 the Association had been formed and he was elected President for 1924 after the first President Lord Mostyn. This was an honour he did not seek; however, he had arranged fixtures with the MCC, South Africa and Lancashire. The sum of £500 was required to run these matches and an appeal was issued but was poorly supported owing to the bad times. He had great difficulty arranging the South African fixture and it was only by the South African players' willingness that the match was to be played. The only ground suitable was at Llandudno. He personally undertook the financial responsibility for the match and carried this out. The visit of the South African and Lancashire teams from a playing point of view were a great success but the bad weather had an effect on the gates. With regard to the fixture with the MCC the games at Llandudno and Rydal School were so successful the probability was they would become annual fixtures. The MCC had made it clear that they did not want to play on the Colwyn Bay ground and preferred Llandudno. He went on to say that the task of maintaining the truest spirit of the game could be greatly enlightened if the atmosphere of suspicion, innuendo and provocation was at all times rigorously discouraged. It was well known that two or three persons had, during the past season, either through jealously or the creation of fancied grievances, made totally unwarranted attacks upon the sportsmanship of the officials of the Association. The game was too important to be associated with conduct of this kind and he trusted that this spirit of petty meanness and spite would cease. Grousing in Colwyn Bay was not confined to the Association but to the Denbighshire Association as well. Colwyn Bay officials had also levelled further criticism at the

MCC side that it did not include any players of note. Mr Rowland felt that the comment was unfair because the side did include J.T.Hearne, England Test player, three ex-County captains and two members of the MCC committee. There were also three men who were entitled to wear the All-England blazer.

Not much is known today about the President Mr C.E.Rowland who had borne a large share of the cost of bringing to North Wales the South Africans, the MCC and Lancashire teams. He had not only taken a great interest in cricket in North Wales but in South Wales as well. He had been instrumental in arranging a match at the Lord's ground in 1925 between Wales and the MCC and for a touring eleven of the MCC to play at Colwyn Bay and Rydal School the same year including the only North Wales v MCC match at Llandudno.

An extract from a letter in the 'North Wales Weekly News' read:

"It would be disastrous to the objectives of the North Wales Cricket Association if the spirit of nepotism were allowed to creep in and interfere with the judgement of the Selection Committee and whilst there is no suggestion that it exists here, experience proves that it is an insidious evil which must be looked out for in sporting organisations and stifled as soon as it shows its unwelcome presence."

Mr H.Brown (Chairman, Colwyn Bay CC) also wrote to the 'North Wales Weekly News' as follows:

"That there was little enthusiasm cannot be doubted and the cause is not far to see. It is a notorious fact that the best players in North Wales were not selected to play in the matches and consequently many enthusiasts did not think it worthwhile to go and witness a series of probable fiascos on the part of the Welsh side. To my mind there are plenty of scope supporting propositions in North Wales provided that the best available men are selected to represent the home side and this depends entirely upon the Selection Committee. There are plenty of first-class players in North Wales and they should be put in the field strictly according to individual merit and without regard to other considerations. I think these facts are sufficient to justify the Association

that first-class cricket can be successfully played in North Wales without unfairly loading one individual with losses or seeking donations from others if proper regard is had to the players and the popularity of the game."

Mr Farrington said he never had directly or indirectly anything to do with team selection. The Association had written to Mr Brown stating that they had arranged a game at Colwyn Bay for the MCC to play a team representing West Denbighshire, Caernarvonshire and Anglesey. Mr Brown had written back stating that he was grateful but on finding out that Llandudno had been given a two-day fixture he turned down the match because Colwyn Bay had already got a match arranged on that day. Since then the Colwyn Bay club had changed their minds and wanted the fixture but objected to the title which must be 'Colwyn Bay and District'. However, the MCC had made it clear they did not want to play at Colwyn Bay because they objected to playing on a poor pitch which also included other grounds at Holyhead and Porthmadog.

Mr Farrington appealed to Colwyn Bay for the sake of the game to work harmoniously with the Association and to sink their differences. Mr Brown said that he was not prepared for the attack made by the President on his club and he questioned the good taste in disturbing harmony. However, he said he would pass over what the President said and that his club would be pleased to have the MCC match in the future. Anyhow, he said, the Colwyn Bay club had, for the coming season, arranged one of the finest list of fixtures for any club in the land whether they played the MCC or not.

A backlash at club level was being felt at Llandudno when the Secretary, Mr J.R.Evans, reported that there was some difficulty arranging fixtures by the action of the Colwyn Bay club. It was because they were not keeping to an agreement made for matches to be played between the two clubs on Whit Monday and on August Bank Holiday each year. When he communicated with the Colwyn Bay Secretary to confirm the dates he was told that those dates had been filled. Instead he had been given other dates available which included a Thursday and Saturday. In his opinion this seemed to be 'sour grapes'. It was agreed by the members to accept the new dates though.

Llandudno was selected as the venue for the three-day International match between Wales and Ireland in August 1925.

The first county match arranged by the North Wales Cricket Association between a combined Caernarvonshire Anglesey team against Denbighshire was played on the Colwyn Bay ground at Rhos-on-Sea on 24th June 1925. The Caernarvonshire/Anglesey team was C.P.Woods (capt) (Llandudno), C.E.Rowland (Llandudno), A.H.Mallalieu (Llandudno), A.H.Hanlon (Llandudno), R.Dennis Jones (Llandudno), Liet. N.Sotherby (Parciau), W.H.Hughes (Porthmadog), Capt. Lloyd (Woodland School, Deganwy), A.Hall (Parciau), A.Elsby (Llanrwst), A.McDermott (Bangor) and 12th man A.Lockwood (Llandudno).

An extract from an article in The Advertiser dated 4th July 1925:

"The cricket controllers have come to the front during the last two or three years and the branch of sport in Llandudno to the world. The visits of the MCC, South Africa and Lancashire last year did an enormous amount of good and a visit from the Australians is not by any means impossible when they come to the old country next. This year the MCC is sending another strong team and the Wales and Ireland match will be played on the Llandudno ground. Llandudno will also entertain Lancashire again later in the year. These fixtures mean advertising Llandudno to a very large sport loving public and therefore cannot fail to attract people to the town."

An inquest was held in the Borough of Westminster on 25th July 1812 into the circumstances of the death of a five year old boy. Whilst walking with his mother and father on Kennington Common (one of the earliest London cricket venues and is known to have been used for major cricket matches from 1724 to 1785) he was struck on the chest by a cricket ball, several yards from the bat, and killed on the spot. The Coroner's verdict was accidental death.

On 5th July 1890 it was reported that Luke Crompton Bridge, aged 15 years, the son of James Bridge, of Paradise Street, Bury, was playing in a cricket match near his home, when a ball struck him on the side of the head with such force as to cause his death before a medical man could attend to him. The ball struck the deceased near the ear.

On 27th September 1890 the Coroner, Thomas Taylor, told an inquest at Dewsbury of his decision on the body of Edwin Berry. The evidence showed that early in the week he and others were playing cricket in a field at Heckmondwike, West Yorkshire. Edwin Berry was fielding at point. One of the batsmen, a young man named Thomas Bottomley, struck at a full-pitched ball, and the bat, leaving his hands, hit Berry on the forehead. He fell backwards onto the ground but rallied quickly, and was able to follow his usual employment up to the following Thursday night. On Friday morning a doctor had to be called to him, and despite all that could be done, he died during the course of the evening from injury to the brain. The jury found a verdict of "Accidentally killed".

On a Saturday in September 1890 a fatal accident occurred at a cricket match at Willesborough, near Ashford, Kent. Mr Jeal, a well-known resident and member of the Hythe Green Cricket Club, was severely struck on the head by a ball, and concussion of the brain ensued. The unfortunate player was taken to Ashford Cottage Hospital, where he died less than 48 hours after the accident.

In June 1897 a young man named Arthur George Lunn fell dead whilst playing in a cricket match in the village of Runfold, near Farnham, Surrey on a Saturday afternoon. He was at the wickets batting for the Badshot Lea and Runfold Cricket Club against Farnham Ramblers, when he suddenly fell to the ground. When medical assistance arrived life was found to be extinct. The distressing affair caused great excitement amongst both players and onlookers, so the match was abandoned.

A cricket accident occurred on 19 August 1905 when a spectator's eye was knocked out. The Littlehampton Cricket Week had been scarred by that distressing accident. During the progress of the game between the MCC and the Littlehampton CC, an elderly gentleman named Mr Lee, sitting in the front row of the pavilion, had an eye knocked out by a sharp rising ball cut by F.H.Giessen, a Sussex batsman playing for the MCC. The ball bounced only once before hitting the unfortunate spectator.

At the Cricketers Hotel, Swansea, on 22nd June 1907 a coroner's inquiry was held into the circumstances attending the death of Harvey Thomas, aged 31, a builder, who was killed by a blow from a cricket ball while practising on the Swansea cricket field on a Thursday evening. The principal witness was Jack Bancroft, who said that at 7.30 on that fateful evening he was standing just outside the practice net. The deceased was playing out in the field away from the nets but positioned to field any ball that came his way. The incident occurred when a batsman hit the ball hard and high which was going in the direction where the deceased was standing. Unfortunately he was not giving his fullest attention at the time probably because of a distraction. The witness was aware of this and shouted "Look out!" Harvey Thomas did not seem to hear the call and was struck on the head by the ball just behind his ear. He fell down and immediately Dr Anderson was called to the scene to tend to him. He found him conscious, but suffering from a reaction following concussion of the brain. He was able to talk. On the Friday he appeared to be better, but on the Saturday he developed inflammation of the brain and died on the Sunday evening. In answer to the Coroner, Dr Anderson said he did not think anything could have been done to relieve the deceased by means of an operation. Mr Lloyd, a juror, questioned the doctor with a view to eliciting whether it would have been better if the deceased had been taken to the hospital instead of being sent home. The doctor, however, said that he felt no good could have been done by an operation. The Coroner, in summing up, said it was evidently a pure accident, one of those sad cases which happened in the world of sport, and for which no one was to blame. He did not know how the friends of the deceased were situated, but he certainly thought that this was a case where the members of the club and the public generally might assist. The jury returned a verdict of 'Accidental Death', and expressed sympathy with the wife and orphans of the deceased, and subscribed 14s towards any funds that might be required. Mr Perkins, the secretary of the club, expressed on behalf of the club his deep sympathy with the family, and announced that at the meeting of Swansea cricket club on Monday a subscription of 10 guineas was voted for the family and the decision made to open a subscription list immediately for their assistance.

Alcwyn Jenkins, 72, was umpiring a league match between Swansea and Llangennech at the St Helen's ground in Swansea on Saturday 4th July 2009.

The widower, from Skewen, was struck on the head by a ball thrown by a fielder and was airlifted to hospital but failed to recover.

Neil Hobbs, honorary chairman of the South Wales Cricket Association, said it was a tragic accident.

"I've umpired with Alcwyn and he was a great guy. He was well respected throughout the league and everybody knew Alcwyn," said Mr Hobbs.

"He's umpired for the best part of 25 years. He also does junior league matches. I'm led to believe it was one of the most freak accidents you could ever imagine on the cricket field."

Neil Hobbs, South Wales Cricket Association commented:

"Everybody probably in South Wales knows Alcwyn through cricket. It's a very, very sad day and I feel sorry for his children."

The match, which was abandoned, was a league game in Division One of the South Wales Cricket Association.

On 28th November 2014 Australia cricket international Phil Hughes died after being hit on the head by a ball batting for South Australia. He collapsed face first on the ground after being hit by a bouncer from 22-year-old Sean Abbott during a Sheffield Shield game against New South Wales. It was a short ball that bounced up towards his left ear and the ball somehow evaded the cricketer's helmet as he swivelled to play the shot. The match was abandoned. The batsman was taken from the Sydney Cricket Ground to the city's St Vincent's Hospital. He was in an induced coma but failed to recover. The Australian team doctor Peter Brukner said Hughes had suffered a "massive bleed into the brain".

Hughes represented Australia in 26 Test matches. The 25 year old also played for Australia's one day team on 25 occasions, scoring 826 runs.

In the 1924 season Llandudno 1ˢᵗ XI played 27 matches, winning 19, losing seven. Only one match was drawn. The 2ⁿᵈ XI also played several matches and some good junior talent had come to light.

Mr W.Woodhouse (formerly of Redford Town and Stalybridge) replaced Ingham Bell as club professional/groundsman. His contract was for 26 weeks at a salary of £4 a week and to include a Benefit.

Wales v Ireland

This game was a two-innings match played over three days at the Oval on 15th, 16th and 17th August 1925.

There was a large crowd every day to witness this historic event being the first International cricket match played in Llandudno. Glorious weather favoured the event and the wicket was perfection for the batsman. It resulted in a decisive victory for Wales.

Ireland won the toss and decided to bat scoring 151 all out in their first innings. Jack Mercer (Glamorgan) bowled well taking seven wickets for 34 runs. Wales replied with a resounding 287 runs. Opening bat Norman Riches (Glamorgan) scored 114 runs. A.E.Mallalieu (Llandudno) was the second top scorer of the match with 66 runs.

Ireland were all out in their 2nd innings for 100. Kenneth Raikes (Glamorgan), right arm fast/medium pace bowler, took seven for 28.

Wales won by an innings and 36 runs.

Ireland 1st innings

J.C.Walton c & b Ryan	48
J.B.Ganly c Sullivan b Clay	16
M.C.Parry b Ryan	17
A.P.Kelly lbw Mercer	41
R.W.Power b Mercer	2
R.J.H.Lambert b Mercer	0
J.G.Aston b Mercer	0
F.W.Jackson b Mercer	2
A.C.Douglas b Mercer	1

M.Sugden not out   6

W.Allen b Mercer   0

Extras   18

Total (all out, 52 overs)   151

Bowling	Overs	Mdns	Runs	Wkts	Wides	No balls
Mercer	19	7	34	7	-	-
Raikes	7	0	22	0	-	-
Ryan	14	1	54	2	-	-
Clay	12	3	23	1	-	-

Wales 1st innings

N.V.H.Riches c & b Parry   114

J.T.Bell. b Aston   21

A.E.Mallalieu b Allen   66

D.Davies b Lambert   3

H.G.Symonds b Ganly   15

J.C.Clay st Kelly b Aston   22

C.A.Rowland c Kelly b Aston   11

K.C.Raikes c Lambert b Aston   3

J.Mercer c Power b Parry   7

F.P.Ryan not out   4

D.Sullivan c Allen b Aston   0

Extras   21

Total (all out, 107 overs)   287

Bowling	Overs	Mdns	Runs	Wkts	Wides	No balls
Lambert	32	7	58	1	-	-
Aston	31	1	58	5	-	-
Sugden	3	0	18	0	-	-
Douglas	4	1	13	0	-	-
Parry	11	0	31	2	-	-
Allen	16	5	50	1	-	-
Ganly	6	2	12	1	-	-
Walton	4	1	26	0	-	-

Ireland 2nd innings

J.C.Walton b Mercer	4
M.Sugden c Mallalieu b Raikes	3
M.C.Parry lbw Raikes	5
A.P.Kelly b Raikes	2
R.W.Power b Raikes	5
J.B.Ganly c & b Raikes	1
R.J.H.Lambert b Raikes	8
A.C.Douglas c Davies b Raikes	6
J.G.Aston c Mercer b Davies	14
F.W.Jackson not out	44
W.Allen b Mercer	0
Extras	8
Total (all out, 40 overs)	**100**

Bowling	Overs	Mdns	Runs	Wkts	Wides	No balls
Mercer	17	3	28	2	-	-
Raikes	16	6	28	7	-	-
Clay	3	0	16	0	-	-
Davies	4	0	20	1	-	-

Norman Vaughan Hurry Riches (1883-1975) played cricket from 1901 for Glamorgan CCC, initially as wicket keeper. His first major innings was against Monmouth at Swansea when he scored 183 (1904).

Riches continued to represent Glamorgan until 1934, and was captain in 1921 (Glamorgan's initial season in the County Championship) and 1929. He scored nine centuries in his career and was the first Glamorgan batsman to pass a thousand runs in first-class cricket (1921). He was vice-chairman, trustee and patron of the club from 1934 to 1950. Riches also played for Cardiff CC from 1934 to 1947.

North Wales v Lancashire

The last big cricket match of the season took place the following month which was a two-innings match between North Wales and Lancashire 14th/15th September 1925 at the Oval. The North Wales team was specially selected by Mr G.E.Rowland (President of the North Wales Cricket Association) who purposely chose an admirable mixture of youth and experience with the objective to foster the game widely in Wales. The attendances on both days were encouraging.

Lancashire won the toss and elected to bat first, scoring 160 all out. (S.F.Barnes took 7/76.) North Wales 1st innings ended scoring 141. Lancashire scored 129 in their 2nd innings which was not enough. North Wales won by two wickets scoring 151 for 8 in their 2nd innings. C.A.Rowland (Llandudno) batted well for his 60).

Llandudno went through a series of competitive matches (North Wales Cricket Association) without a defeat. They won all their games except three which to all intents and purposes were 'moral' victories in which time only saved the opposition from apparent defeats.

The following is a 'letter to the editor' – The Advertiser 16th September 1925:

> *"Dear Sir – In the cricket season now passed there have been three matches at Llandudno ranking as first-class, the MCC, The Gentlemen of Ireland and Lancashire. On Monday during one of the frequent intervals when watching people strolling around the pretty ground one could not help thinking of it as the coming 'Welsh Lords' (save the mark!!) and feeling proud to be a humble supporter of a club that has won its way by pluck and perseverance. The club has been kept on its feet by a small number of ladies and gentlemen who have spent much time and money on it, but it cannot expect to draw a good crowd to the first-class matches until it pays more attention to the golden rule of punctuality. The delays in the three matches mentioned were nothing less than irritating. On the Tuesday morning I heard a gentleman ask one of the gate-keepers at the lunch interval for a pass-out ticket adding "we may return if you give us a little more cricket and a little less foolery".*

Of course it is difficult but something can be done by a firm hand and a little more thought for the poor and often half-frozen spectator in the wrong side of the pavilion enclosure. Yours etc. – The Rabbit."

It was at the club's Hot Pot Dinner in 1926 that G.E.Rowland said he was very pleased that the Colwyn Bay and Llandudno clubs had finally 'buried the hatchet' and were now working together for the good of the game. He hoped the good feeling would continue and for his own part he would do all he could to further it. Mr Tweedle from Colwyn Bay said he was glad to be present to cement the new bond of friendship between Llandudno and Colwyn Bay clubs. He hoped the rivalry would be in the future as keen as it was in the past on the field but whatever they did, let them play cricket.

Mr J.J.Marks presented the club with a large clock purchased from Forfars of Mostyn Street. A new clock now fixed in full view on the pavilion and a new score board which Lord Mostyn had provided, were for members and spectators to add to their enjoyment whilst on the recreation ground.

The MCC again visited Llandudno and played a two-day match at the Oval on 23/24th July, 1926, defeating a North Wales XI this time by six wickets.

A Cricket Bazaar at the Town Hall

A popular attraction in those days anywhere, and especially in the 1920s, was to hold a bazaar which local people could go to, and to hopefully pick up a bargain of sorts usually by means of an auction.

The club committee decided to hold two such sales and did so on 26th/27th September and 2nd October 1926. The items for auction were surplus food, fruit, vegetables and household items.

Lord Mostyn opened the September Bazaar and said that the main purpose was to raise money to pay off the debt on the new cricket pavilion. He said that the cost of the Pavilion and furnishings, including necessary improvements to the ground, was £1,100. The club had managed to raise £346 by means of revenue from subscriptions but had fallen short of their target. He went on to say that the Llandudno ground was second to none in North Wales and he hoped in due course it would be enclosed all round then hopefully people who looked over the railings would then pay to come into the ground and watch the matches.

The Bazaar held in October was officially opened by His Hon Judge Roberts. He said that this privilege was the first time he had taken part in the public life of Llandudno since his appointment to the area two years ago. He had come to look upon Llandudno as one of the most charming and delightful places he had ever seen. It seemed to him that there was a splendid opening for cricket in Llandudno and he understood that Llandudno had the finest ground and the finest pavilion in the whole of Europe. He hoped that in future he would be able to put in an appearance on the ground and even suggested that a partnership between himself and Lord Mostyn would draw a bigger gate that the club had ever known. In speaking of local cricket he said it was hard to refrain from mentioning the name of G.E.Rowland who was doing much for the game and the club. There was also Chas.F.Farrington too, who was a hard worker. Another speaker, Dr Woodhouse (the club professional), said that he always looked on the cricket club as the greatest asset Llandudno had. He complained that the town did not give the support it deserved. Llandudno, he said, could afford to do a lot more for cricket.

The Bazaars did very well disposing of a great deal of produce and goods by auction which realised over £650.

It was announced on the 7th May 1927 during a match against Bangor that Sydney Barnes, the famous All-England cricketer, had been engaged to act as coach during May because of the injury to Dr Woodhouse that would keep him out of the game for a while.

At a monthly meeting of the Llandudno and District Council a letter was read out from Chas.F.Farrington drawing attention to the visit of the New Zealand cricket team to Llandudno in September. He suggested that the distinguished visitors and the Welsh Cricket Association should be given an official welcome by the town. It was agreed that the matter should be referred to the Finance Committee in the first instance with the idea of the chairman inviting the co-operation of some prominent local businessmen.

North Wales played the MCC at the Oval on 24th July 1927. This was a 12-a-side match. Unfortunately, rain prevented a start being made until after lunch on the first day on a very wet, soggy wicket. However, the MCC scored a massive 327 runs for 10 declared. In reply North Wales scored 111 and then managed 71 for six in their 2nd innings before rain finally stopped play.

Joseph Wells, the father of H.G.Wells, was a professional cricketer who took four wickets in four balls for Kent against Sussex in 1862. Among his quartet of victims was Spencer Austen-Leigh, the great nephew of Jane Austen.

A civic welcome for the New Zealanders

The first meeting of a special committee appointed to welcome the New Zealanders was held at the Town Hall Chambers on the 26th July 1927 presided over by Mr T.Lincoln Evans J.P., Chairman of the Council.

It was decided not only to give a civic welcome to the New Zealanders and the Welsh team but to entertain them to a dinner at the Imperial Hotel. The club had arranged fixtures to include the Wales v New Zealand match in a special cricket week festival as follows:

Sat, Mon, Tue, 2/4/5 September, 1927

> *New Zealand v Wales*

Wed, Thurs, 6/7

> *New Zealand v Welsh Cygnets*

Fri, Sat, 8/9

> *North Wales v South Wales*

(Wickets pitched Wed and Fri at 12 noon, other days at 11.30 am.)

Lunch 1.30pm-2.15pm

Admission for two games 2s, pavilion 3s 6p includes lunch

Boys and girls under 16 (ground only) 1s

Other matches 1s 2p and 2s 4p including tea

The local dignitaries that were present at the dinner with Mr T.Lincoln Evans J.P. were Lord Mostyn and G.E.Rowland (President of the Welsh Cricket Union). The tables had been decorated with fern leaves as a reference to the New Zealand National Emblem.

The menu consisted of:

Grapefruit

Tortue Clare

Crème Sevigne

Filet Sole a la Florentine

Selle de Mouton a la Anglaise

Haricot Verts au Beurre

Pomme Puree

Mazarine a La Russe

Glace Maraschino

Café

Mr Lincoln Evans welcomed the guests. He said that on behalf of the local authority and the people of Llandudno it gave him great pleasure to welcome to Llandudno such distinguished players and officials to the town. He hoped that during their stay they would make full use of the excursions that have been arranged for them to see and enjoy a part of Wales renowned for its beautiful rural scenery. Turning directly to the New Zealand players he said:

> *"When you arrived in the UK you had no brass bands to meet you. You came in quietly to play cricket and not much was expected of you. It was pleasing to hear that you confounded your critics by beating a number of good English county sides. I forecast that in the near future you will be pitted against other cricketing countries in official Test Matches."*

He then welcomed the Welsh players and said that everyone in North Wales was very proud of what Glamorgan had done for the game of cricket in Wales. He concluded by saying it was an honour to entertain all of them as visitors to the town and he hoped the match between the two sides would be a great success.

Mr G.E.Rowland responded to some comment that had been made concerning Syd Barnes (England Test cricketer) appearing in the Welsh side. He said Syd had been resident in Penrhyn Bay for over 20 years and he thought was sufficiently qualified for either country.

Lord Mostyn said of Mr Lincoln Evans that he was a man who had been away from the town for some years but had come back and was then devoting his time for the good of the town. He sympathised with him as Chairman of the Council as the work would have increased enormously from the days when he was Chairman of the cricket club. During the last few years cricket in Wales had revived wonderfully thanks to the hard work of G.E.Rowland who had been the leading factor in developing Welsh cricket and to Glamorgan who had also led the way.

The best cricket bats according to popular belief are always made from the wood of the female of a certain species of willow tree. Experts now state that this is not the case, but that the male, as long as it is not a hybrid of inferior timber, is just as good for the production of bats.

Wales v New Zealand

Fine weather favoured the match. Wales won the toss and batted first scoring 182. New Zealand followed and were all out for 130.

Wales followed this with their second innings scoring 183 for 9 declared. New Zealand replied and had scored 124 for the loss of only two wickets when bad light stopped play, much to the disappointment of the spectators. The game ended in a draw.

Umpires R.D.Burrows, T.W.Oates

Wales first innings

W.E.Bates b Allcott	29
J.T.Bell c McGirr b Dacre	52
*N.V.H.Riches c Page b Henderson	22
C.F.Walters c and b Allcott	18
C.A.Rowland run out	2
D.Davies c Dempster b Henderson	6
K.C.Raikes c Dempster b Allcott	5
S.F.Barnes b Henderson	5
S.T.Jagger c Page b Allcott	9
A.E.Thomas c Blunt b Allcott	16
D.Sullivan not out	2
Extras (8 b, 8 lb)	16
Total (all out, 67.5 overs)	**182**

Bowling	Overs	Mdns	Runs	Wkts	Wides	No balls
McGirr	9	0	33	0	-	-
Bernau	4	0	11	0	-	-
Lowry	9	2	17	0	-	-
Allcott	19	5	46	5	-	-
Blunt	7	1	17	0	-	-
Dacre	3	1	10	1	-	-
Henderson	14	5	28	3	-	-
Dempster	2	0	4	0	-	-

New Zealand first innings

C.C.R.Dacre b Thomas	7
H.M.McGirr c Rowland b Barnes	0
E.H.L.Bernau b Barnes	0
*T.C.Lowry c Sullivan b Barnes	21
J.E.Mills c Jagger b Thomas	18
R.C.Blunt c Jagger b Thomas	10
C.S.Dempster lbw b Barnes	14
M.L.Page c Jagger b Raikes	14
K.C.James b Jagger	23
C.F.W.Allcott c Walters b Raikes	4
M.Henderson not out	1
Extras (14 b, 4 lb)	18
Total (all out, 83.3 overs)	130

Bowling	Overs	Mdns	Runs	Wkts	Wides	No balls
Barnes	35	12	47	4	-	-
Thomas	30	15	39	3	-	-
Jagger	11	3	24	1	-	-
Davies	1	1	0	0	-	-
Raikes	6	4	2	2	-	-

Wales second innings

W.E.Bates b Henderson	18
J.T.Bell b Henderson	10
*N.V.H.Riches c James b Lowry	25
C.F.Walters c Lowry b Allcott	11
C.A.Rowland c and b Page	14
D.Davies c McGirr b Lowry	42
K.C.Raikes b Henderson	33
S.F.Barnes c Bernau b Henderson	2
S.T.Jagger c Dempster b Lowry	2
A.E.Thomas not out	1
Extras (10 b, 15 lb)	25
Total (9 wickets, declared, 67 overs)	183

D.Sullivan did not bat

Fall of wickets:

1-35, 2-54, 3-78, 4-88, 5-108, 6-172, 7-180, 8-181, 9-183 (67 overs)

Bowling	Overs	Mdns	Runs	Wkts	Wides	No balls
McGirr	4	3	1	0	-	-
Lowry	20	5	41	3	-	-
Allcott	14	7	27	1	-	-
Blunt	5	2	8	0	-	-
Henderson	7	1	29	4	-	-
Page	17	4	52	1	-	-

New Zealand second innings

C.S.Dempster c Raikes b Thomas	70
J.E.Mills b Jagger	27
M.L.Page not out	15
*T.C.Lowry not out	6
Extras (5 b, 1 w)	6
Total (2 wickets, 49 overs)	**124**

Fall of wickets:
1-79, 2-116

Did not bat: C.C.R.Dacre, H.M.McGirr, E.H.L.Bernau, R.C.Blunt, K.C.James C.F.W.Allcott, M.Henderson

Bowling	Overs	Mdns	Runs	Wkts	Wides	No balls
Barnes	8	0	30	0	-	-
Thomas	19	8	30	1	-	-
Jagger	13	4	36	1	-	-
Davies	4	1	11	0	-	-
Raikes	5	1	11	0	-	-

The following day New Zealand played the Welsh Cygnets. The Welsh batted first and scored 350 for six declared. In reply, New Zealand was dismissed for 195.

In the last match of the Cricket Festival Week North Wales beat South Wales comfortably by an innings and 15 runs. Syd Barnes bowled magnificently for North Wales taking seven wickets for 40 runs in the South's first innings.

Mr G.E.Rowland thanked Mr Farrington for all the hard work done by the club members. He said that for their first attempt it had been a very successful festival and the arrangements laid on for the spectators had been excellent. The cricket on the field was first class and he thought that Wales had proved its right to meet other countries at the game. With regard to one or two matters that had arisen concerning the hours of play which had confused some people, it was the experienced umpires on the day that decided that the light during September would not permit play before 12 noon and after 6pm. Another reason for the early stoppage was that the sight screens were not high enough to hide that part of the Great Orme which was wooded.

A few days after the New Zealand match a letter appeared in 'The Advertiser':

"Dear Sir – I beg to lodge a protest to the shortening of the hours during the cricket match and also to the wasting of time during the game. What justification was there on Monday after the innings of the New Zealanders which terminated at 3.50pm in taking a tea interval and not returning to the field until 4.45pm?

In view of the admission charge of 2s I consider that the public should be given, weather permitting, a full day's cricket with a chance of a definite result to the match.

If the idea of these first class matches is to encourage the public to patronise cricket in North Wales the tactics pursued during this match was more likely to discourage support in the future. The advertised hours of play for Monday and Tuesday were 11.30am to 6pm and three quarters of an hour for lunch.

On what grounds were the times altered to 12noon to 6pm?

In conclusion and in fairness to the public I beg to urge the authority in charge to insist that the motto 'play cricket' is adhered to in the future.

Thank you for your kindness for publishing my complaint. – 'Tyke'"

Sir Arthur Conan Doyle played cricket for the MCC. He hit a century on his debut, had bowling figures of seven for 51 against Cambridgeshire at Lord's in 1899 and once bowled out W.G.Grace. Moreover, he took the name of Sherlock Holmes from the Derbyshire cricketer F.Shacklock. Another Derbyshire player, Thomas Mycroft, inspired the name of Sherlock Holmes's brother Mycroft.

A Civic Reception for the West Indies Test team

The West Indies and the Welsh teams were given a civic welcome at The North Western Hotel on 25th July 1928. The Chairman of the Council presided and welcomed both teams on behalf of the people of Llandudno. He said there were two good reasons for the warm welcome. The first was a business reason for the town depending entirely on visitors and the second was that they were always glad to welcome real sportsmen and women who played the game in all corners of the world. He was convinced sport played a part in cementing the British Empire together. Mr Cheetham sketched the many attractions on offer, winding up with a reference to the Happy Valley. Mr G.E.Rowland commented that the West Indies team had brought sunshine with them that day and he hoped it would continue to shine on them in the next test match against England later that month.

Mr C.K.Nunes on behalf of the West Indies team said they had come from a land of ancient mountains and lovely dales to another land of ancient mountains and lovely vales. He thanked everyone for the splendid welcome and great kindness. He felt that it was a great honour to be at the head of a body of men, mostly young men, from the islands which had shown great loyalty to the throne on this visit.

Mr Rowlands said that only 2,500 people had attended the first day of the match. When he said that a crowd of 10,000 had been present at a match previously in the North of England against the West Indies in spite of a depression in that area he felt that 2,500 was a little disappointing.

Wales v West Indies

This match ended in a great win for Wales. The game opened on the first day in glorious weather and over 2,500 spectators paid for admission into the ground. West Indies batted first and Syd Barnes bowled well taking seven West Indies wickets for 51 runs. The world famous West Indian cricketer L.N.Constantine batted at number seven and scored 24 in his first innings and 16 in his second innings.

West Indies 198 and 137, Wales 229 and 107 for 2.

Venue the Oval, Llandudno on 25th, 26th, 27th July 1928 (3-day match)

Balls per over 6

West Indies won the toss and decided to bat.

Result Wales won by 8 wickets

Umpires A.Morton, W.R.Parry

West Indians first innings

G.Challenor lbw b Barnes	50
C.A.Roach c Ryan b Barnes	4
W.H.St Hill lbw b Barnes	20
*R.K.Nunes b Ryan	25
O.C.Scott b Barnes	7
C.R.Browne b Barnes	0
L.N.Constantine c Barnes b Ryan	24
E.A.Rae c Ryan b Barnes	0
J.M.Neblett b Barnes	17
C.V.Wight not out	16
G.N.Francis b Ryan	3

Extras (21 b, 11 lb)   32

Total (all out, 60 overs)   198

Bowling	Overs	Mdns	Runs	Wkts	Wides	No balls
Barnes	27	9	51	7	-	-
Dolman	4	1	19	0	-	-
Jagger	10	3	28	0	-	-
Ryan	19	5	68	3	-	-

Wales first innings

*N.V.H.Riches c Roach b Constantine	12
D.Boumphrey b Francis	6
C.A.Rowland b Constantine	6
C.N.Bruce run out	10
A.Ratcliffe b Neblett	71
V.A.Metcalfe c Rae b Neblett	18
S.T.Jagger c Neblett b Francis	30
C.E.Dolman c Neblett b Browne	35
S.F.Barnes not out	25
W.H.Rowland b Browne	0
F.P.Ryan c and b Browne	0
Extras (6 b, 6 lb, 4 nb)	16
Total (all out, 63.5 overs)	**229**

Bowling	Overs	Mdns	Runs	Wkts	Wides	No balls
Francis	17	4	70	2	-	-
Constantine	14	4	44	2	-	-
Scott	4	0	19	0	-	-
Browne	15.5	6	26	3	-	-
Neblett	13	2	54	2	-	-

West Indies second innings

G.Challenor lbw b Barnes	26
C.A.Roach c Ryan b Barnes	30
W.H.St Hill c Ratcliffe b Ryan	7
* R.K.Nunes b Barnes	17
O.C.Scott c Ryan b Barnes	4
C.R.Browne lbw b Ryan	1
L.N.Constantine c Jagger b Ryan	16
E.A.Rae b Ryan	11
C.V.Wight c Riches b Barnes	1
J.M.Neblett lbw b Ryan	2
G.N.Francis not out	0
Extras (17 b, 3 lb, 2 nb)	22
Total (all out, 41.1 overs)	**137**

Bowling	Overs	Mdns	Runs	Wkts	Wides	No balls
Barnes	21	5	67	5	-	-
Jagger	5	0	31	0	-	-
Ryan	15.1	6	17	5	-	-

Wales second innings

*N.V.H.Riches c Browne b Francis	4
D.Boumphrey b Constantine	4
C.A.Rowland not out	52
C.N.Bruce not out	42
Extras (4 b, 1 lb)	5
Total (2 wickets, 22.5 overs)	107

Did not bat: A.Ratcliffe, V.A.Metcalfe, S.T.Jagger, C.E.Dolman, S.F.Barnes, W.H.Rowland, and F.P.Ryan.

Bowling	Overs	Mdns	Runs	Wkts	Wides	No balls
Francis	4	0	29	1	-	-
Constantine	2	0	15	1	-	-
Scott	3.5	0	28	0	-	-
Browne	9	2	9	0	-	-
Neblett	4	0	21	0	-	-

Sir Learie Constantine (1901-1971)

He played 18 Test matches for the West Indies before the 1st World War. A lawyer and politician, he served as Trinidad's High Commissioner to the United Kingdom and became the first black peer. He was Wisden's cricketer of the year in 1939. He became a life peer in 1969. He played for the Lancashire league club Nelson. In his final years he served on the Race Relations Board of the Sports Council and was on the Board of Governors at the BBC. Sir Learie Constantine died of a heart attack on 1st July 1971.

The West Indies in the early days were still dominated by English expats and the team's success was patchy. The real turning point came in the 1950s and 1960s when players like Gary Sobers, Wes Hall, Frank Worrell and Everton Weekes came through the ranks to establish the team's identity as a mixture of powerful stroke play and ferocious bowling. This reputation was further enhanced in the 1970s and 1980s when the fast bowling attack, spearheaded by players like Malcolm Marshall, became feared around the world for short-pitched bowling on hard surfaces. Meanwhile, batsmen like Viv Richards were demonstrating the fearsome art of aggressive batting that would make the West Indies the number one side in the world in the mid-1980s. Although the team's fortunes have dipped in the past 20 years they have continued to produce some of the world's greatest cricketers, most notably Brian Lara, who still holds the record for the highest score in Test Match cricket of 400 runs.

North Wales v MCC

At the end of the West Indies week, North Wales met the MCC which provided some splendid cricket and a triumph for the young Llandudno player A.H.Mallalieu who scored 122 for North Wales out of a total of 257. The MCC had scored 264 in their first innings and were 234 for 7 in their second innings before rain stopped play and the game ended in a draw.

For some years prior to 1928 The Railway Cup Final (London, Midland and Scottish Railway – became known as British Railways from 1948) was always played on the Oval and that year on the 18th August Wolverton beat Harwich by five wickets. Mr J.E.Morris, club chairman, presented the cup to the winners.

It's worth mentioning that for many years the committee had always welcomed visitors to the town and, if it was possible, invite cricketers to play and would join a team if selected. This happened often. J.J.Marks received a letter from F.P.Sawyer of Sheffield who joined the club as a visiting player in several games in the early part of August 1928.

"Dear Mr Marks – I wish to thank you personally and through you to the committee and members of the club for the extremely pleasant time I had with them during my short holiday.

Although I was an absolute stranger to the majority of the players they went out of their way to make me feel at home at once and I thoroughly enjoyed every game I played in. The spirit of all the members would do much for the glorious game if it was obtained in more clubs. Will you please convey to them all my thanks for their courtesy. Kind regards and best wishes to you – Frank P.Sawyer"

Although cricket has been played in England since the seventeenth century; test cricket is widely regarded to date back to 1877, marking the moment when cricket moved away from England to being an international sport. The first test match was played between England and Australia in 1877 and the success of the competition gave rise to the Ashes, first played at the Oval in 1882. Today there are ten cricketing test nations, and test cricket is widely regarded as the ultimate measure of ability, 'testing' the strength of the best cricket teams in the world.

North Wales cricket mourns the death of Lord Mostyn

The sad news was received in Llandudno of the death of Lord Mostyn on Thursday night, 11th April 1929, at a nursing home in Hove, Brighton. Following an operation it was understood that up to the Thursday morning it seemed as if the operation was to prove successful but there was a change in his condition and he rapidly sank to pass away late that night. The funeral took place on the following Wednesday at the Ancient Church of Llanrhos, just outside the town of Llandudno. This has been the family burial place for generations with a vault under the south transept. In the Mostyn enclosure there are two crosses. The crosses are a Celtic one to the memory of his mother, Lady Henrietta Augusta Nevill Lloyd Mostyn, and a white marble one in memory of his first born child who died at the age of two years.

Mr O.A.Lowe and Mr Cyril Rowlands attended the funeral representing the Welsh Cricket Association.

A memorial service was also held in the Holy Trinity Church, Llandudno. Mr and Mrs J.J.Marks attended on behalf of the Llandudno Cricket Club.

*

Five Llandudno players were chosen to play for Caernarvonshire against Denbighshire at Llandudno on 21st June 1929. They were C.P.Woods (captain), E.Eldred, J.Wooller, Capt. Lloyd and D.E.Jones. Match was drawn.

Members of the 1st XI had an alarming experience when returning from a match against St Asaph on 15th June 1929. As the team coach was travelling up the hill near Llanddulas just behind a bus, a saloon car attempted to overtake both vehicles; just at that moment the bus suddenly stopped causing the saloon car to also pull up. The driver of the team coach had to avoid running into the car by swerving onto the side of the road and in so doing crashed against a wall badly damaging the front of the vehicle and the front axle. Fortunately, none of the passengers required medical attention but they were all badly shaken. They continued their journey home in another coach that was sent to rescue them.

During the 1929 season Llandudno played 35 matches of which nine were won, 15 lost and 11 drawn. The club professional then was a Mr Woodhouse who was given lots of praise for the work he had done on the ground. However, for some reason to this day not known and "in the interest of the club" it was felt a change had to be made for the coming season so A.B.Creber of Swansea was engaged. He was already a young professional at 21 years of age, a right handed batsman and a medium/fast bowler who had played for Glamorgan. The club announced a record programme of matches for the 1930 season which included some strong touring sides.

At the end of the 1929 season the club still owed £59 on the pavilion and the balance sheet showed a loss of £104. Some concern was that certain players had failed to pay their subs, the tea receipts were down and expenditure had increased because of the painting work on the pavilion that had to be paid. Also some Vice-Presidents had not come forward with their usual support. It was decided to shame some members by putting up a list in the pavilion of those members who had paid their subscriptions in full.

Some criticism was also directed at a few committee members who did a lot of talking but took no action.

In pursuance to endeavour to brighten up the game for the spectators it was decided that there would be no tea interval in home matches. Play would proceed continuously except for the interval allowed between innings and the MCC rule as to time would be observed.

Cricket Maxims

In Lord Hawke's 'Recollections and Reminiscences' published in 1914 the following maxims for cricketers were taken from his scrapbook written in 1897.

"Cricket is a fine game and the one that does most good. It is characteristic of cricket that while you make runs you make friends. There is no game in the world that requires less training. You cannot drink hard and keep playing. Alcohol must tell on you in the long run. Practise your fielding as much as batting and bowling, and when playing obey the captain cheerfully. Victories are gained generally by the united efforts of the whole team and seldom by any one man."

Most cricketers in pre-war days will recall the fact that Lord Hawke was on the Test Match Committee at Lord's and on five occasions he was chairman which he considered the most thankless position imaginable. He said the honour of being selected to represent England at home is the greatest that can be paid to the merits of any British cricketer.

It was in the 'Good Old Days' members of the Llandudno Pier Orchestra figured prominently in local cricket. Such stalwarts as A.Halstead, A.Nicholls and F.Foulds regularly played for Llandudno who were members of the band. At one time the Orchestra played regularly against the club team but the fixture was dropped in the early 1920s. The date of the very first match is debateable but three games were played in 1889 and the very first match Llandudno played on the Gloddaeth Avenue Recreation Ground (The Oval) was against the Pier Orchestra.

The re-appearance of the Pier Orchestra on 19th June 1930 was when they played a match on the Oval against the Conservative Club and won by 15 runs.

D.E.Jones, Llandudno fast bowler, playing for Caernarvonshire against Flintshire on 14th August 1930, took nine wickets for 12 runs.

During the 1930 season Llandudno did play 25 matches and won 14, lost five and drawn six. The club professional, A.B.Creber had a good season. He had worked hard on the ground and on the field of play he was only four short of 100 wickets. It was felt his engagement had been justified and he was re-engaged for the 1931 season.

There had been some good attendances by the general public at home matches and despite the cold weather the gate receipts were up by £32. 1930 was a good year for cricket and a good advertisement for the town. For the first time for many years the club had a surplus.

Praise for Llandudno Batsman A.H.Mallalieu

'A lover of cricket' wrote the following article in the Colne Valley Guardian of the Llandudno player A.H.Mallalieu who had, on 26th June 1931, scored 93 runs in a match against Llanrwst.

> "Mallalieu had played evening games for Slaithwaite and hard luck to Slaithwaite not to have the services of the brilliant batsman for Saturday games, such a pleasure being reserved for the Llandudno club. I was strongly reminded of Arthur Richardson by this fine amateur's style, particularly in the forceful back play and full blooded front of the wicket strokes. Often he made a defensive stroke crash through the covers and the drive was executed with ease and little apparent effort. Such players in club cricket are rare and well worth watching for an object lesson seems to accompany each shot. I have played on the Llandudno ground and can well imagine an innings played by the brilliant batsman on what may be called a batsman's paradise."

During the interval at the match against St Asaph on 18th July 1931 the club chairman, Mr A.E.Mallalieu J.P. presented D.Emrys Jones, a popular member of the team, with a chiming clock with an inscribed silver plate to mark his wedding which had taken place the previous Saturday. Mr Mallalieu said the presentation showed the esprit-de-corp which existed amongst the members and players of the club.

Llandudno's new professional for the 1932 season was Harry Hall. A medium to fast right arm bowler, he had recently done good service for Crewe Alexandra.

Llandudno played Bangor on 4th July 1932 at home and won by eight wickets. A.H.Mallalieu scored 100 not out which included a six and 14 fours.

The visit of HMS Norfolk to Llandudno

A naval visit of HMS Norfolk arrived in Llandudno on 16th June 1932 and anchored in the bay for 10 days. HMS Norfolk was built on the Clyde by the Fairfield Shipping and Engineering Company and was launched on the 12th December 1928 by the Countess of Leicester and was first commissioned at Devonport on the 14th May 1930. The official tonnage was 10,000 tons with an overall length of 633 feet. In the Second World War she was part of the force that finally sank the German battleship Bismarck in the Atlantic in 1941. The ship's complement consisted of 650 officers and men. HMS Norfolk was attached to the 2nd Cruiser Squadron under the command of Rear-Admiral E.A.Astley-Rushton C.B., C.M.G.. She was met on arrival by Mr R.C.Baxter J.P., Chairman of the Council, and there was a civic reception given at the Imperial Hotel for her Capt. Somerville and officers with other members of the town council present.

A cricket match between the ship's XI and Llandudno took place on the Oval on the following Tuesday, 20th June, in glorious weather. Llandudno batted first and ran up a score of 218 runs. HMS Norfolk fell short on 142. Harry Hall, Llandudno's professional, took eight wickets for 75 runs. The top scorer of the day was Lt. Commander Moore 42 not out.

Other events arranged for the ship's men included a crown green bowls competition at Craig y Don, tennis on the Queen's Road courts and a football match against Llandudno Town on the Council Field. The final event was a Naval Gymkhana on the Council Field which included 14 events and the ship's brass band was also in attendance.

In a local derby match Llandudno were well and truly trounced by Colwyn Bay at Rhos-on-Sea on 1st August 1932. The whole team were dismissed for 31 runs in under an hour. Colwyn Bay had batted first and amassed a total of 244 runs. The famous Test and County player Wilf Wooller was top scorer with 60 runs. Edge took five wickets for nine and Barlow four for 19.

An unusual incident occurred on the pitch during a match against Prestatyn on the Llandudno ground on 28th August 1932. One of the Prestatyn men, whilst facing a ball from D.E.Jones, the home team's fast bowler, suddenly burst into flames when the ball flew past his pad and hit his thigh. The batsman was seen thrusting his hand into his pocket and throwing something away. The flames went out and play continued with no further incident. It was only when the players returned to the pavilion after the match that the spectators were made aware what had happened when one of the umpires produced for all to see a spent box of matches.

Wilfred Wooller (1912-1997)

Wilfred Wooller was a sportsman par excellence who displayed, on and off the field of play, a combative spirit shot through with self-belief. An all-rounder, he was capped 18 times for Wales at rugby. He captained Glamorgan County Cricket Club for more than a decade and played soccer briefly for Cardiff City. He represented Wales at squash rackets and the Cardiff Athletic Club at bowls.

Wooller was a man of charm and a man of arrogance. He was born at Rhos-on-Sea on the North Wales coast and attended Llandudno County School and Rydal School, one of Wales's few public schools, where a shrewd rugby coach switched him from the pack to the back division. At Cambridge he took a degree in Anthropology and won three rugby Blues in 1933 to 1935 and cricket Blues in 1935 and 1936.

Wooller survived incarceration by the Japanese in the Changi prisoner of war camp in Singapore during the Second World War.

On the cricket field he swung the ball worryingly, batted tenaciously and excelled as a close fielder at a time when protective gear was almost non-existent. He first took the field for Glamorgan in 1938 and played his last match for the county 24 years later. He captained the side from 1947 to 1960, with 1948 a golden year when

Glamorgan won the County Championship for the first time. He became secretary of Glamorgan County Cricket Club in 1961 and was elected president 30 years later. Although never called up for service with England he was a Test selector from 1955 to 1961.

During the 1960s and 1970s his uncompromising support for keeping sporting links with South Africa when apartheid was at its most intense sat uneasily with Wales's tolerant culture – a culture made real by the rich ethnic mix of African, Somali and Chinese communities in Cardiff's docklands. Yet, in print and on the air, he never wavered in propounding a point of view some felt gave aid and comfort to an enemy.

There was a special Cricket Week held in 1933 which commenced on the Monday 7th August when the home team played Colwyn Bay. The match was drawn. The following day Llandudno played the 'Visitors' touring side and won that game. On the Wednesday it was the turn of Nantwich and at this game Harry Hall, the club professional, took his Benefit. Nantwich included Dick Tyldesley, the former Lancashire fast bowler, in their side and won handsomely. Undoubtedly, the 'man of the match' was Tyldesley who took seven wickets for only 19 runs. The following day a Lancashire team (Colonel Lawrence XI) were the guests which attracted a very large crowd made up mainly of Lancastrians who were taking their holidays in Llandudno that week. The Cricket Week ended on the Saturday with a game against Bangor.

A Ladies v Gentlemen match was played on 14th September 1933. The ladies' team captain, Miss Mallalieu, met a set of men selected by the club captain, Tudor Roberts. The rules were the usual ones for such matches but in spite of their handicap batting left-handed, or right-handed if a natural left hander, the men scored 176 runs. The Ladies followed and batted very well with a respectable score of 142.

The 1933 season proved to be a successful year for both on and off the field, and also a year to remember in other sports. The club's finances were in good order and the 1st XI had played 36 games and only lost seven. Fifteen were won and 14 drawn. This was no mean feat because captain and 'star' player A.H.Mallalieu was only able to play a few times owing to an injury. The glorious weather that summer was ideal for cricket and greatly enjoyed by the spectators, resulting in an increase in the gate revenue. Harry Hall had another good season establishing a record for the club amassing 1,139 runs and taking 44 wickets in the season.

In the same year England won the Ashes by four games to one. This was the tour when the actual competition was overshadowed by an unfair controversy caused by the Australians, who protested against fast leg stump bowling, known as 'bodyline' bowling. The players and the authorities 'down under' claimed this was dangerous and unfair. Yorkshire won the County Championship for the third year in succession. Arsenal won the First Division (Premier League) while Everton beat Manchester City in the FA Cup Final at Wembley. Lord Derby's horse Hyperion won the Epsom Derby. Cambridge won the Boat Race for the tenth successive time, and Wales won the Rugby Championship. 1933 is certainly a year to remember.

Lord Hawke (Martin Bladen) 1860-1938
England and Yorkshire right-hand batsman.

There can be few, if any, whose services to cricket have more deserved acknowledgement and recording in the pages of Wisden than Lord Hawke. He was associated with the MCC as chairman, president and secretary over the years and was a great administrator of the game. He was also president of the Yorkshire County Cricket Club. What service he may have rendered to cricket and cricketers was for him a labour of love. He gained his greatest pleasure from playing cricket and doing what he believed to be in the interests of the game.

The club held another Cricket Week in 1934 and matches were played against Colwyn Bay, Kendal, Manchester YMCA; Col. L.Willams XI, Wigan and Bangor. Kendal was the fixture set apart for Harry Hall's Benefit match.

Tributes were rendered in respect of Albert Mallalieu J.P. (father of the club's star player) who died in November 1934. He had given close on 30 years to the club and had by reason of ill-health resigned as chairman at the start of the season.

Throughout the 1934 season the committee had received many letters from visiting teams stating how much they had enjoyed their games in Llandudno and thanking the members for their courteous reception. This response proved that cricket was undoubtedly in those days an attraction to Llandudno. It was also reported that again the club was in a happy financial position and that there had been a good attendance at matches.

Michael Vaughan and Andrew [Freddie] Flintoff, now elderly, 85 and 82 years old, are sitting on a park bench outside Lord's cricket ground feeding pigeons and talking about funny cricket moments, past Ashes series, and tours, like they do every day.

Michael turns to Freddie and asks, 'Do you think there's cricket in heaven?'

Flintoff thinks about it for a minute and replies, 'I dunno. But let's make an agreement: if I die first, I'll come back and tell you if there's cricket in heaven, and if you die first, you do the same.' They shake hands on it. Sadly, a few months later, poor Freddie passes on.

One day soon afterwards, Vaughan is sitting there feeding the pigeons by himself when he hears a voice whisper, 'Michael...Michael.'

Vaughan responds, 'Freddie, is that you?'

'Yes it is, Michael,' whispers Freddie's ghost.

Vaughan, still amazed, enquires, 'So, is there cricket in heaven?'

'Well,' says Freddie, 'I've got good news and bad news.'

'Gimme the good news first,' says Vaughan.

Freddie opines, 'Well... there is cricket in heaven.'

Vaughan says, 'That's great! What news could be bad enough to ruin that?'

Freddie sighs and whispers, 'You are going to open the innings this Friday.'

For many years the LMS (London, Midland and Scottish) Railway had held their final on the Llandudno Recreation Ground (it was in this year 1935 that it became called the Oval officially, after houses that had been built around the field and where a new road was built for access to these houses was called the Oval). The 1935 final was played on 17th August between Carlisle and Euston. The cup was presented to Euston, who won by five wickets, by Sir William M.Letts. There were replicas and medals presented to the players and umpires. Sir William referred to the excellent support in which the railway company supported the game of cricket and for bringing the event to the town every year. He was glad LMS took a keen interest in all sport and his thanks were extended to the Llandudno Cricket Club for their hospitality and use of their fine ground.

Carlisle played Euston in the final again in 1936 at the Oval. On that occasion Carlisle won by 67 runs.

Harry Hall was again re-elected professional for the 1936 season.

An interesting occasion held on 4th November 1936 was a cricket club dance held at Paynes's Majestic Ballroom (now a Peacocks store) in aid of club funds. As well as dancing there was a whist drive and cabaret given by the Jose Craven Dance Troupe.

It was on 13th August 1935 Montgomeryshire won the North Wales County Championship for the first time beating Flintshire by 38 runs.

The 1936 Annual General Meeting of the club was held in the Anti-Room of the Town Hall on 22nd December 1936. Mr W.Bolton presided. It was reported the club had had another successful season especially from a playing point of view. The 1st XI played 33 matches and won 19, lost eight and drawn six. Three of the victories were over old rivals Colwyn Bay ending a long spell of defeats under the captaincy of Mervyn Griffiths. G.H.Brown topped the batting averages whilst Harry Hall was the top bowler with 137 wickets. Comments had been made at the splendid work by Hall in coaching the juniors.

The ground and the pavilion were being improved each season and it was considered that the square and outfield was second to none in North Wales, praised by all the clubs affiliated to the North Wales Cricket Association. The election of officers that year included Lord Edward Llewellyn Roger Lloyd-Mostyn (4th Baron) who had taken over as President from the 3rd Baron on his death in 1929.

An interesting fixture list for the 1936 season amongst the usual local matches, i.e. Bangor, Rydal, Colwyn Bay, Denbigh, St Asaph, included some interesting opposition – University of Liverpool, Ashfield, Clubmoor, Wellington, Wrekin College, Wellington, Leeds Zingari, Old Oswestrians, Bury, Viatores, London County Council, Woodcops, The Leather Jackets, LMS and Epworth College.

On the 30th June 1936 in a match against Llanrwst the Llandudno skipper, Mervyn Griffiths, scored a brilliant 101 punishing the Llanrwst bowlers unmercifully for nearly an hour. Llandudno scored 186. Llanrwst were all out for 64.

On 8th May 1937 at the Oval, Llandudno played Prestatyn. R.Thomas, bowling for the Prestatyn side, took all ten Llandudno wickets. Llandudno did go on to win this match by 148 runs.

In the Annual Colwyn Bay Knockout Competition Llandudno (1936 winners) beat Colwyn Bay NALGO on the way to the final. The highlight of the match was R.R.Pole's hat-trick for Llandudno taking altogether four wickets for nine runs.

Llandudno ended the 1937 season with a good win over the LMS Railways team from Crewe. G.H.Brown scored 72 runs for Llandudno. He had totalled 404 runs in his last previous four innings which included three successive centuries. To commemorate this feat the members of the club presented him with an inscribed silver cigarette case. The presentation was made by the High Sheriff of Caernarvonshire Mr Herbert Wood who said Brown's feat was one of outstanding merit and without parallel in the annals of the club. He had scored over 1,000 runs in the 1937 season.

Professional cricketers have been slow to take women's cricket seriously. However suitable it might have been for schoolgirls in those days, the hierarchy at Lord's would not accept that women should be playing a man's game. But in 1937 it was said that women had been playing first class cricket in England for years and it was a fact that a women's England team was in the 1936 season sent out to Australia by the Women's Cricket Association. In 1937 the Australians came to the UK and played return matches. The MCC, the governing body of the cricket world, at last took notice and actually contributed £25 to the hospitality fund which the Women's Cricket Association was raising for entertaining the Australian visitors during their stay.

A regular first team player, The Rev A.E.Parry, B.A. received an invitation to conduct a 'Cricketer's Service' at Shotton Parish

Church on the evening of the 10th August 1938. The occasion was the dedication of a font presented by the cricketers of Flintshire in memory of one of their most faithful supporters, Mr Philip T.Parry.

It was against Shotton at the Oval on 20th August 1938 that Llandudno's popular professional, Harry Hall, was given his Benefit match. He had served the club faithfully for six seasons and each year up to 1938 Hall had taken more than 100 wickets. A large crowd attended the match which resulted in a win for Llandudno and some money 'in the pot' for Harry Hall.

The junior members of the club held their annual match at the Oval on 23rd August 1938. This was the fourth match they had played over the years and had proved to be very popular with the young players, senior club members and spectators. Mr J.J.Marks (President) who was the instigator of this event felt strongly that something should be done to encourage the young members, who regularly practised in the nets, to give them the opportunity to play a match on the sacred square. For this event the lads turned up in white flannels and took their places on the first team's pitch where the match was supervised by white-coated umpires, in the approved style. The teams were selected by Harry Hall who made sure that every lad who wanted to play had a game. Mr Marks observed:

> *"I was impressed by the sportsmanship displayed by these lads who, if only playing 6-a-side, insisted on observing all the rules of the game. Some hold distinct promise and as for the fielding, well, it would do some of the first team eleven good to watch their keenness."*

Mr and Mrs Marks provided the tea with the help of Mrs Ben Morris and Mrs Hywel Hughes. One of the boys called "three cheers for Mr Marks for a lovely tea".

After which play was resumed and the whole atmosphere was one of cheeriness and the event informal as it ought to be to encourage the lads. It was proven that some were good enough eventually to play in a senior side and for years to come.

On the same day this match was being played Len Hutton was making history scoring 364 runs in a Test Match against Australia which still remains an England Test record. It's also interesting to know that when he was just 17 years of age at Colwyn Bay playing for the Yorkshire 2nd XI against Denbighshire he made his first county century.

Mr J.J.Marks

He died on 25th March 1939. He was a founder member of the Llandudno Cricket Club in 1890. Mr James Jones Marks M.A., LL.B. was a Llandudno solicitor and Registrar for the County Court. Mr Marks's body was recovered from the sea on 25th March 1939. He had fallen into the water from the Llandudno Pier.

He had recently undergone an operation at the Llandudno hospital and had been seriously ill for months. A keen sportsman, and especially cricket, he was also considered one of Llandudno's outstanding citizens. It was known then that he had been suffering with depression. The Deputy Coroner's report stated that there was a small cut to his neck probably caused by a razor blade. Some blood was found on the pier near a hat and coat, with the initials and name 'J.J.Marks' neatly folded and placed just behind one of the pier kiosks. An empty razor blade case holder was also found. It was said the cut to the neck could not have been fatal. The cause of death was drowning.

The death of Chas F.Farrington was reported on 15th April 1939. A keen sportsman who was a particularly enthusiastic cricketer and for many years he was a member of the Llandudno cricket club. When he ceased active participation he continued to show his interest in an executive capacity. At one time he captained the 1st XI. He was the first chairman of the North Wales Cricket Association and at one time he was chairman of the Colwyn Bay cricket club. He was also an efficient umpire.

Playing for Nottinghamshire against the MCC at Lord's in June 1870, George Summers died after being hit on the cheekbone by a ball from John Platts, a Derbyshire fast bowler making his first-class debut. Above George Summers' grave in Nottingham the MCC erected a memorial tablet 'testifying their sense of his qualities as a cricketer and regret at the untimely accident on the Lord's ground'.

1939-1945

2nd World War – The War Years

It was generally said that the Second World War began on 1st September 1939 with the invasion of Poland by Germany and subsequent declarations of war on Germany by France and the United Kingdom. On 3rd September 1939 Prime Minister Neville Chamberlain in his famous speech to the Nation said:

> *"I am speaking to you from the Cabinet Room at 10 Downing Street. This morning the British Ambassador in Berlin handed the German Government a final note stating that, unless we hear from them by 11 o'clock that they were prepared at once to withdraw their troops from Poland, a state of war would exist between us. I have to tell you now that no such undertaking has been received, and that consequently this country is at war with Germany."*

The outbreak of the Second World War brought the evacuation of government departments from London to the safer areas in North Wales. The civil servants of the Treasury took over all Llandudno hotels. Many brought their families with them.

During the 1939 season Llandudno's 1st XI played 31 matches, won 17, lost four and drew seven. They opened their 1939 season against Prestatyn with a new captain, Mr T.Taylor, who was also the secretary and treasurer. They did beat Prestatyn but the interesting point about this game was the introduction of the 8-ball over.

The following is some interesting cricket data in 1939 (mid-season) of the performance of clubs in North Wales, including that of Llandudno.

	P	W	L	D
Llandudno	14	11	2	1
Northop Hall	9	7	0	2
Prestatyn	10	5	5	0
Llanrwst	9	5	3	1
Halkyn	10	5	4	1
Portmadoc	7	4	2	1
Parciau	9	4	2	3
Buckley	11	4	3	4
St Asaph	13	4	7	2
Bangor	12	4	3	5
Bryn y Neaudd	6	3	1	2
Ruthin	9	3	4	2
Colwyn Bay	14	3	5	6
Shotton	9	2	2	5
Bangor University	7	1	2	4

When Llandudno met the Old Oswestrians at the Oval on August 11th 1939 it was Harry Hall's great day. He not only attained his 100 wickets for the season but had also attained a grand total of 1,029 wickets for the period he had been professional at the club. When asked which was his best year he said it was when he had taken 178 wickets and made 1,000 runs. At the time it was a record in North Wales.

Lord and Lady Mostyn were bereaved under particularly distressing circumstances with the loss of their second son The Hon John Llewelyn Lloyd Mostyn R.N.. He was 28 years old and a Midshipman in the Royal Navy. On 10th January 1940 he lost his life as a result of a shooting incident. He was on leave in Glasgow when he was shot dead by a fellow midshipman who had pointed a pistol at him as a prank. The latter was put on trial but acquitted of culpable homicide (manslaughter). Lord Mostyn told the inquest that nobody was to blame for the death, which had happened when his son and comrades had been working with a revolver, apparently thinking it wasn't loaded. Lord Edward Llewelyn Roger Mostyn (4th Baron) had taken over the role of President of the Llandudno cricket club in 1929.

Causing a lot of concern in 1940 was the club's bank overdraft. At the time the tenancy of the ground was still on a year to year arrangement and that being the case little security was being offered to the club's guarantors. Communication with the landlords, Mostyn Estate, on this matter had been ongoing for some years. They were only prepared to grant a lease when the club could show that its finances were in order. The club had been told to improve their finances as the position was now becoming serious.

There was some doubt, because of the war, whether the club could continue because they had lost many of the regular players to the HM Forces. Some of the regular visiting sides had been unable to arrange fixtures as they had no team. However, it was felt that with the presence of the Civil Service having moved offices to Llandudno from London and with several good players available amongst them, some matches could be arranged. Other arrangements were made that a Civil Service Cricket Club could have the use of the Oval for their matches, including the pavilion, and for some Llandudno players to join them. The civil servants who were keenly interested in cricket were thankful to be in Llandudno as they knew there would be little club cricket in the London district during the war.

The Civil Service played their first match at the Oval against Bangor University on 27th April 1940. In the following month they played Colwyn Bay twice. The Llandudno batsman George H.Brown played for the Civil Service and hit two centuries (127 and 103). In a match immediately following and playing for Llandudno against the Inland

Revenue he missed his third century by two runs. Llandudno won that game by 189 runs.

In the last game of the season on 1st September 1940, Llandudno played their final game and were defeated this time by the Inland Revenue.

It was reported on 7th September 1940 that Lieut. The Hon. Roger Edward Lloyd Mostyn of the Royal Armoured Corps (Lancers) had been badly injured. The 20 year old was the direct heir for Lord Mostyn and did become 5th Baron in 1965. A few months before the incident when he was on active duty in France, his tank was knocked out by a direct hit when advancing against the Germans. He died in 2000.

The 1941 season opened at the Oval on 4th May. That year there was an amalgamation, and the club was then known as the Llandudno and Inland Revenue Cricket Club. Owing to the war the number of Llandudno cricketers available to play had been sadly reduced but the Inland Revenue cricketers had come to the rescue and were playing to keep the club going until the return of peace. The teams were therefore a combination of Llandudno players and the civil servants who had made temporary homes in Llandudno. Harry Hall had been re-engaged as club professional.

Llandudno player Sergeant Gordon Wooller (Wilf Wooller's brother) had been posted as missing on 19th July 1941.

The 1942 season opened at the Oval on 2nd May 1941. The Inland Revenue Sports Association had now leased the Oval from Mostyn Estate and by arrangement with the War Department the military in the town would be sharing the ground.

For Saturday matches entrance to the ground was 6p. Members of the forces were admitted free to all matches. Season tickets were available at 10/6d each which admitted the holder and one lady to all the games.

In a match at the Oval on 9th May 1942 between the Army Garrison XI against Colwyn Bay, Gunner Private Gill took all ten Colwyn Bay wickets.

A cricket match played on 24th July 1943 at the Oval had been arranged in aid of the Red Cross Prisoners of War Fund by the Inland Revenue Sports Association between an Association of North Wales Clubs and the Combined Services. Just £25 was raised from 800 spectators present which was one of the largest gates on record at the time for a cricket match at the Oval. John Hardman (Rydal School), E.W.Holt (Colwyn Bay), D.E.Jones (Bangor) and W.E.Edmond (Colwyn Bay) played for the North Wales team. There were no players from Llandudno. North Wales won by 15 runs.

The Inland Revenue Women's Cricket Club played their first match at the Oval on 21st March 1944 against the Ministry of Food Women's Cricket Club. The game was drawn but another game between the two sides played the following month was won by the Inland Revenue. This was to be the first of many women's matches played at the Oval during the war years.

Lieutenant Peredur V.Morgan Thomas joined the Royal Navy in 1944 when he was 18. He was the only son of Police Constable Robert Thomas and Mrs Morgan Thomas. They lived in Maelgwyn Drive, Deganwy. He was a pupil at the John Bright School. His first station was on HMS Glendower based at Pwllheli. Within six weeks he became a cadet and served on HMS Marattah which was torpedoed in a Russian convoy off the Norwegian coast. After having been at the Royal Naval College at Gosport, he went to Canada and the USA and qualified as a pilot. He served on the aircraft carrier 'Theseus' in the Mediterranean until the war ended. He was appointed instructor in aerial combat and ground attack at headquarters of the Naval Air Fighter School, Helston. Whilst taking part in exercises, two planes from the Royal Naval Air Station, Helston collided, five thousand feet up over the English Channel. Lieutenant Thomas did everything possible to bring his crippled plane to base although part of the wing had been ripped off. His machine crashed into the sea off the Lizard. Lieutenant Thomas did not survive. He was 25 years of age.

It is interesting to trace how some of the laws of cricket came into being. For instance Law 6, which lays down that the bat should not exceed 4 1/2 inches in its widest part, was passed in the early 1800s following the appearance of a player named Mr White of Reigate who brought to a match a bat the width of the stumps which proved a veritable 'barn door' to the bowlers. Probably there may be some players today who wish the law had never been passed.

Today one can scarcely visualise a cricket ground without a marked boundary but there was a time when even Lord's was without. W.G.Grace had recorded that in those pre-boundary days the ball very often was fielded amongst the spectators. During one match in the 1970s A.N.Hornby playing for Lancashire chased a ball into the crowd scattering spectators in the process. Unfortunately one elderly gentleman was not quick enough to get out of the way of 'charging bull' Hornby and was badly hurt. This unfortunate occurrence caused the Lord's authorities to give the matter serious consideration and as a result a boundary line was instituted.

1946-1972

Efforts to revive Llandudno Cricket Club fail

Thanks to the enthusiasm of the departments of the Inland Revenue, cricket on the Oval was assured during the 1946 season. Efforts had been made to revive the former Llandudno club but this had failed.

The Inland Revenue Association took over the Oval again in 1947 for the cricket season. However, they had hoped the long cricket tradition at Llandudno which had been maintained during the war years should continue. The Inland Revenue had always welcomed resident players who were not on the Revenue staff to play. They now felt very strongly that the time had come when Llandudno cricketers should come forward and accept the Revenue's invitation so that to form the nucleus of a future Llandudno club which would carry on that unbroken tradition.

The future of cricket in Llandudno was discussed at a full Town Council meeting on 15th August 1947 when the whole matter was referred to the Pleasure Grounds Committee for consideration.

The subject at that meeting was raised by Alderman Arthur Hewitt O.B.E. who said:

> *"We used to have the finest cricket club in North Wales but now we are in danger of having no cricket at all in Llandudno. The game has been kept alive during the last few years only by the enthusiasts of the Inland Revenue. The Pleasure Grounds Committee should consider whether this council can do anything to preserve and keep alive the game of cricket in Llandudno and secure for that purpose the ground on which for 60 years this club has played. It seems a great pity that we should hand over the laurels to Colwyn Bay."*

Councillor James Payne said that matches played in Colwyn Bay were mainly because permission had been refused for them to be played in

Llandudno on Sundays. *"We have the finest ground in North Wales and we ought to have a good team in Llandudno,"* he added.

As a result of what was said at that meeting there were welcoming signs to follow of a general interest amongst locals in the attempt to ensure a revival of cricket in Llandudno. A suggestion put forward by Mr John Tipton was that a council meeting should be called at an early date to re-establish the Llandudno cricket club. He suggested the idea that the Council's Publicity Association should be asked to assist and that an effort be made to get 100 Vice-Presidents to subscribe £2.2s a year and in time a special annual cricket week be organised.

> *"The establishment of a good club would in my opinion be of distinct benefit to the town as a holiday resort and that is why the Publicity Association should give their aid," said Mr Tipton.*

At a meeting of the John Bright Grammar School Governors, it was agreed that boys should be given the opportunity to be associated with a new town club so that they could learn to play cricket on a good wicket. They had been advised by the headmaster that consent had been given by the Inland Revenue for the boys from the school to play matches on the Oval.

Letter received from Allan Owen of Clifton Road, Llandudno:

> *"It is not for the lack of enthusiasm that Llandudno is without a good team. Admittedly, the Inland Revenue has kept cricket going in Llandudno during the war years and the reason is obvious to all. Alderman Arthur Hewitt was quite right when he said that we did have the finest club in North Wales but he did not mention the period when the club was in being. I would venture to say that not for a good number of years has cricket been on a high level in Llandudno. This was indicated by the number of cricket followers in the town compared with the number of spectators seen at every pre-war match. Real talent was wasted because boys could not afford to join the club or buy the necessary equipment that is vital to the game. The number of boys that play cricket at school with definite talent is quite a large percentage but how*

many do we see with the bat after school? Is the standard of school cricket low? The answer to that question is certainly not. I've seen school cricket teams in Llandudno far better than the so-called Llandudno team. I suggest that when a committee is formed to take this question further it should include members who know something about cricket and how to pick a team worthy of Llandudno. Let the working man's son be a true representation of the town's cricket talent. If the team member cannot afford to buy 'togs' then let the supporters of good cricket come forward and help. Let us have a Llandudno team of Llandudno men who can display talent with the next, providing that they are managed in a good democratic way."

A letter to the editor of the Llandudno Advertiser 6th September 1947:

Dear Sir

May I, as an old playing member of the Llandudno Cricket Club express my appreciation at the way the Inland Revenue members have looked after the ground and pavilion during their tenancy. I have been a playing member of the club for the last 28 years with a break from 1942-1946 and hope to join the club again this season. I was afforded every facility for net and match play. A few people, not connected with the club, are aware of the great amount of purely voluntary effort the Inland Revenue members (men and women) have put in. I understand that they are now preparing a fixture list for next season with a view to it being used either by themselves or by a local revised Llandudno club side. I am well aware that some old members of the Llandudno cricket club do not see eye to eye with the Inland Revenue members but surely the main point is that the club and ground have been kept alive and are ready for the 1948 season.

G.H.Brown

Victoria Drive, Llandudno Junction

It is interesting to note how far back it is since some of the things which are now an integral part of the game came into being.

The first detailed score sheet made its appearance in 1744. Even then it did not always record how a batsman was out. This was also the year when the first 'Laws of Cricket' were published.

In 1829 the length of stumps increased from 24 to 27 inches and the length of bails from seven to eight inches.

Did you know that the Association of Cricket Umpires has its own special tie? The tie has salmon pink stripes with the beady eyes of an owl of wisdom perched beneath the Scales of Justice. We know of some players today who would swear that the owl has its eyes closed.

The occasion of the Annual Meeting of the Inland Revenue Cricket Club in September 1947 contained sufficient evidence to prove that the members of the Inland Revenue staff, when their stay in Llandudno ended, would be pleased to hand over cricket at the Oval as a going concern to the new club.

The Chairman Mr C.R.Pledger C.B.E. said:

"We don't know where we shall be next season. That remains in the lap of the gods but if we do go we shall leave things in good order and the fixtures already arranged will be handed over to local players who we hope will keep the cricket club flying in Llandudno."

The headmaster of John Bright Grammar School, Mr S.O.Rees, had been invited to the meeting because it was well known that he was very interested in stepping up cricket in Llandudno being a keen player himself in the past. Mr Rees thanked the Inland Revenue club in allowing the boys of John Bright School the facilities to play on the Oval for they had no suitable ground of their own. He said some of the Inland Revenue staff in Llandudno had been educated at his school and he welcomed their support in the effort made to re-establish the old club in the town. The chairman made the point that he had always supported the policy of inviting local players to join hands with the Inland Revenue in keeping the game alive.

It followed there was uncertainty at the time in forming a club in readiness for the 1948 season because local enthusiasm was lacking. Fixtures had been arranged with a number of clubs who were keen to play in Llandudno mainly because the Oval was still regarded as one of the best grounds in North Wales. In the circumstances that the organisation of a local club should fail it was decided a deadline for a decision to be made would be 5th January 1948. If the fulfilment of fixtures was still in doubt the clubs would be informed so that they could go ahead and arrange an alternative fixture elsewhere.

In the meantime the decision to reform the Llandudno Cricket Club by the town council was unanimously agreed. The welcome news came out of a meeting called by the Pleasure Grounds Committee on the 8th January 1948.

Alderman Hewitt who was elected as chairman of the new steering committee of the club was pleased that the right decision had been made as he felt it would have been an everlasting disgrace to the town if they were to allow cricket to die without some effort being made to resuscitate it and arouse some keenness among the younger men. They had probably the finest ground in North Wales to play on.

> *"Let us not start with the idea that we are setting off a damp squib that will go up and come down again, but on the basis that it will be once more a permanent club," he said.*

Mr Tom Taylor pointed out that they would be faced with several difficulties because they had no essential kit and no professional player/groundsman which would require financial support.

Alderman Hewitt expressed a thought that they were leaning too much on the local council. He suggested that the council should assist the new club for the first season but not let the council permanently run the club. He suggested that the Pleasure Grounds Committee should be asked to assist in maintaining the ground for the forthcoming season to give them a good start. It was emphasised that unless they got good support from the locals they would have financial difficulties and it was pointed out that the cost of a cricket ball had risen from 13/6d to £1.13s.6d. The Inland Revenue had promised to help by handing over the sight screens and other equipment and items.

Mr S.O.Rees said that he would like to see the boys of his school develop an interest in the game.

> *"I think the great thing is having the spirit," he said. "If you get that, other things will follow. If you make it a selective club then it will be doomed. I think the school would be willing and glad to make some small contribution to the upkeep of the ground."*

In the 1948 John Bright School Magazine a poem written by Pat Byron (Class 4A) appears which highlights the plight of enthusiastic pupils at the school who do not have their own cricket field to play on:

The grammar school now is in a state of despair,

The cricket enthusiasts all tear their hair,

The reason for this is abundantly clear,

Our cricket's been banned for the whole of the year.

Though our hopes, at first, were really quite high,

An appeal was issued to all those inclined,

To give cash to our cause – the best you could find!

We've almost lost hope of an offer from one

Who would give us the chance of a great deal of fun

By giving a field intended for cricket –

We would show him our skill in defending the wicket.

Still we'll try not to be too gloomy and mope,

And one motto remains, "We won't give up hope".

It was agreed to invite Lord Mostyn to become President. Alderman Hewitt was appointed as Vice-President and Councillor P.I.Dutton was asked to act as temporary Chairman. The following were appointed to the committee. They were Messrs S.O.Rees, J.H.Cadman, N.J.Meyor, N.White, Emrys Jones and David A.Roberts. Mr A.R.Hughes was appointed Press Secretary.

The 'Father of Cricket' W.G.Grace was once bowled first ball in an exhibition match. 'They have come to watch me bat, not you bowl,' he said, before replacing the bails and resuming his innings.

A notice appeared in the press on 24th January 1948 as follows:

Are you a cricketer?

Players invited to join town club

Lovers of cricket in Llandudno will be pleased to know that the recently elected committee, entrusted with re-establishing the local club, have started in their tasks energetically. Negotiations for the lease of the Oval have been initiated and the committee are in a position to report to another general meeting of the council, convened for Thursday 29th January 1948 in the Council Chambers of the Town Hall. The help promised by the Town Council was greatly appreciated for the committee have to face heavy expenditure on equipment. The Honourable Secretary will be pleased to enrol prospective members and give any information regarding the proposed activities of the club. The club have taken over the fixture list arranged by the Inland Revenue cricket club.

After a few days following the notice in the press, a letter was received from the Secretary of The International Refrigeration Co, Ltd. Llandudno Junction (known later as Hotpoint). It stated that there were several good cricketers in the firm who wished to obtain the use of the ground. All these players had expressed a wish to join the new club.

A meeting was arranged with Mostyn Estate Ltd. with regard to obtaining the use of the ground at the Oval. Unfortunately, the conditions laid down by Mostyn Estate were not accepted. This led to the decision that the attempt to re-instate the club be shelved for at least the 1948 season because of the ban by Mostyn Estate on Sunday cricket and the fact that the rent of £50 was considered too high. This decision caused the Coldrator Refrigeration Sports Club of Llandudno Junction to withdraw their support. This meant that the number of prospective playing members had halved and that the estimated loss of revenue to the club (£250-£300) would be too much.

Mostyn Estate had originally asked for £70 rent and only agreed after tough bargaining to reduce it to £50. It was pointed out that the reason for the ban on Sunday play was because of a clause in the lease agreements of the recently built houses surrounding the Oval ground.

Coldrator Cricket Club secure the Oval for the 1949 season

Coldrator Cricket Club of Llandudno Junction had secured the Oval for the 1949 season and their first match on 7th May was against the Victoria Cricket Club of Deganwy – they won by four runs.

During the season they played matches against Crosville, Rydal School 2nd XI, HMS Conwy, Ruthin, Mochdre, Colwyn Bay Colts, Willows XI, Penmaenmawr, Ministry of Foods and Braids Garage Group.

It was announced in September of the same year that there would definitely be a Llandudno Cricket Club playing at the Oval in the 1950 season. An inaugural meeting of the club was held in the Council Chambers on 13th October 1949.

At this public meeting it was unanimously decided to re-form the club which had not functioned properly since 1939, before the war. Alderman Arthur Hewitt was appointed chairman at this meeting. Messrs S.G.Bullen, Howell Hughes and E.Lee were appointed Secretary, Treasurer, and Fixture Secretary respectively. The following were elected to the committee with power to co-opt. They were Messrs David A.Roberts, H.Travers, J.Knott, R.Wildblood, C.Brown, N.Batley, N.Meyer and J.P.Jones. At a meeting that followed J.P.Jones was elected Chairman.

There was an item in the local Advertiser from the Chairman and Treasurer following the meeting appealing for funds for equipment etc.

"There should be no need to stress the fact that an attractive cricket club would be an asset to Llandudno in addition to providing recreation for the youth of the town and pleasure for cricket enthusiasts."

Dennis Lillee once commented that the arrogant natured Yorkshire man Geoff Boycott was, 'The only fellow I've met who fell in love with himself at an early age and has remained faithful ever since'.

An Extraordinary General Meeting on 21st March 1950 was held to formally agree to the new rules and adopt the constitution for the new club.

Net practice sessions commenced on 15th April 1950 to welcome all playing members.

The season officially opened on 29th April, with the first team away to Northop Hall and the second XI at home to Rhyl. Both games were cancelled because of rain. The following week a first team game against Kinmel Garrison was also cancelled because of rain.

Three Llandudno players selected to play for Caernarvonshire against Denbighshire at the Oval on 20th May 1950 were John Humphreys, H.F.Adams and C.R.Tooth. The match ended in a draw.

In a match at the Oval against Rydal School on 3rd June John Humphreys attained the distinction of being the first player to score a century for the newly formed club. His innings of 104 not out took under three hours and steered Llandudno to a 42 runs win.

The Llandudno Town Council received a written protest from the Welsh Free Church Council against the playing of cricket on the Oval on Sundays. Without comment the council on 16th June 1950 adopted a recommendation of the Pleasure Grounds Committee that cricket should be allowed on Sundays on the Oval from 2pm.

Before a record crowd of 500 spectators Llandudno beat a strong Flintshire XI at the Oval.

In reply to a letter from Mr S.O.Rees (Headmaster of John Bright G.S.) the council's Pleasure Grounds Committee gave permission for the boys of the school to have use of the Oval on dates in June and July. They decided to allow the use of a practice pitch at 30s per afternoon for up to four hours. The school did have a cricket team but owing to the fact that they had no home ground at their disposal all their fixtures were played away.

Llandudno CC held the first of their Annual Buffet Dance evenings at the Grand Hotel on 18th October 1950. It was announced at the event that the club's post-war season had been a success. The 1st XI had played 41 matches, won 18, lost 15 and drawn eight.

Arthur Meyrick, a pupil at John Bright Grammar School, wrote a prize-winning essay which won the Lily Wartski Memorial Prize for 1950. It was on 'The Importance of School Games' and the following excerpt from his essay describes his thoughts on cricket and the values of just taking part:

"It may be a mud-churned field in winter, or the fresh sparkling grass echoing to the crack of bat upon ball or the drab timbers of the gymnasium floor – any one of these can teach the ways of a gentleman, the essence of sportsmanship, the goodwill of friendship. They can also relieve the strain of lessons. What a refreshing thought it is when I have just had a lesson which has been boring and strenuous. I come out of the main door with my boots in my hand. I must rush into the dressing room, change into my kit and get onto the field and join in the game. After the end of every match, walking off, either victorious or defeated, the school captain's cheerful voice breaks in with: "Three cheers for…" and then everybody congratulates each other. I think that the dressing-room atmosphere counts a lot. There is always the cheerful, joking spirit there, endless chatter and the room echoing long after it has emptied.

Cricket is regarded as the Englishman's game and it's quite true. What Englishman will pass a cricket field without looking on for at least a few moments? The thrill of expectancy is there as in soccer. Every boy has a thrill when he is called upon to bowl or to make the long trek from the pavilion to the wicket. He is aware of the eyes of the spectators following him and of the confident attitude of the fielders as they lounge about. He feels hot under the collar, perhaps he is walking too fast. He holds his bat more tightly and pulls his pads nervously. At last he reaches the crease and calls for guard. He tries to obtain some position of ease while the field is set. Down comes the first ball which he plays carefully and at last the over is finished; he is full of confidence and ready to distinguish himself but oh! How long the wicket seems as he scampers along watching the flight of the ball which seems to be reaching the wicket before him. Walking back to the pavilion after his innings he either receives cheers for a gallant innings or unspoken sympathy for a 'duck' but whatever happens he is always ready for the next game. That is where sportsmanship comes in, if he has a bad innings it does not matter – he is still popular because it is all part of the game and nobody minds if he has a bad game now and again. Manners count a great deal and this comes from the field of sport as well. We are taught not to argue but to accept decisions and play the game, to control tempers if we are unjustly penalised and take it with civility. I myself have found a lesson in games. They help us to develop our characters, our personalities and bring forth friends old and new. Handshakes and claps on the back all round while the setting sun casts lengthening shadows on a scene of a day's play... ."

Fixtures for the 1951 season included matches against teams from Lancashire, Yorkshire, Cheshire and Staffordshire.

The Oval was again let at a rent of £50, as for the previous year.

The square had been enlarged to prevent the wicket becoming 'overloaded'.

Efforts were being made for caps, pullovers, ties, and blazer badges to be available.

The professional/groundsman for the 1951 season was John Trevor Gibson from St Anne's on Sea, Lancs.

The fixtures arranged for the 1951 season included 49 matches.

1st XI captain – George Heap, 2nd XI captain Norman Batley.

There were junior practice nights during the week and junior matches played during the season against John Bright G.S., Colwyn Bay and Mochdre.

John Trevor Gibson, in his only year as professional for the club, finished the season with 1,115 runs with the bat and he also took 116 wickets. In a match against Old Maricollians (a Liverpool touring side) he scored 112 runs and rounded off a great day by achieving a hat-trick. His bowling figures were five wickets for 18 runs.

Mr J.Knott, Secretary, announced that for the 1952 season a cricket festival on the lines of the Colwyn Bay Festival would be held during August. It was anticipated there would be a two-day match against a Northants team which would include H.R.Brown, the England Captain.

The 1952 cricket season started on 26th April.

1st XI – C.R.Tooth (captain), N.Batley, R.Beswick, W.Housley, H.Hughes, E.S.Robinson, Rev. D.G.Taylor, R.Wilde, J.Williams, H.Yates and J.Shaw.

2nd XI – C.C.Brown (captain), A.C.Abbott, Z.Brierley, P.Fitton, P.B.Greenwood, J.Knott, B.Langley, R.A.Noke, J.M.Smith, J.Taylor and R.C.Williams.

W.Housley, one of Llandudno's promising young cricketers in 1952, and a John Bright G.S. pupil, played in the trials for the Welsh Schools XI which was held in Cardiff.

In a match for Caernarvonshire against Flintshire held on the Oval on 12th July 1952, the club professional Jack Shaw, took 5 wickets for 54 runs and then went on to make the top score (47) to win the match. Two other Llandudno players contributed to this win which assured Caernarvonshire winning the North Wales County Cricket Championship. They were Howell Hughes (Woodwork teacher at John Bright G.S.) and G.Heap.

When Llandudno met the Rover Cars Co. CC on 19th July 1952 they made their highest score up to then in post-war cricket while Jack Shaw hit an unbeaten 127 which included 96 in boundaries. Llandudno made 210 for four dec. Rover Cars were bowled out for 154 with just five minutes to spare.

Mr Huw Tudno Williams was an energetically active and highly respected club member for all of his 40 years, both on and off the field. He was an Honorary Life Member for a number of years. He played his first match recorded for Llandudno in a 2nd XI game against Wigan on 29th July 1952. Batting at no.11 he was out for a 'duck' but it was reported his contribution to the game deserved high praise in the field. Mention was made of "his grand fielding who handled every ball that came his way cleanly and dived for anything in his reach". He developed into a fine right arm medium pace bowler who captured lots of wickets over the years and who was highly praised as a 2nd team captain. He was a hard-working committee member and a fund raiser who, unselfishly, made thousands of pounds for the club with his self-adapted '250' club. He found time as the press reporter on matches in the 1960s ,1970s and 1980s for the Llandudno Advertiser and the North Wales Weekly News. He was also a famous and respected local historian who had been a member and chairman of the Llandudno Historical Society. He was also a founder member of an exploratory group into the copper mines on the Great Orme. He enjoyed other sports and especially table tennis, becoming one of the best and finest top players in North Wales. He had also played football for Llandudno and the Llandudno Youth Club. During the 1980s he was a team member of the Craig y Don Bowling club. Huw died after a long illness in 1992 at the age of 64 years.

The last unofficial fixture of the 1952 season at the Oval on Sunday 21st September resulted in a nine wicket win for a Reg Boase's XI (Colwyn Bay) against a Clem Brown's XI (Llandudno).

There was an interesting comment in the Llandudno Advertiser which singled out a 17 year old named Rene Clayton who had certainly played his part in securing victory for the visitors. He followed up his five wickets for 26 runs by carrying his bat for 37. It was said on the day that the Bay certainly had an up and coming cricketer in the youngster.

Jack Shaw in his only season with the club as professional took 134 wickets and scored 1,230 runs. The new man for the 1953 season was Frank Lees from Slough, a fully qualified MCC coach.

The club was grateful to Zac Brierley for his gift of a new scoreboard.

The Publicity Committee had worked hard in 1952 and succeeded in raising membership from 183 to 266.

Work commenced on the preparation of a concrete playing strip at one end of the cricket square.

E.S.Robinson, J.Chilton and J.Rhys Williams were each presented with an inscribed cricket ball for accomplishing a hat-trick during the 1952 season.

The incoming club captains for the 1953 season were 1st XI C.Birch and 2nd XI Clem Brown.

A spectator's season ticket cost half a guinea entitling the holder to all matches considered as 'cheap cricket' even in those days.

Visitors to the Oval on 28th May 1953 numbered 600 and they were treated to a thrilling game against Courtaulds. After Llandudno had batted scoring 230 for five declared, Courtaulds followed with their innings and it was not until the last ball of the final over of the match did Llandudno snatch victory. It was the bowling of Stan Pounder who captured that last wicket and finished with three for 25. It was Ronnie Tooth for the home team who was the man of the match after scoring 109 not out which included 14 boundaries.

The 1953 season ended with the 1st XI having played 30 matches, won 16 and lost six, with eight drawn. The 2nd XI played 11, won five, lost three and drew three.

After a long illness John Humphreys of Ffordd Penrhyn, a prolific batsman for Llandudno for a number of years, died on 14th September 1954 aged 34 years. He was the first player to score a century for the newly formed cricket club in 1950. He was also a Caernarvonshire County player. He played football for Everton making his debut for the club in 1946 and made 61 appearances for the top division side. He obtained his Welsh Cap against Ireland in 1947 and finished his footballing career with the Llandudno town club. His son, Gerald Humphreys, a well-known local taxi driver followed in his step-father's footsteps and also played for Everton from 1963-1970. Gerald never actually played cricket for the club but at one time was often seen with bat and ball 'giving it a go' in the nets.

The late Mr Howell Hughes was a fine batsman and wicket-keeper. He was chosen to play for Caernarvonshire on many occasions and was Llandudno's 1st XI opening bat. He was Woodwork teacher at John Bright Grammar School from 1949 and was affectionately known as 'Woody Mallet' by his pupils. The success of many of his pupils on the cricket field was because he was responsible for the school cricket and the boys who were keen were encouraged to play for the town team as a means of stepping up their game. Before 1953 the school had no field to play on and in association with the Llandudno CC had practice sessions on the Oval during week days. For a number of years it was quite common for boys to play for the school on Saturday morning and to go on and play for Llandudno 1st or 2nd XI in the afternoon. In a school magazine written to celebrate 'One Hundred Years of Quality Education 1896-1996' the following is an article by Mr Hughes which includes the names of 99% of players who went on to play for Llandudno CC:

"Cricket during my first years at the school was played at the Oval and it is thanks to the Llandudno Cricket Club that we were able to have school and house matches played there.

My memories of those early days are mainly of the late Derek Harrison. He was an excellent all-round sportsman and an exceptionally good fast bowler, who also turned out for the town XI. After him come such names as I.G.Williams, Peris Edwards, Geoffrey Evans, P.J.Nevitt, H.K.Roberts, M.H.Sharpe and Bill Housley who became the best all-rounder to play for the 1st XI.

In 1953, for the first time since the war we were able to play cricket on our own ground. We had a first class wicket in 'the middle' and what is more we had first class nets for practice. Cricketers from this era I recall are John Joule, Ken Jones and Joe Cosgrove, who was to become the best seam bowler to play for the school. Vaughan Rees was a Welsh school boy cricket trialist and one of the best cricketing captains to lead the team. Others include Keith Pritchard, Alan McIntosh, John Hughes, Brian Baister, Ronnie Williams, Geoffrey Rees, Gareth Roberts, Alan Hughes and Graham Edwards. John Owen and Roger Latham were very effective leg-break bowlers.

Later, two outstanding batsmen came on the cricketing scene – Anthony Neville, a Welsh Schools international who also played for the Minor Counties. He went on to play for the Glamorgan 2nd XI. Geoffrey Ellis who captained the Welsh schoolboys, went on to play professional cricket for Glamorgan, and later captained the Welsh Minor Counties side. Other good cricketers at this time were Robert Hughes, John Breeze, Dudley Hare, David Collins, Roger Major, Colin Abbott, Henry Owen and John Newnham whose father played a very important part in the development of Colwyn Bay Cricket Club.

In the beginning of the 1960s another crop of good cricketers represented the school including Max Shone – a very good fast bowler who was a Welsh Schools trialist – Bill Llewelyn, John Robertson, David Evans, Philip Millican, R.Elwyn Williams – a very good batsman and an excellent hockey player (recently appointed Director of Education for the new Aberconwy County Council) – Chris O'Mahoney and David Holt, who did well in the shadows of Geoffrey Ellis. One name however will remain in my memory, Mr Alun Hughes, Head of English at the school whom I have known for some years now. He was a great enthusiast who always tried his very best and considered himself quite a bowler. He fooled quite a few batsmen with his variable length – I will not say anymore!"

An Extraordinary General Meeting was held at the Town Hall on 2nd February 1955 to give approval to a recommendation for increased subs.

Full members 21s to 25s

County members 10/6p to 12/6p

Junior members 7/6p to 10/-

It was decided at that meeting not to increase the subs.

An item in The Advertiser appeared on 11th July 1955.

"It came as a pleasant surprise when Mr Frank Ash (Snr) learned that one of his guests at his boarding house in Caroline Road was Harry Hall, former professional of the club in the 1930s. Mr Ash was Assistant Secretary at the time. Mr Ash managed to get him to talk about the old times and his days at Llandudno in particular. His best year for the club was in 1934 when

he took 175 wickets and scored 1,500 runs. The two outstanding boys he remembers in his day were John Humphreys and David Pardon. He recalled that David played for the county at the early age of 13.

For some big hitters he remembered C.P.Woods, A. Mallalieu and J.P.Jones who gave very creditable performances which excited the crowd, many of them coming back wanting more. As a fast bowler Ronnie Russell was good to watch and not forgetting such men as George Brown and Dr Cole who always gave their best.

Referring to touring sides that played at the Oval, a Dodd's XI (team of doctors) and Col. Lawrence Williams's XI always provided exciting cricket for the spectators. With regard to skippers none impressed him more than Llandudno's own Tudor Roberts."

Mr Ash wrote: *"When Harry visited the Oval to watch a game on June 5th so many people came forward to shake his hand and especially from some of the old boys he coached. There were some real hearty handshakes that afternoon which showed admiration and respect at its best."*

In 1955 W.Housley was chosen as skipper of the Caernarvonshire Schools Cricket XI. He also played in a Welsh Secondary Schools trial game and was selected to play for the Caernarvonshire County Cricket XI. He was captain of the John Bright School XI. Keith Jones and Joe Cosgrove were also chosen to play for the Caernarvonshire Schools Cricket XI.

Pakistan's Misbah-ul-Haq scored the fastest 50 in Test cricket and equalled the record for quickest century. He reached 50 in 21 balls on the fourth day of the second Test against Australia in 2014, eclipsing Jacques Kallis of South Africa who took 24 balls in 2005.

The Pakistan captain went on to match the 56-ball century mark set by West Indies legend Viv Richards in 1986.

Concern was expressed again at the financial position of the club in February 1956. The treasurer reported that there was a considerable loss on the cricket side of the club and members were urged to pay their subs as soon as possible. The situation had worsened because it was only 12 months previously when it was decided not to increase the subs. It was decided on this occasion for the 1956 season the rate for full membership should be increased to 30/- and country members to pay 12/6p. Subscription rates for juniors would remain the same at 7/6p.

Horace Chetwyn was the new professional for the 1956 season; 1st XI Captain – Jack Riley and 2nd XI Captain – Ron Beswick.

After giving excellent and devoted service for some years as Secretary, Archie Abbott relinquished his post for business reasons. It was not long afterwards that he was made a Life-Member – an honour bestowed to just a few deserved members who had given outstanding service over the years recognised by other members of the club. His successor was J.P.Jones who joined the club in 1912. An active playing member for 25 years having played in the company of such stalwarts as A.Halstead, Chas Farrington, Ted Hobson, Albert Mallalieu, C.P.Woods and a host of others. In his prime he was a bowler of considerable pace and had many excellent performances to his credit and as a batsman he could grace the 'long handle' with considerable effect. Probably the proudest moment in his cricketing career was on that memorable day when he was a member of the Llandudno XI which dismissed Colwyn Bay on the Oval for just 12 runs.

The charge for hiring a deck chair was increased from 6p to 7p with the deposit of 3p to remain the same.

A London visitor to the town and a staunch Middlesex supporter came to watch a match at the Oval on 1st July 1956 when the 1st XI were entertaining Styal CC. He got chatting with some members and had some very interesting things to relate about some Middlesex personalities and had intimate knowledge of the Lord's ground. Having inspected the 'square' he gave his opinion that it was a far better wicket than that at Lord's in spite of all the lavished attention on that ground. The re-marling carried out by the council groundsman during the closed season had undoubtedly improved the playing pitch. Micklehurst CC players who had played on the ground on a recent visit that season said it was the best wicket they had seen that summer.

Two very promising young players, Vaughn Rees and Geoff Rees, still pupils at John Bright G.S., were available to play for the club in 1956. Vaughn, the son of Mr S.O.Rees, Headmaster of the John Bright School, was Head Boy and captain of the school XI. He was already a very useful wicket keeper and highly praised by no less an authority than Howell Hughes who was the wicket keeper for Caernarvonshire and Llandudno at the time. Geoff, the son of another headmaster, Mr Garfield Rees of the Llandudno Secondary Modern School, had all the makings of a good cricketer at a very young age and was beginning to shine as a bowler but in later years proved to be a very good batsman. He was also for a time an active member of the club who served on the committee and for a number of years held the position as chairman.

Some bowling terms

Leg break – a ball which turns leg to off after pitching.

Off break – a ball which turns from off to leg after pitching.

Good length – a ball bowled which pitches at such a distance that the batsman is undecided whether to play back or forward

Maiden over (you ladies out there have nothing to worry about!) – this describes an over of six balls bowled from which no runs are scored by the batsman

Googly – an off-break with a leg-break action

In swinger – a ball swinging in flight from the off across to the leg side of the wicket

Chinaman – a left arm bowler's delivery bowled over the wicket with the ball breaking from the off to a right-handed batsman

Yorker – a ball which pitches almost beneath the bat of the striker as he plays at it

---

During 1956 there had been concern at the late starts in several matches played on the Oval. In one or two instances this had been due to the late arrival of the visiting team but on some occasions it had been the home team who had made late appearances. Evidently cricket had suffered from this sort of thing for many years and as far back as in the minutes of the Hambledon club for 27th July 1773 the following appeared:

> *"That for the future the wickets shall be pitched at half an hour after 10 o'clock in the morning and the players that come after 11 o'clock are to forfeit 3p to be spent amongst those that come at the appointed time."*

There is a shrewd assumption where the men of Hambledon spent the forfeited money because adjoining the ground at Broad Halfpenny Down was and still is the famous 'Bat and Ball' Inn.

Before the commencement of the 1957 season the chairman, Mr David Roberts, appealed for new members because of the steady decline in the recent years. He also said that more young members should take it upon themselves to join the committee and fill official positions in the club otherwise, in his opinion, there would be no future for the club.

In view of the outstanding services to the club in both a playing and administrative capacity over 44 years, Mr J.P.Jones was appointed an Honorary Life Member. He had been involved with the club since 1912.

Horace Chetwyn was re-engaged as professional/groundsman.

Tony Spencer gets the first century (102) of the season against Connahs Quay on 23rd June 1957.

Matches during the 1957 season attracted good attendances at the Oval of between 300 and 500. The ring of spectators sitting in colourful deckchairs around the ground and pretty ladies in bright summer dresses made for an exciting atmosphere. This is something lacking all too often today and, unfortunately, the expression 'one man and his dog' is often the case.

A foreign visitor to Llandudno was once given the following explanation by club member John Breeze, with the aid of Elias Thomas (ex-umpire), who was well-known amongst the players for his knowledge of the game.

> *"There are two sides, one out in the field, one in. Each man on the side that's in goes out and when he is out he comes in and the next man goes in until he is out. When they are all out the side that's been out in the field comes in, and the side that's been in, goes out and tries to get out those coming in. Sometimes you get men still in who are not out. Then when both sides have been in and out, including not outs, that's the end of the game..."*

Before John Breeze was able to finish his explanation the foreign gentleman had hurriedly left the Oval and was last seen running down Lloyd Street towards the town in a very confused state!

The innovation of a licensed bar during the 1957 season had proved to be a success. Viewed with some disdain by some members at first, it was soon welcomed unanimously because it proved to be a financial success.

Mr B.H.Morgan was re-appointed President for the 1958 season. The captains elected were 1st XI Ron Beswick and 2nd XI Ken Lowndes.

Ken J.Williams, a slow leg-break bowler, took all ten wickets at the Oval on 17th May 1958 against Mochdre. He finished with 10 for 39 in 14 overs. At the request of his captain he was asked to bowl at a quicker pace than usual which Ken keenly obliged. But after capturing the first two wickets and in order to conserve his energy he took it upon himself to revert to his normal pace and got the next eight wickets, much to the delight of his captain and team mates. In the same month another Llandudno player, 15 year old Allan Hughes, made history capturing 10 wickets for the John Bright G.S. 2nd XI against Llanrwst G.S..

Peter Greenwood was the guest professional who was engaged to play just one match a week during 1958. He was not involved with any of the cricket coaching.

The club committee in 1958 obtained an electric generator for supplying lighting for the first time in the pavilion.

An interesting reminiscence of cricket in days gone by was when a wealthy gentleman staying in the town during the summer months became a member of the club and during the week attended net practice sessions at the Oval. He had a small tent erected nearby within which his wife would sit combining her knitting with the job of timing the players whose turn it was to bat. At intervals the gentleman's personal butler would appear carrying a silver tray upon which liquid refreshments were arrayed and all the players present were invited to partake.

Those were the days when the wealthy cricket enthusiast brought an aura of breeding and dignity to the cricket fields of our land.

The new chairman for the 1959 season was Archie Abbott.

Subs were increased as follows:

Playing members – £1.10.00

Non-playing members – £1.15.00 (included a deckchair for every match and also to include all the amenities of the club including spending their money at the bar)

Ladies 12/6

Juniors 7/6

A 'friendly' match at the Oval on 7th June 1959 against Great Chell came to a sensational premature end following the home umpire Johnson's refusal to continue umpiring to what he considered ungentlemanly conduct on the part of some of the Staffordshire club's fielders, including their captain. The first incident was when Arthur Johnson (son of the umpire) played a defensive shot which left the ball motionless at his feet. As there was no fielder near to pick up the ball he picked it up and returned it to the bowler. When the Great Chell skipper appealed umpire Johnson had no hesitation in giving him out. At that moment the Great Chell umpire walked over to the skipper and asked if his appeal was serious and was most positively assured that it was. Following this, there were several lbw appeals made by fielders as far apart as gully and square leg. There was also an appeal for a catch behind the wicket which was obvious it was from a ball the batsman did not touch. There were also some comments made by some fielders which might have tended to disturb the batsman. The culminating point came when the opposing skipper appealed for a catch when the batsman edged a ball to the slips which fell well short of the fielder's hands. The fielder did not appeal but the skipper did. Umpire Johnson made it clear that he had had enough, took off his white coat and invited skipper Schofield to continue the game with another umpire and quickly marched off the field and into the pavilion. Apparently the captain was not prepared to accept another umpire and immediately led his men off the field. It was felt by everyone present who witnessed the scene that such frivolous appealing was uncalled for in a friendly game and many spectators commented on Great Chell's unsportsmanlike attitude. Efforts were made to resume the match after tea but the Great Chell captain would not agree.

Mr Johnson afterwards commented that in his opinion a point is reached were 'gamesmanship' becomes 'unfair play' and the visiting side had gone far beyond that point before he decided to retire from the scene. The club committee met a few days afterwards to discuss the circumstances of the match and its result was unanimously confirmed that the action taken by the club's umpire was perfectly justified.

During the 1959 season Raymond Williams became the first amateur player of the club to take 100 wickets in a season. He finished with 120 wickets. In previous years some of the professionals including Shaw, Gibson, Lees, Hartley, Woodhouse, Pell and Harry Hall had reached the century mark and beyond.

During the years Harry Hall was at the club he had no fixed abode except every night he slept on the 'catching cradle' in the pavilion with the blessing of the club committee.

In the 1959 John Bright School magazine, the late Mr Howell Hughes gave the following advice to all players:

> *"Every game calls for ability, fitness, concentration and courage and, should any one of these be missing, a player may not gain all the enjoyment, which he should, from playing games. If a player is not gifted with all the necessary ability, he may succeed, because by combining the other three, he can improve his technique and thus automatically become more able at the game.*

Cricket, in particular, is a game where the non-gifted player may be just as good a player as the gifted one, because of a determined approach to improving himself.

It has been said by cricketers, nearing the end of their playing days that if they could start their game again and combine their knowledge they gained over the years with the agility and fitness of their younger days, how much more they would have enjoyed the game of cricket.

Cricket is a game which always sets new problems for the players, and it is this fact which makes it such a fine game. The leading players are always trying to improve themselves so if you wish to enjoy your game take every possible opportunity you can to improve your standard of play."

J.B.G.S. Team 1950's

J.B.G.S. Team 1953

J.B.G.S. Team 1957/58

J.B.G.S. Team 1960

J.B.G.S. Team 1961

Club Members 1960's

Club Members 1960's

Llandudno mid 1960's

Huw Tudno Williams (3rd right) and Glamorgan 1980's

Committee 1960's

Llandudno 1966

Ron Beswick

Tom Barlow

Brian Baister, Raymond Williams

Clive Stock, Rene Clayton, Roger Bower, Max Shone, John Collier

Vaughn Rees, Brian Baister

John Collier, Rohan Kanhai

On Tour

On Tour 2

Team photo 1960's

HMS Whitby And Llandudno 1970's

Collis King

Andrew Roberts

Stephen Nicholls

Cricket Pavilion is saved from being burnt down

The cricket pavilion had a narrow escape from being burnt down in early May 1960. Some very young children broke into the store shed and took a can of petrol. They proceeded to soak some timber baulks lying in the space below the pavilion floor and set them alight. Fortunately the smoke attracted the attention of the groundsman who immediately called the Fire Service and prevented what would have been, in a few minutes, a very serious conflagration. Fortunately the damage was not extensive.

It was in 1960 that Mr J.A.Edwards, Surveyor to the Llandudno Council, submitted to the Pleasure Grounds Committee sketch plans for providing an improved entrance to the Oval ground from the Gloddaeth Avenue end and the construction of new storage accommodation, public conveniences and a car park. The committee approved the plans and the buildings and improvements are what are used today.

Three John Bright G.S. boys who were regular playing members of the club were selected to play for the Caernarvonshire Schools XI against Anglesey on 4th June 1960. They were Tony Neville (captain), Geoff Rees and Colin Abbott.

The Llandudno CC was represented by the chairman Eric Johnson at the opening on 8th July 1960 of Colwyn Bay's new pavilion by HRH the Duke of Gloucester. Archie Abbott was also present representing the Caernarvonshire Cricket Association of which he was vice-chairman.

Peter Greenwood, the club's professional, scored 100 not out against a touring Wolverhampton side, Mandor Bros., at the Oval on 19th June 1960. Llandudno won that match by 85 runs.

The 1960 season provided several very promising players – two of which worthy to note were youngsters like 16 year-old John Breeze who could send down his left arm deliveries at quite a speed and Eric Goldsmith who on his day could cause batsmen quite a bit of trouble.

Archie Abbott was made a Life Member on 4th March 1961 in recognition of many years' service to the club.

The club suffered a severe setback in early June 1961 when the big-end of the diesel generator which gave light to the pavilion broke down and would prove a very expensive item to replace.

At the same time a mass invasion of the Oval by local children during the evenings was giving considerable worry. Not only was damage being done to property but the square was being trampled on unceremoniously. Several turfs which the groundsman had laid had been deliberately and senselessly torn out and thrown carelessly to all parts of the ground.

Well-earned commendation was extended in 1961 to the club's vice-chairman Owen Jones for his valuable voluntary work in taking charge of looking after the lawns and flower beds in the pavilion enclosure. He also spent time during a match taking around the collection box, thus gaining valuable revenue which was badly needed in 1961.

Young Anthony Neville, already in 1961 a very successful opening bat for the club, was selected to play for the Wales Schoolboys XI. He was also selected to play for the Welsh Clubs XI to play against Glamorgan at Neath. Later in the same year he played for a Glamorgan XI against Cheshire.

Peter Greenwood performed the hat-trick in a match against Halkyn at the Oval on 20th August 1961. He narrowly missed taking a fourth wicket with his next ball which missed the off-stump by a 'whisker'. Llandudno won by eight wickets. He topped the 1st XI averages in both batting and bowling.

G.C.Robinson topped the 2nd XI batting averages while Colin Thomas topped the bowling.

Colin Thomas was an outstanding table tennis player and during his career he won numerous tournaments at both senior and junior level in England, Scotland, Northern Ireland and Wales. He represented Wales in both senior and junior level in 1961. Colin was also a keen golfer and represented North Wales as a junior. He was also an excellent football, tennis and squash player. He was a pupil at John Bright G.S. and during the summer holidays he worked the theatre spotlights at the Llandudno Pier Pavilion and made friends with many of the show business stars appearing on stage at the time. Tommy Steele, the UK's first rock'n'roll teen idol, topped the bill and appeared there for one week. To pass the time in between shows, Colin would be called upon to make up the numbers required around the table and play cards with the great entertainer. There were some nights he would make more money playing cards than what he could make in wages!

For many years the Easter Hockey Festival was held on the Oval. At the 1962 'gathering of hockey sticks' the usual 30 clubs from all over the UK would take part on three prepared pitches which always encroached the cricket pitch outfield. The cricket square, as always, was fenced off during the winter months. The hockey club was always proud to be playing on the Oval because of the wonderful condition of the playing surface, well-grassed and well prepared pitches, which the visiting teams were often heard to praise. This of course was the care and attention the cricket groundsman gave to the outfield during a season and credit was due to their efforts over the years.

Club playing member, Alan Macintosh was selected in January 1962 to play for Wales (amateur football) for the 16th time! He also represented a Great Britain side on two occasions. Alan made his debut in the First Division (Premiership) football league for Cardiff City against Nottingham Forest on 17th February 1962. He later signed professional forms for Cardiff City.

In February 1962 Llandudno Town Council made available three tennis courts for the club to use for practice purposes.

The Llandudno Rugby Club let it be known that they were interested in obtaining playing facilities on the Oval ground. The cricket club was delighted to co-operate with the rugby club in any way they could. However they made it clear that it was important that the cricket square was not touched. The possibility of an amalgamation of various clubs using the Oval which might become a real sports centre was a fact the officials of the cricket club thought a matter worth considering in detail.

The club had its first practice match before the start of the 1962 season on 2nd May 1962 and the players were introduced to Rene Clayton, the new club professional, who would be holding coaching sessions every Tuesday and Thursday throughout the season. At 27 years of age Rene Clayton had already made his name in Welsh cricket circles. Born in Rhos on Sea he learnt the game as a boy at the Colwyn Bay Cricket Club. At the age of 13 and in his first game for the Colwyn Bay 1st XI he scored a memorable 50 runs. He went on to play for Glamorgan for a number of years before returning to the Colwyn Bay club. He played many times for a select Wales XI, played for Denbighshire and Caernarvonshire throughout his playing career and often for a North Wales Select XI when required. He was fortunate to be in many of the Glamorgan touring sides and played cricket in the West Indies and Australia against the greatest cricketers of all time. Rene Clayton was an all-rounder who was outstanding on his day with both bat and ball and renowned as a brilliant fielder at second slip, regarded as a key role in any team placing.

Electricity was finally installed in the pavilion in May 1962.

On 9th June 1962 at the Oval a magnificent batting performance by Rene Clayton scoring the first century (109) recorded against Colwyn Bay for many years excited the Llandudno spectators and players. The home team won by a convincing 140 runs. This was Llandudno's first win for 23 years against Colwyn Bay since Whit Monday 29th May 1939. Credit was also given to the two bowlers Ray Williams 6/30 and Max Shone 2/41 which made it a memorable day.

Llandudno 2ⁿᵈ XI followed this up the following week by inflicting another win against the Colwyn Bay 2ⁿᵈ XI at the Rhos ground winning by two wickets in a low scoring game. Man of the match on that day was Brian Baister. Batting patiently and intelligently he was top scorer with 30 runs. He was the mainstay of the Llandudno innings that won the match for the away team.

It was Brian Baister who organised and arranged for a Pakistan touring side to visit Llandudno in 1978 which played matches against a North Wales Select XI at the Oval and at Colwyn Bay. This resulted in Rashid Israr, Iqbal Sikander and Anil Dalpat playing for Llandudno in the North Wales League during the 1979 and 1980 seasons. Iqbal and Anil went on to play Test match cricket for Pakistan in the early 1980s.

A Llandudno lad 'born and bred', Brian was a pupil of John Bright G.S. who played both cricket and rugby for the school and for the Llandudno town clubs in both sports. He was previously a pupil of Lloyd Street Primary School where the young Baister was a member of the football team that won the Llandudno Cup and the league Shield in 1952-3. He joined the Metropolitan Police and rose rapidly through the ranks to eventually become Deputy Chief Constable of Cheshire. In 1993 he was awarded the Queen's Police Medal for his work in dealing with the IRA's bombing campaign in the North West of England. He has been a member of the Commonwealth Games Committee. Although a proud Welshman, in July 1998 he was elected chairman of the English RFU (Rugby Football Union) Management Board in London. Brian is now retired from public life and lives in Cheshire. He often visits Llandudno and stays with his life-long school pal Jimmy MacMullan. Whenever they can Brian and Jimmy meet up with John Llew Evans (ex-Cardiff first team Rugby Union player) and Peris Roberts (all ex-John Bright Grammar School boys) for a drink and a chat about the 'old days'. He is a keen golfer and plays when he can at the Llandudno Maesdu Golf Club.

In a Llandudno Junior match played at the Oval on 25ᵗʰ July 1962 against Mochdre Juniors, seven of the young Llandudno players went on to aspire at senior level and to provide the backbone of the Llandudno CC with their services on and off the field of play. They became hard working officials in their day at all levels including president, chairman, secretary, committee member, 1st XI and 2nd XI captains. They were Graham Gibbons, Roger Latham, Eryl Williams, Adney Tingle, Peter Harpin, Andy Roberts and Richard Fowler.

In a match against Llanddulas at the Oval on 4th August 1962, Joe Cosgrove for Llandudno gave a superb display of bowling taking 9/54 including a hat-trick. Llanddulas were all out for 116. The match was abandoned because of rain.

Llandudno finished the 1962 season unbeaten at home. Rene Clayton finished the season with over 100 wickets.

At the 1963 Annual General Meeting held at the Town Hall in February it was agreed to confer Life Membership status on B.H.Morgan (President), K.G.Williams, James Payne and Peter Greenwood.

At the cricket club's Hot Pot Supper night on 8th March 1963 the sad news was announced of the sudden death of B.H.Morgan. He was to have received his Life Membership certificate on that night. Members and officers stood in silent tribute.

A new drinks bar was installed in the pavilion thanks to the generosity of the brewers of Ind Coope Ltd. New flooring was also laid that year.

It was announced that Rene Clayton had taken on the duties of groundsman.

Eric Johnson, the club and county umpire, retired from his white-coated duties. His understudy for several seasons, Elias Thomas, took over at the Oval. Eric Johnson became the new club president elect.

Gwilym Roberts, Roger Latham and Max Shone were chosen to play for the Caernarvonshire Schools XI. Max Shone had also been chosen to play for the North Wales Schools Cricket XI against South Wales.

On 15th July 1963 Chairman Tom Barlow presented Clive Stock with a club centurion tie to commemorate his century (100 not out) in a 2nd XI match against Rydal two weeks earlier.

Clive Stock was an entertainer, producer, and chairman of the internationally famous Grand Order of Water Rats. He appeared in West End musicals. He appeared in Oklahoma at the Drury Lane Theatre. He went into partnership with Robinson Cleaver and produced shows and pantomimes at the Arcadia and Pier Pavilion in Llandudno sharing starring roles with his wife Gwen. He played cricket with Keith Miller and Ray Lindwall when he was working in Australia. As a school boy he was selected to go to Lord's cricket ground where he received valuable batting coaching from the famous Essex and England player Dennis Compton. He played cricket for Caernarvonshire and had a spell of captaincy for the club. In his youth he won the London Junior Table Tennis Championship one year. He became the first manager of the Theatre Cymru, Llandudno which was then called the Aberconwy Conference Centre. He was host and producer of the original Welsh Medieval Banquet at the 13th century Gwylch Castle in Abergele.

In his book, which is available at the Llandudno Public Library, he wrote:

"In 1962 I came to Llandudno to play at the Arcadia Theatre. During rehearsals I was asked to go to the Llandudno Cricket Club. I had written to the club in the hope they might consider me to play in a team for the summer season. I had given them references including centuries scored and clubs I had played for. I arrived at the Llandudno Cricket Club where the president, chairman and full committee were waiting. I kitted up and then the captain led me to the nets where the first team were practising. I remember clearly the officials lined up in front of the wooden pavilion with its white picket fence and the Llandudno flag flying in the breeze. I was expected to bat and

bowl to show them if I was good enough for a place in the very strong 1st XI side at the time. I went into bat to face the bowling of all types. My stomach was in knots. This was far worse than appearing on stage in front of 3,000 people. I was so nervous I kept saying to myself you have faced Lindwall and Miller, this is easy. I batted well and dealt with the bowling hurled at me. I was asked to bowl and hit the stumps at regular intervals. I passed the audition and the president said that I would fit in well with the current side. I then told him that I could only play on Sundays and if they wanted me on a Saturday I would have to leave at 7.30pm at the latest. This was not acceptable so I resigned myself to Sundays only. I was put in the 2nd XI for the first match against Rydal Public School. As I scored 100 not out and took a wicket they had a re-think in playing until 7.30pm. I then became a regular member of the first XI and the antics that went on when I was still batting at 7.15pm and trying to get myself out to get to the theatre was hilarious. I would dance down the wicket to have a swipe it would come off the edge and go for four. I would go forward and play an air shot so that I would be stumped but the wicket keeper would miss it altogether. Many times I would go on to try to get myself out. Needless to say my wife Gwen would be 'chomping at the bit' but when the curtain was about to go up I somehow never failed to make my entrance. What happy times."

Clive goes on:

"Playing cricket in 1971 for Llandudno I had a good season. At the end of the final fixture that year there was a special trophy meeting. David Roberts who had been president of the club had sadly passed on. In his place, his son, Andrew Roberts presented the batting, bowling and promising newcomer awards. I was presented with the batting award. The trophy was in his father's name. As the trophy was being presented, Andy said, "This is not for the 100 you scored against the Cheshire Offices; it's for the 58 you hit against Styal. The side's batting was collapsing and only two players had reached double figures and your innings was exceptional in eventually winning the match when all was lost – well done!"

Clive Stock is now retired and at the time of writing he is well into his 80s and continues to enjoy good health.

At the start of the 1964 season the club had acquired a motor roller at a cost of £145.

Subs for full playing members were increased to £2.5.0.

Rene Clayton hit a superb unbeaten century (100 not out) against Manchester League competitors Moorside at the Oval on 17th May 1964. Seven days later he followed this up with another century (101 not out) against Coseley Crusaders.

Five Llandudno players were chosen to play for Caernarvonshire in June against Merionethshire – John Collier, Keith Jones, Rene Clayton, Ray Williams and Max Shone. Against Flintshire the following week – John Collier, Rene Clayton, Roger Bower, Clive Stock and Max Shone.

The 1964 season ended with the President and Chairman's Sevens Tournament which became an annual event for some years. The teams were called The Grasshoppers, The Pixies, The Taverners and The Crossbats. This always provided great entertainment for players and spectators. At the end of the tournament Rene Clayton and Huw Tudno Williams were presented with mounted balls to commemorate their hat-tricks during the season.

On Monday 14th June 1964 Llandudno beat Bangor University in the final of the prestigious Caernarvonshire Knock-Out Competition.

There was a royal visitor to the Oval ground on 26th June 1965. Arriving by helicopter and in readiness before the landing, the groundsman Rene Clayton had cut and rolled the pitch to perfection. It was felt the Duke of Edinburgh must have noticed and been very impressed with the Oval. He spent a few minutes inside the pavilion before leaving in the royal limousine which had arrived to meet him for his next appointment in the town.

Sportsmanship must come first

In a match at the Oval against Marchwiel on 26th June 1965 the age-old question of "should a batsman walk" when he knows that he has had a touch and been caught occurred. Marchwiel's last man was in. He played a ball and got an edge and wicket keeper Roger Bower held the catch. He appealed only to be turned down by the umpire. Two balls later the batsman hit the winning runs giving Marchwiel victory with the last ball of the last over to end the match. It was at the bar later the batsman calmly admitted with a smile on his face that he did get an edge. Of course in today's professional game sportsmanship doesn't always count!

Walking is a contentious issue, with the cricketing world split along two lines – those who feel it's the batsman's responsibility to admit he is out and those who feel it is the umpire's duty to make the decision. Some argue that too much is at stake in the professional game for individuals to willingly give away their wicket.

There has never been a more conventional aspect of the game of cricket than umpiring. With technology being used more and more these days for the benefit of the men in the white coats, the ICC have had the task of bringing umpiring into the 21st century. Their skills are being monitored in international matches so there can be regular assessment of their performances. Amongst the list of technologies are included:

A snickometer: A difficult decision for any umpire. Did the ball come off the bat? The pad? Neither? Both? Often it's very hard to detect by sight alone. The sound can often provide more than a clue. Using microphones in the stumps, the snickometer can study tell-tale noises and can illustrate them on screen. An edge is shown by a long thin line extending almost from top to bottom of the snickometer box. Ball hitting pad is a much more 'chunky' picture.

Hawkeye: Six cameras around the ground track the path of the ball as it is bowled. The data goes into a computer and emerges with a prediction of where it would have finished. It has turned out to be a valuable coaching tool for umpires and players.

On 14th August 1965 against Marchwiel Hall Rene Clayton scored another century (112). Llandudno won by just five runs.

The club held a 'Centenary Celebration' dance in the winter of 1965 to commemorate being one of the oldest clubs in North Wales. Although the club was in existence in 1849 they played a match well recorded at that time against Conwy on the Great Orme. Later they moved to The Warren in the West Shore. The celebration in 1965 seemed to have been belated.

A young John Bright G.S. boy, Geoff Ellis, played his first game for Llandudno in a 2nd XI match against Colwyn Bay. Huw Tudno Williams reported that he was the best junior prospect he had seen for years locally and prophesied a great cricketing future for him.

Rene Clayton scored 105 against a touring side Monsanto on 23rd July 1966.

Glamorgan v North Wales XI

This match was played at the Oval on 28th August 1966 and ended in a draw. Glamorgan batted first and scored 217. North Wales were unable to finish their innings on 133/5. The Glamorgan players commented on how amazed they were at the organisation and hard work that had been put in by club members. Ossie Wheatley, the Glamorgan skipper, remarked that he had never seen people work so hard and efficiently for a game of such calibre by such a small club. The members were rewarded by the largest crowd seen at the Oval for many years. Both teams provided some excellent entertainment which was in aid of Test player Peter Walker's Benefit year.

On 17th February 1967 Owen Jones, a former chairman and treasurer, was elected Honorary Life-Member of the club. The new president elect was Mr Cecil Manson.

Vandalism on the Oval had become a major concern at the start of the season in 1967. A break-in and another attempted effort had caused damage to the pavilion. Also a further break-in of the groundsman's hut, which resulted in the theft of tools, was thought to be the work of local youths.

The formation of a joint Amateur Sports club at the Oval took a step forward in 1967 at a meeting set up by the Llandudno cricket and hockey clubs. Agreement was reached in approving a Constitution and Rules format and that the club was to be named 'The Llandudno Amateur Sports Club'.

A match against Winnington Park of Manchester in July 1967 certainly highlighted the greatly appreciated work Miss Bebb had been doing for the club for many years. There had been an intensive advertising campaign to get more spectators to the ground which had paid off. Every deckchair was sold and the crowd were strewn right around the ground. Miss Bebb was in her glory frantically racing around trying to find more seating and taking the collection box with her, getting as much money as she could for the benefit of the club. She did this for many seasons, 'week in, week out'. Ladies of her character and willingness, including all the ladies over the years who take on the task of making and preparing match teas, are the backbone to any cricket club and always deserve a big thank you each time for their efforts.

Llandudno won the Caernarvonshire Knock-Out Trophy in 1967 for the second time in three years when they defeated Bangor University at Bangor. They won the trophy again the following year in a repeat final against the University.

It was in 1967 that some talk was going around at the possibility of calling several of the North Wales clubs together to discuss the formation of a Saturday cricket league in North Wales.

There was another break-in at the pavilion which was viewed with great concern. A window was broken and damage was caused inside the building. Police were sure the damage had been caused by young vandals. They had also destroyed the remaining sight screen and damaged the pavilion clock.

Lord Mostyn (5th Baron) Roger Edward Lloyd Mostyn received spinal injuries in an accident riding his horse when it fell in the Groom Hunter's Chase at the Worcester Races on 12th March 1968. He had succeeded to the title on the death of his father in May 1965. He was educated at Eton and entered Sandhurst Military College joining the 9th Lancers in 1939. He served in France and was wounded and mentioned in despatches afterwards. He served in the Western Desert and was also wounded there during the defence of El Alamein. He went to Italy in 1944 and was with the 8th Army when the war ended.

Geoff Ellis, along with Rene Clayton and Roger Bower, was selected to play for Caernarvonshire against Merionethshire in 1968. Just a few months later, 18 year old Geoff Ellis, still a pupil at John Bright G.S., was presented with a statuette by headmaster Mr S.O.Rees to mark his achievement in being the first Welsh schoolboy to score a century against England. His progress and his performances for both

Welsh Schoolboys XI and Glamorgan 2nd XI made every member of the club and pupils of the school proud of him. He continued to play for the club as the 'star' player in a formidable sixties line-up regarded as being one of the best teams Llandudno has ever produced. Such talented cricketers he played alongside were: Tony Neville, Rene Clayton, Mike Manson, Keith Jones, Ray Williams, Max Shone, Stan Pounder, Graham Gibbons, Alan Gibbons, Ron Beswick, Clive Stock, Roger Latham, Roger Bower and Doug Rossington. Geoff Ellis was a right-handed batsman who bowled right-arm medium pace. It was as a batsman he made his first-class debut for Glamorgan against Oxford University in 1970. His final season for Glamorgan was 1976. He had scored 3,759 runs in both first-class (2,673) and List A (1,086) matches. In 1974 he scored a century (116 runs) against Middlesex at Sophia Gardens, Cardiff. In a match against Nottinghamshire in Cardiff on 30th May 1970 he was 20 not out at the close. He was paid a great tribute by Gary Sobers after helping his side to a fine victory by hitting the winning runs off his bowling. The legendary Wilf Wooller was also impressed. He played for Wales in the 1979 World Cup against the Netherlands, Israel and the United States. Nearly a decade later, the Wales Minor Counties team was formed, which he often made appearances for until retiring from first-class cricket in1989.

The 1968 season was a very good year for the club with some fine performances from individuals which are worth mentioning. Rene Clayton, the club professional, passed 1,000 runs; Graham Gibbons had turned out some match-winning bowling performances; and Tony Neville had also revealed some excellent form with the bat. The 2nd XI also did well that year with Peter Owens making startling progress with both bat and ball. Mention was also made at the skill of Mike Squire as wicketkeeper who was regarded well-above average and an excellent cover when required for the 1st team wicket keeper, Roger Bower, who was undoubtedly one of the best in the whole of Wales. Tom Barlow had again set an example to the young players with his excellent fielding when he took well over 20 catches in the season.

The Llandudno Amateur Sports Club

On 1st April the Llandudno Amateur Sports Club embracing cricket, hockey football and rugby came into being. It was hoped that through a series of fund-raising efforts enough money would be made to build a new pavilion. Plans had also been made to provide football and rugby pitches on the Oval by 1971. The chairman elect of the new club was Geoff Rees who was also secretary of the Gwynedd Sporting Club and recently retired secretary of the cricket club.

Llandudno annihilated Ruthin at the Oval on 7th June 1969. On that occasion pace-bowler Graham Gibbons destroyed the Ruthin batsmen by claiming seven wickets for a meagre 12 runs. Ruthin were all out for 27 after Llandudno had scored 124 (Rene Clayton 62).

John Player League – Glamorgan v Leicestershire

Played at the Oval on 22nd June 1969, this was an historic sporting event with over 3,500 supporters on the ground. The whole game was televised 'live' and nationwide by the BBC giving the resort valuable publicity. There was no doubt that the Oval had the best crowd-pulling potential over any other North Wales ground at the time. The outfield and square were in superb condition as Ray Ilingworth, the England and Leicestershire captain, and his players testified. Favourable comments were passed on the state of the wicket by knowledgeable personalities present such as Jim Laker, Richie Benaud, John Arlott and both umpires. All agreed that it was a better wicket than the one at Rhos-on-Sea. This was due to the hard work and expertise of the groundsman Rene Clayton, the ex-Glamorgan player.

Glamorgan won by 10 wickets (with 14 balls remaining) (revised target)

Leicestershire innings (40 overs maximum)

M.R.Hallam c Cordle b Williams	11
M.E.J.C.Norman c E.W.Jones b Williams	3
B.J.Booth lbw b Majid Khan	28
C.C.Inman c Shepherd b Wheatley	3
P.T.Marner lbw b Shepherd	15
R.Illingworth* b Walker	31
B.R.Knight c E.W.Jones b Cordle	39
G.D.McKenzie b Majid Khan	0
C.T.Spencer not out	3
R.J.Barratt not out	1
Extras (b 5, nb 2)	7

Total (8 wickets; 40 overs) 141 (3.52 runs per over)

Did not bat R.W.Tolchard

Fall of wickets 1-13, 2-20, 3-33, 4-50, 5-62, 6-125, 7-134, 8-138

Bowling	Overs	Mdns	Runs	Wkts	Wides	No balls
O.S.Wheatley	8	4	16	1	-	-
D.L.Williams	8	2	26	2	-	-
D.J.Shepherd	8	2	22	1	-	-
Majid Khan	8	1	26	2	-	-
E.A.Cordle	6	0	30	1	-	-
P.M.Walker	2	0	14	1	-	-

Glamorgan innings (target: 74 runs from 27 overs)

B.A.Davis not out	29
A.Jones not out 32	
Extras (b 8, lb 3, w 1, nb 1)	13

Total (0 wickets; 24.4 overs) 74 (3.00 runs per over)

Did not bat A.R.Lewis*, Majid Khan, P.M.Walker, K.J.Lyons, E.W.Jones, E.A.Cordle, D.J.Shepherd, D.L.Williams, O.S.Wheatley

Bowling	Overs	Mdns	Runs	Wkts	Wides	No balls
G.D.McKenzie	4	1	4	0	-	-
C.T.Spencer	5	1	12	0	-	-
R.Illingworth	4	0	15	0	-	-
B.R.Knight	7	0	17	0	-	-
R.J.Barratt	1	0	1	0	-	-
P.T.Marner	3.4	1	12	0	-	-

Match details

Toss – Leicestershire, who chose to bat

Points – Glamorgan 4, Leicestershire 0

Umpires – H.Mellows and C.Petrie

It was a great honour for the club when Rene Clayton was selected to play for Wales against the famous International Cavaliers which took place at Rhos-on-Sea on 29th June 1969. Players of the calibre of Fred Trueman, Ted Dexter, Godfrey Evans and many other internationally renowned cricketers played for the Cavaliers that day.

A century (105) by opening bat Eryl Williams clinched a resounding win for the Llandudno 2nd XI against St Asaph 2nd XI at the Oval on 9th August 1969 by 112 runs.

Caernarvonshire clinched the county title defeating Anglesey at the Oval on 15th August 1969. Ron Beswick, Rene Clayton, Roger Bower, George Roberts, Stan Kidd and Geoff Ellis played a prominent part in turn to gain the county the honours.

The junior elevens had fulfilled their fixtures by the end of August and there were several exciting prospects who were reported as 'on their way up'. Keith Thomas, son of Elias Thomas the senior club umpire, had already been 'blooded' in both first and second eleven matches with considerable success. Dave Robertson had also been promoted to the senior game for both his batting and bowling skills and was regarded as a player with a bright future.

In a low scoring match at the Oval on 5th September 1969 Rene Clayton stole the show taking nine wickets for 37 runs against Ruthin. Not satisfied with that he also had a hand in the 10th wicket when he caught the last man in the slips off Roger Latham's bowling. To finish off a great memorable day for him and for Llandudno he was top scorer with the bat. Ruthin will never forget Mr *Rene* Clayton!

Roger Bower hit the first century of the 1970 season against Liverpool NALGO on 3rd June.

The Glamorgan coaching team selected Llandudno youngsters Dave Robertson and Keith Thomas for special coaching lessons in Cardiff in January 1971.

Gwilym Roberts scored a century (101 not out) in a win against Llanrwst on 11th June 1970.

A match against St Asaph seconds played on the Oval on 8th August 1970 was marred by an incident on the field when a Llandudno batsman walked off the field following a dispute. Some harsh words had been spoken by both sides which led to the match being abandoned.

The dilapidated condition of the fencing around the Oval was referred to the Town Council in October 1970 by Councillor Algwyn Hopkins. He was quoted as saying "It is like a derelict army camp". Councillor Doherty agreed and the cost to carry out the repair was included in the Town Council committee's Estimates of Requirements for 1971-1972.

The fire which burnt down the hut destroying the club's deckchairs in the winter of 1971 was the reason for an appeal to the public, through the local media, who might have some unwanted deckchairs to give to the club.

In June 1971 the Llandudno Amateur Sports Club was disbanded after attempts to form a proper club had failed. It had been hoped that adequate funds would be raised to build a new sports pavilion. Just as important would be for a lease of not less than 29 years to be sought from the Town Council so that a grant could have been applied for from the appropriate body. Unfortunately this venture had little support as shown by the fact the club, after four years, only had a balance of £95 which was not sufficient for the cause.

He was once described as the 'hostile' Graham Gibbons after his eight wickets against Chester College two weeks earlier; he followed this up on 5th June 1971 taking seven Llanrwst wickets for 21 runs. As time has gone by and 'age hath withered' Graham's hostile approach relinquished amongst his friends who now regard him as 'grumpy' Graham but still a loveable character by everyone.

Since the departure of Rene Clayton to the Colwyn Bay club the decline of the Oval wicket was causing concern. With no official groundsman having the skill required to prepare a decent wicket some members tried their best to fill the role. The committee was grateful to Andy Roberts for his time in watering the square when required and to organise heavy rolling which did bring about some improvement.

During a Test Match at Edgbaston in 2004, England's Andrew Flintoff hit a mighty six into the crowd, where a spectator made a gallant attempt to catch it. But, very publicly, with the world's TV cameras on him, he dropped it. The hapless individual turned out to be Flintoff's father.

The progress of junior players during the 1971 season had been most heartening. Many had developed considerably under the watchful eyes of Graham Gibbons and Ron Beswick who both spent many hours coaching the youngsters. Glyn Gibbons, Kevin Gibbons, Malcolm Beswick and Michael Pounder had been performing well in the 2nd XI. Other young players that had been attracting attention included Joe Coe and Stuart Everall. Keith Thomas was already playing regularly for the 1st team.

In September 1971 tributes were paid to the late David A.Roberts and his son Andrew Roberts. David A.Roberts, who had served the cricket club before and after the war so magnificently and who left a gap that can never be adequately filled, would have been delighted with his son Andrew Roberts. The year 1971 had been a dismal and difficult period for the club and it was noted then that Andrew's unending exuberance and loyalty had been his most outstanding quality. During those difficult times with a paint brush in his hand, a heavy roller pushed around the ground, or handling a motor mower preparing a wicket, he was always in the thick of things. He was also emerging as an excellent committee member, just like his dad, and who later followed in his footsteps becoming Chairman and President. His excellent temperament and gentlemanly conduct earned him the respect and confidence of all, as did his father before him.

It was learnt that the Llandudno Town Council had plans afoot in 1972 to extend the Oval ground increasing the area by approximately 15 acres. There was also the possibility of a new pavilion to replace the existing one. In a report by the club chairman, Geoff Rees, he made it clear that because of the bad state of repair of the pavilion he was anxious that something should be done. He said that vandals had been responsible for some of the damage but that over a length of time the construction of the building had fallen into a dilapidated condition. He also felt that the time was right to press the council once again in obtaining a lease on the ground to replace the unstable annual tenancy.

In June 1972 further damage was caused to the pavilion and to the score board. Some expensive accessories that were locked inside an outbuilding had gone missing. The motor mower had been clumsily dismantled and the engine stolen. The wooden fencing surrounding the members' enclosure in front of the pavilion had been recklessly damaged. All caused by vandalism. A meeting with the police took place and steps were taken to keep a 'round the clock' vigil on the premises.

It was not all doom and gloom in 1972 though. Tributes were paid to Andy Tingle on doing a great job during the season behind the bar and to hard-working Cliff Potter who spent many hours of his leisure time giving the interior walls of the pavilion a dabble of paint. Both members played regularly for the 2nd XI.

A match against Conwy 2nd XI at the Oval on 2nd September 1972 was highlighted by an unbeaten century (102) by the youngster, Dave Robertson, which helped to snatch victory for the home side by 19 runs.

It's just not cricket – used generally to mean something is unfair or against normal rules of behaviour.

Play a straight bat – to behave in a decent and honourable fashion.

Bowled over – completely overwhelmed, possibly in a very positive context, as in 'I was bowled over by her smile and charm'.

Stumped – confused and utterly bewildered.

On the back foot – behaving in a defensive manner.

Caught out – deceived or misled, as in 'The students were caught out by the trick question in the exam'.

Hit for six – taken completely by surprise, as in 'The news has hit me for six, to be honest'.

1973-2001

North Wales Cricket League

An announcement was made in February 1973 that Llandudno's first and second elevens had entered into the newly formed competitive North Wales Cricket League commencing in the 1973 season. There were 12 clubs in the first division and eight in the second division.

Scoring System

Each match will consist of 90 overs.

Not more than 45 overs will be available to the side batting first.

The toss of a coin will give the winning captain the option to bat first or second.

The side batting first can declare "innings closed" at any time up to the 45 overs available, in which case the balance of overs up to the 90 total must be used up by the side batting second.

Any side declaring "innings closed" is considered all out.

If the side batting first is all out before 45 overs expire the side batting second must use the balance of overs up to the total of 90.

Incomplete overs count as full overs.

If, owing to the weather or other circumstances a game cannot start on time or it is considered that the full 90 overs cannot be played the captains have the option to agree mutually on a match of a lesser number of overs down to a minimum 50 overs.

Such reduced over matches shall count under the points scoring system as if the full 90 overs had been played.

For an outright win i.e. the defeated side are all out – winners 7 points, losers nil.

For a win when the defeated side is not all out – winners 5, losers 2.

For a tie when one or both sides all out with total runs level – 4 points each.

For a draw when neither side is all out with total runs level – 4 points each.

For a match cancelled or abandoned – 1 point each.

It was in 1973 that Mr J.G.Gibbons had been elected president of the club.

A recommendation to approve outline plans for the future development of the Oval was made by Llandudno Council's Amenities Committee. A sub-committee had been appointed by the Finance and General Purposes Committee to consider capital schemes. The lay-out of the scheme provided for three hockey pitches, a cricket pitch, rugby and soccer pitches, tennis courts and a proposed access skirting the actual playing area. The sports pavilion plan which had already been approved by the Amenities Committee provided for a two storey building situated on a site just to the rear of the existing building. The pavilion, it was proposed, would comprise men and women's changing rooms and showers, together with stores accommodation on the ground floor. The upper floor would include a clubroom, office kitchen and bar. The plan incorporated a built-in scorebox and an outside stairway to an open veranda. The cost of the new pavilion was estimated to be £59,000 and expected to be ready for the 1974 season.

The existing building erected 40 years ago had been targeted by vandals and hardly a pane of glass remained. The balcony was a dangerous place and broken floorboards were becoming a hazard. A member, David Holt, crashed through to his thighs on a plank which gave way and had to receive hospital treatment. Later a small boy entered the building and suffered a minor injury.

Prince Philip, Duke of Edinburgh, landed by helicopter on the Oval for the second time in eight years on 6th May 1973. He was greeted on arrival by a crowd of about 300. The Prince was in North Wales to attend the Association of River Authorities Conference at the Winter Gardens, Llandudno.

Pavilion destroyed by fire

It was on the night of the 5th November 1973 that the fire started which completely gutted the pavilion. The fire started a few minutes before 9pm and 12 firemen using two appliances fought the blaze for nearly two hours. A fire engine from the Conwy Fire Brigade 'stood by' in case it was required. The main part of the pavilion roof was completely destroyed as were all the fixtures and fittings. The blaze was confined principally to the bar and lounge areas. Chairs and tables were destroyed as were drinking glasses, pottery, a stove, an urn and two electric fires which had just recently been installed at a cost of £160. It was estimated that 70% of the building and its contents were damaged. Lying amid the wreckage was a telephone call box that had been targeted by thieves a couple of weeks before.

The cricket tea has evolved from the fact that the earliest games involved a great deal of feasting on the part of the spectators. Tents would be erected for the ladies (and a separate one for the gentlemen) to take tea while the game was in progress. It's no surprise that the players decided to get in on the act.

An article in a well-known national newspaper on Monday 7th May 1974 headed 'Llandudno Rap?' reflected the club in an unfavourable light.

The article was written as follows:

"Llandudno could be in hot water with the North Wales League for failing to show up for their scheduled game against Wrexham. Llandudno called the match off 24 hours before the scheduled game after pleading that they were unable to muster a side. The rule was invoked which provided for this contingency giving Wrexham the maximum seven points and Llandudno none. But with relegation introduced for the first time commencing in the

1974 season the league committee were unlikely to let the matter rest there. The seven points could save Wrexham from the drop at the end of the season and some other innocent club would go down."

An official from the Llandudno club defended the issue by saying the facts were far from normal at the Oval. The newly built pavilion was still incomplete and facilities were not available for the players to enter their names into the 'availability book'. The records of names, addresses and telephone numbers of players had been destroyed in the fire. The North Wales League committee had been notified of the unusual circumstances and did view the matter with some understanding and sympathy.

Worse was to come! For the first time since 1891 the Llandudno club found themselves batting on a really 'sticky wicket' and it had nothing to do with the weather. It came to light that the proposed plans set out by the town council were to re-site the square so as to accommodate rugby, football and hockey pitches at the expense of cricket. The proposed plan of a sporting complex as envisaged by the Parks Superintendent had been approved by the Aberconwy District Council. The plan ensured that the outfield would include the penalty area of a football pitch in one direction, a rugby pitch in front of the pavilion in the other and a hockey pitch in between. In simple words the plan was to provide sports pitches enveloping the sacred cricket square. The situation was causing deep concern to the cricketing authorities who had held occupancy, peacefully, for over 80 years during which time they had invested £8,000 in the previous four years in maintaining the pitch and providing necessary facilities.

Letters of protest were sent to the town council officials regarding the nonsensical proposal. There was no doubt at the time that the sports complex intended was absurd and impracticable as far as the cricket club was concerned, threatening their very existence and which could deprive the town of its only major summer sporting attraction.

The battle was on! In an all-out concerted and united effort the club launched its counter attack with the full intention of meeting the

Aberconwy Borough Council, face to face, setting out the reasons and explanation for why the sporting complex would be unplayable and that it would not only jeopardise cricket but the other sporting factions as well. It would also do harm to the lush Oval itself which had been described as the finest sporting arena in North Wales. It was envisaged that cramped and crowded pitches would prove very annoying to players and create serious maintenance difficulties. It was felt the Oval was not large enough to comply with most of the requirements set out in the planning. The welfare of Llandudno sport and the whole situation needed to be revised. It was felt the powers to be needed to intervene and limit the number of pitches otherwise the dream of a combined Llandudno sports association at the Oval would die a death.

It seemed at the time that the objection had 'fallen on deaf ears'. Therefore Plan B, introduced by Huw Tudno Williams, came into effect with the help of the media and television. Support for the amendment of the plan and the survival of cricket in Llandudno came flooding in from all quarters. The television cameras came down to the ground to cover the 'Save our Square' campaign.

At last the council sat up and listened and due to the efforts of the public and members of the cricket club an amendment to the plan was adopted. For a while football, rugby, hockey and, most important, cricket were able to share the Oval ground without any hindrance.

However, the battle was not completely won. The decision to pull down the fencing surrounding the ground in order to proceed with the 'open planning experiment' still stood. In the meantime the participant clubs (rugby, hockey, cricket and football) did form a combined Llandudno Sports Association with each club responsible for running its own affairs.

Whilst this was all going on Llandudno 1st XI was relegated to the second division of the newly formed North Wales League.

The Association were very angry and accused the Aberconwy Borough Council of a scandalous waste of ratepayers' money. The local sports clubs held a special meeting to 'take the lid off' alleged council mismanagement and lack of co-operation. Mr Ernest Jones, chairman of the Llandudno football club, said that thousands of pounds of public money had been spent at the Oval ground including £59,000 on a new pavilion but efforts to get the sports complex working smoothly had repeatedly been blocked by the council's indifference and lack of co-operation.

An Aberconwy spokesman replied that they were still awaiting confirmation that the Sports Association had adopted the draft constitution and had also not heard from them about a Justice's Club licence which was forwarded some months before.

A meeting did take place between representatives of Aberconwy Borough Council and the Llandudno Sports Association in February 1976 about the future use of the Oval pavilion. Councillor Harold Gott, who was chairman of the Leisure and Amenities Committee, did report back to the Borough Council on 19th February 1976 as follows:

> *"The suggestion is that we should set up a management committee to run the Oval and the pavilion. The committee should comprise of four representatives of the Borough Council, four representatives from the Town Council and seven representatives from the Sports Association. We do not intend at this stage entering into a Lease Agreement with the Association."*

By the year 1976, sport at the Oval was suffering badly because of the 'open plan' and because the area was no longer a showpiece recreation ground. The cricket club was in a pretty sorry state because of the 'open plan' experiment. It was once a great ground but was now a dismal failure with people using the acreage to exercise their dogs who were fouling the place. Cycles, motor cycles and even horses were causing havoc to the playing surface. No longer did several hundred spectators each week make their way down to the ground to lounge in deckchairs and watch the day's play. Since the removal of the tins, trees and fencing there was no longer shelter from the prevailing winds and gradually another amenity which undoubtedly brought much revenue to the town was dwindling away. It had become unfit to play any sport and was a health hazard. It was reported that four Sunday fixtures had to be cancelled because of the poor state of the ground.

Unfortunately, this sad state of affairs had caused slackness and apathy amongst cricket club members – all due to an experiment removing the fencing. The Oval was a mess and had been brought down to an all-time low and the goodwill and respect built up over decades was being badly damaged, almost irrevocably.

There were some highlights during the 1975 season which are worth mentioning. Johnny Johnson grabbed five wickets for nine runs in a 12 over bowling stint against Pilkingtons, guiding the home team to a five wickets win at the Oval on 28th June 1975. He followed this up scoring 117 in a return match against Pilkingtons on 7th September.

Prior to the 1975 season during the winter months indoor nets commenced from 29th January for the first time at John Bright G.S..

Llandudno v Glamorgan

The sun shone brightly when Llandudno played Glamorgan at the Oval on 28th September 1975. Glamorgan batted first and scored 247 for six declared (K.Lyons 100, A.Francis 73. Johnny Johnson took three wickets for 49).

Llandudno replied 122 (Glyn Gibbons 24, Graham Gibbons 21).

Umpires were Elias Thomas and Geoff Rees.

The caterers were Mr and Mrs C.Potter.

The Glamorgan players were entertained in the pavilion after the game. It was the Glamorgan captain, Eifion Jones's Benefit year. Geoff Rees, club chairman, presented him with a cheque for £150. An autographed bat signed by the Glamorgan players which had been raffled for many weeks was won by club player Emyr Parry.

In 1969, John Inverarity of Western Australia was bowled by a delivery from South Australia's Greg Chappell that hit a swallow in mid-air and was deflected on to the stumps. The umpires signalled a no ball and Inverarity, who had yet to score, went on to make 89.

The most expensive dropped catch was made by Durham wicketkeeper Chris Scott who put down Brian Lara when the West Indies batsman had made just 18 for Warwickshire at Edgbaston in 1994. Lara, who had earlier been bowled by a no-ball, was in his prime at the time. Lara went on to make 501 not out, the highest innings in first-class cricket.

There was no doubt the club at that time was going through a very difficult period in its history. The effect it had on and off the field was becoming critical. An alarming decline on both playing and administrative fronts over the last two or three years had seen this once proud cricketing stronghold crumble sadly. Stalwart members of the club realised something had to be done to arrest the slide and lift the club to its rightful status in the cricketing world.

Mini-Cricket for the U/11s age group

In came an inspired scheme from John Breeze, a former Llandudno 1st XI captain and an enthusiastic committee member, who had identified there was a need to re-capture the youth of the town which had been lacking in recent years. For some reason the local secondary schools had pushed cricket into the background. In fact no cricket was being played on the school playing fields anymore. This had been damaging to the club. In the past the cricket club had benefited from this wealth of talent, but now the new recruits were drying-up from this previously unending source of supply. His scheme was to initially approach primary schools within the area, and explain to headmasters the proposals and facilities that would be made available at the Oval. It was hoped the schools themselves would be encouraged to promote the game or at least consider it as an extra-curricular activity outside school hours. The idea would be to introduce youngsters up to the age of 11 years old to the game of cricket by initially using soft balls and small bats, eventually introducing a hard ball.

The response from members, after listening to all the proposals set out by John Breeze, was promising. The club recognised that there was a need for a fully qualified professional to eventually organise proper coaching needs but in the meantime the idea to get the youngsters onto the field was the priority. The main aim would be to instil the 'fun' aspect of the game and introduce them to bat and ball and to the discipline and eventually to the competitive spirit of the game.

The committee endorsed the plan. A short while before there had seemed little hope for the club until John Breeze came up with this idea which aroused a lot of interest amongst the few hard-working club members that were left and still willing to give up their time and energy. Under the guidance of John Breeze and with a determined and united effort from the promised support it was felt that the scheme was worth trying.

It was not long after the 'go ahead' was granted that approaches were being made to the primary schools and at the same time John Breeze was also organising fixtures, bringing back to the Oval many 'old faces'. These were ex-players who did so much for the club, during the decades of the fifties and sixties.

In just a few weeks, John Breeze's scheme in revising interest in local cricket was beginning to work. Already it was a heartening sight watching in the region of 40 youngsters enjoying themselves with soft balls and bats, being introduced gently to the fine arts of cricket. It became a regular sight each week with the numbers growing and the keenness showing amongst many of the youngsters. With the help from regular 1st and 2nd XI senior members especially from Dave Robertson, Allan Hughes, Jeff Nicholls and later Graham Gibbons, the sessions became a great success. Coaching took place every Sunday morning and mini-cricket matches were being introduced and organised by John Breeze.

An event took place at the Oval on 31st July in a match between a Show Biz XI and The All Stars. The purpose was to raise money for the formation of a Mini-Cricket League for the 8-12 age groups in Llandudno which was part of John Breeze's scheme. The game and the afternoon went very well. The weather was ideal for such an event. On the ground the 2,000 or so spectators were well entertained by the efforts on the cricket field by local stage personalities and their opponents including Dai Davies (Welsh champion boxer), John Clarke and Clive Stock. The town mayor, Councillor Jim H.Milbourne, tossed the coin watched closely by the club president, Mr Gordon Gibbons. The club members who helped to organise the event were disappointed when unfortunately sporting stars, including footballers Francis Lee, Mike Summerbee and Welsh International Gareth Davies, had to cancel at the last moment. However, the crowd were kept well amused by a number of side stalls on the ground and some side shows including Llandudno's own Morris Dancers, the Gaytones.

More needed to be done to make the teachers of the local schools aware that steps needed to be taken to halt the decline of the sport at grass roots level locally. There was a very good response when 16 schools were invited to a seminar held at the Oval which included the showing of two short films. The first outlined the basic methods of introducing cricket at primary school level and the other provided an insight, giving details of the Test and County Cricket Awards scheme. Mr Breeze, who presented the seminar to the many teachers attending, stressed that due to the recent apathy from schools, cricket could die in the locality. In order to take steps to correct this misdemeanour he said cricket should be as much part of school curricula as maths and English. He explained how committed the club was to put in place a plan to rectify the situation with hopefully the support of teachers and in doing so would provide all the facilities available to help those schools who agree to include cricket in their curriculum. Mr Breeze announced that at the start of the next season a primary school mini-cricket league would commence. The club facilities would include an umpire, scorer and transport when required. The matches would consist of 12 overs per innings played on the Oval every Monday night during the season. He also announced that the club had obtained the services of a professionally qualified coach from Tasmania, Robert Knight, who would be very much involved in the scheme.

Thanks to John Breeze, the primary mover of the schools cricket league, the competition was initiated and noticeably became a great success. There were seven schools involved – Ysgol Maelgwyn, Loretto, Craig-y-Don, Llandudno Junction, Dyffryn Road, Deganwy and Bodafon. An abundance of talent emerged from the ranks of the various teams in the league. There were enthusiastic youngsters at all sizes and ages batting away as though their very lives depended on the outcome. Julian Breeze, Stephen Nicholls, Mark Lambe, Darren Vernon, Melvyn Kelly, Martin Richardson, Gareth Wynne, J.Fernandes, Andrew Collis, Gareth Hughes and D.Roberts were amongst the many others who were showing the ability to do well in the game.

It was reported that in 1979 Llandudno's promising junior cricketers, so carefully and patiently mustered over the last couple of years by John Breeze, had all had a successful season. The scheme now included boys at U16 level as well as the U11s. Graham Boase, Gary Talbot and T.Bretton were showing lots of promise. Also youngsters Bryn Kyffin, Robin Hunt and Andrew Boddis, all in the U11 age group, were doing really well.

Organised cricket at the amateur level is the grassroots game whether it is school competitions, local league cricket, village cricket or just a group of friends in a public park or playing on a beach which has truly been the lifeblood of many followers. It is true that the age group in a side may span 50 years or more and the level of ability may be similarly widespread. Especially in evening league cricket it is not unusual to have included in a team two teenagers, a 60-year-old, a man with one arm and a couple of keen ladies. In truth, the recently developed Twenty 20 is just a professional version of the game that evening cricketers have been playing for decades – 20 overs a side, four overs per bowler and as many runs as possible in whatever way you can get them. Ok, so there are no cheerleaders and fireworks, but evening cricket must lay claim to the original, exciting short form of the game. Players are chosen not just for their skills but for other qualities such as reliability or usefulness. For example maybe they have a big car to carry the team's kit or they serve behind the bar in the local pub. It might be determination because they are prepared to spend hours chasing up all the other players to get a team together each week. What other game allows such an inclusive team line-up?

The rituals of amateur cricket mean that it's a whole-day activity. In a weekend game the ritual begins at midday with a meeting at some bar and a drink to catch up on the week's news. The team then goes onto the ground to inspect the pitch, plays the game and then returns to the bar to celebrate or to drown their sorrows. All of this can take nine hours or more out of the day especially if the team is playing away. What better way to reduce the stress of a hectic working schedule than to have an enforced day-long focus on playing games? Without the constraints of league rules most truly amateur sides don't have to worry too much about the condition of their kit or whether they've got two recognised umpires. As long as there is a pitch, a bat and a ball, there's a game of cricket in the offering.

In the 1976 season, Llandudno won the Colwyn Bay Wednesday Evening Cricket League. Bill Ward (captain) was presented with the trophy by the League President, Reg Boase.

Club captain Phil Warburton scored a brilliant 128 not out against Norton (Runcorn) in May 1977. He hit 10 sixes and 9 fours in 66 minutes. This was a record fastest century for the club at that time.

Llandudno bowler Jeff Nicholls, introduced at a late stage in a 2nd XI match against Blaenau Ffestiniog at the Oval on 28th May 1977, had only six deliveries and in his last three bowled out the last three Blaenau Ffestiniog batsmen to end their team's innings. This feat has not been equalled. After the game, club captain Phil Warburton presented Jeff with a hat-trick tie.

The continuing saga over the state of the Oval ground because of the 'open plan experiment' was still raising serious concern throughout seasons 1976, 1977and1978. It became very serious when the North Wales Cricket League officials wrote to the club complaining about the dangerous state of the outfield at the Oval. The club felt there was little they could do to improve the situation because of the number of sports organisations using the Oval. The Caernarvonshire County Cricket officials had also told the club that they would no longer play at the Oval because of the state of the playing area. The outfield had for many years been used by the Hockey Club but since the allocation of a rugby pitch and for Sunday football the outfield was badly damaged and left in a bad state for the cricket season. It was realised that the ground was in such a bad condition it needed time to be brought back to an acceptable and safe standard. The once lush area was then a dismal park-like eyesore not fit for first-class cricket. Since the departure of Rene Clayton the cricket club had been without a professionally qualified groundsman and despite the efforts of certain club members and the council's own groundsman the once magnificent square had deteriorated rapidly and the outfield become a disgrace. The introduction of rugby and football had had a disastrous effect and it was estimated then that it would take two years for the turf to be restored.

Thankfully, in 1978 the Rugby Club moved to its present ground at Maesdu. Football pitches were re-allocated to other parts of the Oval away from the cricket playing area. In 1978 the club was now seen to be making determined and progressively ambitious plans for the future.

The signing of the new club professional from Australia, Robert Knight, arrived in the UK in April 1978 and was warmly welcomed by the committee and club members. He soon got stuck into the tasks waiting for him including coaching duties in the nets with both senior and junior members. It was not long before he was showing a remarkable talent with the bat on the field and before the end of May he had already recorded four centuries which brought his tally of runs to over 500. In his first game for the 2nd XI against Carmel on 22nd April he scored 109 not out and took five wickets for 51 runs. The following week against St Asaph for the 1st XI he hit another century (136 not out) and his bowling figures were four for 11. On 27th May against Bethesda at the Oval in a North Wales League match, Robert Knight (114) and Glyn Gibbons (110) made a fantastic opening partnership of 237. This created an all-time club record partnership and also for an opening pair to hit a 'ton' a piece.

By 17th June that year Robert Knight had scored over 1,000 runs for the season. In the match against Denbigh he achieved that by scoring 122 not out, and had recorded his sixth century.

Not to be overshadowed by Mr Knight, the club's own Glyn Gibbons scored 100 not out against Brymbo the week before and in the same match Dave Robertson took five wickets for 46 runs.

North Wales Select XI v Pakistan (PIA)

This was a match which had been eagerly awaited. It had required a lot of hard work for weeks by club members arranging and organising the visit. However most of the credit in staging this special event went to Brian Baister, ex-club member, who at the time was a high ranking Metropolitan Police Officer in charge of security at the CID offices at Heathrow. His duties as Detective Chief Inspector put him in contact with officials of all the airlines with offices at Heathrow. The Station Manager for Pakistan International Airlines was Captain Abdullah Baig who, in his flying days, held several World records for the fastest commercial flying times between various airports. He had also experienced the misfortune of being hijacked on one occasion, when 'sky-jacking' was in its infancy. He was a man Brian Baister got on well with and they became friends. It wasn't long before they realised that they both shared a passion for the game of cricket.

At the time, if you became an International cricketer in Pakistan you could be rewarded by being given patronage and sponsorship by becoming an 'employee' of PIA. Most of the Pakistan Test cricketers were on the PIA books. It was Brian Baister and Captain Baig who together organised a tour of Pakistan of a cricket team of British police officers in 1976. Agreement for the trip was only possible after consultation with Scotland Yard and the Foreign Office. The following year Brian Baister and a police colleague were invited to tour Kenya with the PIA team.

It was in 1978 that the PIA cricket team was scheduled to fly over and play the Metropolitan Police cricket team in London. Captain Baig was keen that the PIA team play other matches while they were in the UK and asked Brian Baister if it was possible could he arrange a weekend tour of North Wales. Plans were set in motion to play two one-day matches against a North Wales Select XI at the Oval and Rhos-on-Sea grounds.

The first was at the Oval on Sunday 27th August 1978 followed by a second match the following day at the Colwyn Bay club on their Rhos-on-Sea ground.

The Pakistan Test players were besieged by autograph hunters when they arrived at the Llandudno railway station a few days before the game at the Oval.

On the day of the match, despite the dull weather, the crowd swelled to about 1,500 and were given an entertaining display in a showpiece clash with some superlative fielding by both sides. Pakistan batted first and scored 193/7 dec. The top scorer was Shafkat Rams (50). Robert Knight took two wickets for 16 runs. North Wales were dismissed for 126. Robert Knight was elected 'Man of the Match' and presented with a radio.

The following day on the Monday Bank Holiday at Rhos-on-Sea, Pakistan hit 256/8 dec. with Talat Ali Malik scoring 163 which included 11 fours and four sixes. North Wales replied with a respectable 190/7 (Geoff Ellis 86 not out). The 'Man of the Match' prize of a radio on this occasion went to Talat Ali Malik.

Captain Abdullah Baig and the PIA party stayed at the Hydro Hotel, Llandudno. Throughout the whole trip, PIA picked up all of their own travel and accommodation costs, leaving the cricket club with a handsome profit. In the first game at the Oval, in an effort to take advantage of the biggest gate the club had experienced for many years, a raffle was organised for which the tickets were a mere 50p. Out of the blue, and just before the first ticket was drawn, Captain Baig announced to the waiting crowd that PIA would donate the first prize of two return flights from Heathrow to Tokyo.

The prize was won by Miss Pat Boase, the daughter of local businessman and vice-president of the club, Mr Reg Boase.

The Pakistan party included all Test players except Rachid Israr and Salim Anwar. They were:

S.Alouddin, Shafkat Rams, Naeem Ahmed, Aftab Baluch, Anil Dalpat, Rizwanuzzaman, Salim Anwar, Rachid Khan, Ikbal Sikander, Majid Khan, Hanif Mohammed, Saleem Altaf, Hassan Jamil, Mudassar Nazar, Wazim Bari and Talat Ali Malik.

The North Wales Select XI was:

Robert Knight (Tasmania –
Australian Sheffield Shield and Llandudno CC)

Don Wilson (Yorkshire and England Test player.
Head coach at Lord's cricket ground)

Collis King (West Indies Test player,
a Kerry Packer star, Pontblyddyn)

Kevin Brookes (MCC)

Kevin Lyons (Glamorgan)

Geoff Ellis (Glamorgan, Wales, Caernarvonshire and Llandudno CC)

Rene Clayton (Glamorgan, Wales, Caernarvonshire,
Denbighshire, Colwyn Bay CC and Llandudno CC)

Dominic Burke (Leicestershire)

P.J.Dunkley (Liverpool)

K.Jones (Liverpool)

Glyn Gibbons (Glamorgan, Caernarvonshire,
Colwyn Bay CC and Llandudno CC)

Dave Robertson (Caernarvonshire, Mochdre CC and Llandudno CC)

Neil Radford (Glamorgan)

Bradley Jones (Tasmania – Australian Sheffield Shield)

John Newnham (Derbyshire and Colwyn Bay CC)

G.Gunning (Pontblyddyn)

On 3rd September 1978 Robert Knight notched up his ninth century (105 not out) of the season against Chance Pilkingtons' XI and became Llandudno's most prolific batsman scoring the highest number of runs in a season.

Robert Knight went back home to Australia (Tasmania) at the end of the season. The club members were all sorry to see him go but were pleased to hear later that he had been selected to play for Tasmania in the Sheffield Shield in 1978 and continued to do so until 1982. During that period he scored 742 runs and his top score was 114. He did return to the UK in 1979 and played during the summer for Redcar in the North Yorkshire and Cheshire League.

At the Annual General Meeting of the club in December 1978 the President, Mr J.G.Gibbons, spoke of the fortunes of the club's 1st XI and how sad he felt that they had missed promotion to the 1st Division by only nine points. He announced that the club's new groundsman for the coming season was Keith Elphick, a former Colwyn Bay and Sussex player, who was playing for Mochdre during that season.

It was reported that Mr Reg Boase, for many years a vice-president of the club, had died on 18th March 1979.

As a direct result of the visit of Pakistan (PIA) in 1978 Llandudno were fortunate in signing Rashid Israr as professional for the following season – he had expressed a wish, when on tour with PIA, to return to Llandudno and play for the club. As an added bonus he brought along with him Ikbal Sikander and Anil Dalpat who had also wished to return and play in the 1978 season for the club.

Rashid Israr

He was a prolific right hand opening batsman and medium pace bowler. His name appears in Wisden's list of high individual scores when he hit 330 runs in a Pakistan competition in 1977. He played first-class cricket for five years in Pakistan including a period with PIA. In the 1980/1981 season he played for a Pakistan Combined XI.

Anil Dalpat

He was the first Hindu ever to play Test cricket for Pakistan. Dalpat was a lower-order batsman and wicket keeper and represented Pakistan in the early 1980s. On his debut, against England at Karachi in 1983/1984, it was reported Dalpat kept well, behind the stumps, to the spin of Abdul Qadir as Pakistan won by three wickets. In his nine Tests he made 25 dismissals and his highest score was 52 against New Zealand at Karachi in 1984/1985. In 1983/1984 Dalpat dismissed 67 batsmen as wicket keeper, a Pakistan domestic record.

Iqbal Sikander

He was a right-hand batsman who bowled leg-breaks and googlies. He played for Pakistan in the 1992 Cricket World Cup and was part of the Pakistan squad that won the competition, but he was never selected again for Pakistan in either Tests or ODIs. For a while he was coach for the Afghanistan national cricket team.

He is now the ACC Development Officer for six up-and-coming cricketing nations which are Kuwait, Afghanistan, Singapore, Iran, Saudi Arabia and Qatar.

Just recently he was asked what was most rewarding about his position on the Asian Cricket Council. He replied: *"What I find most fulfilling about my job is that the countries that I am looking after have developed and prospered both in their administrative set-up as well as their performances on the field. Another aspect that is highly pleasing is the development of the general cricket infrastructure over the past four years."*

He was also asked what the biggest difference is with cricket played now and 10 years ago. He replied: *"The game of cricket has changed dramatically primarily because of the number of one-day Internationals being played and this is what has resulted in an overall change. Back when I was playing, the game seemed to be more technically correct. Today, cricket is more on an entertainment level and now with the introduction of Twenty20 it's only going to get more popular."*

About the 1992 World Cup – was winning it the ultimate achievement? Could there be anything greater?

"At that stage the World Cup was the ultimate. To win the World Cup is a dream come true for any cricketer and I was fortunate enough to be a part of that team. For me personally, it was the ultimate achievement."

In January 1991, playing for Karachi Whites against Peshawar in a one-day match, he recorded the extraordinary bowling analysis of 6.2–3–7–7; no other Pakistan domestic cricketer has ever taken seven wickets in a first class game for the cost of fewer runs.

After his 1978 season at Llandudno he went on to play for Prestatyn in the North Wales Cricket League and then went on to play for Leigh CC in the Liverpool Competition League. In 2001 he took over 100 league wickets for Leigh.

There was some good news circulating in 1979 when it was learnt that five junior members had gained club scholarships to attend advanced cricket courses at Lord's. They were Joe Lambe, Richard Williams, Gary Talbot, Graham Boase and Tim Bradley.

Aberconwy Council were told on 16th May 1979 that a disco planned for the hockey Easter Festival had been called off because consultants had said the upstairs club room could not hold more than 60 people. The cricket club, during their season that year had held, successfully, two discos a week for EF students strictly adhering to the 'no more than the 60 people limit'. In doing so they raised a lot of money at the door and at the bar for the purpose of club funds.

Rashid Israr hit his first century (128) against Carmel on 20th May 1979. His bowling figures were 4/14. Glyn Gibbons in the same match scored 74 not out. The following week against Thrybergh Park Israr scored 113, emphasising his talent.

Iqbal Sikander made his debut for Llandudno on 9th June and Anil Dalpat against Colwyn Bay on 16th June.

In July 1979 tributes were paid to the efforts of the club committee in obtaining the services of Pakistan cricketers, Rashid Israr, Iqbal Sikander and Anil Dalpat to play for the club. Since their arrival an improvement was seen in Llandudno's general standard of play on the field. They were winning matches. Promotion to Division One of the North Wales League was then a possibility. With the help of these 'star' players in addition to the experienced John Barlow, ex-Lancashire League player, and youngsters like Paul Hughes (sponsored by the well-known cricketing company Duncan Fearnley), Tim Bradley and all-rounder Jed Hughes they were contributing tremendously in keeping the cricket flag flying for Llandudno. Other cricket club members, especially Ron Beswick, were highly commended too for their work. Phil Warburton and Barbara Whitehead were mentioned for their hard-working efforts in organising functions and looking after the general running of the club. Praise was also extended to Eryl Williams, 2nd XI captain, in boosting morale in the 2nd team squad.

The 1979 season was certainly a very good year for the club.

Opening the batting with Rashid Israr against Menai Bridge on 28th July 1979, Allan (the milk) Hughes (father of club stalwart Mark Hughes) scored a superb 104 runs. He and Rashid put on 221 for the first wicket. Allan, in his youth as a pupil at John Bright G.S. had already made his mark in the archives of Llandudno cricket by taking all 10 wickets in an innings.

Rashid Israr scored over 2,000 runs in the 1979 season for the club.

As expected Llandudno did gain promotion to the Premier Division of the North Wales Cricket League and it had to be said that the club's success was very much due to the performance of the three Pakistan players. At a Club Dinner on 7th September 1979 the chairman, Andrew Roberts, congratulated all the players for their 100% efforts which made for a very successful season. He went on to say that the season's success merited continued support and effort in another direction. He warned that without full support the club could easily fold altogether and made the point that fundraising went hand in hand because one could not exist without the other. Despite an excellent playing season he said the year had been a continuous running battle with town hall officials to ensure that the club's interests were not neglected. Regrettably in that direction only minimal support materialised.

Club president, Mr J.G.Gibbons endorsed the chairman's comments and expressed satisfaction at the progress of the club over the past two years.

There were also glowing comments in the room on the standard of umpiring by Elias Thomas.

The 1st XI captain, Graham Gibbons, said it had been an excellent season for all the players. The skills and enthusiasm of professional Rashid Israr and colleagues Sikander and Dalpat had rubbed off onto the remainder of the squad. He highlighted the performances of Gwilym Roberts, Neil Gallagher and thanked vice-captain John Breeze for his help and support.

John Breeze added that through the Primary School League competition the amount of cricket being played at John Bright G.S., once the club's breeding ground, was gradually increasing and this was encouraging.

There were many members present who expressed concern at the poor support from the Town Council. The Oval ground, once the show piece of North Wales, was in a deplorable condition. It was also agreed that the 'open planning' scheme initiated some years previously had been a dismal failure and had contributed greatly to the present shabby appearance of the Llandudno Oval.

Rashid Israr was welcomed back as professional for the 1980 season. He was not accompanied this time by Iqbal Sikander who had joined Prestatyn, and Anil Dalpat who chose to stay in Pakistan. By July he had already passed the 1,000 runs milestone in the North Wales League when he scored an unbeaten 102 not out against St Asaph on 5th July 1980. Llandudno snatched the maximum 10 points with thanks also to Glyn Gibbons who bowled superbly with figures of 8/41.

The following day Llandudno trounced Welshpool and earned their place in the Zone A Final (effectively the quarter final) of the Welsh Cup against Newtown. This resulted in Newtown going through to the semis only to be defeated by St Fagans, who, in turn, were defeated in the final by Maesteg Celtic.

On 23rd August 1980 in a league match between Llandudno and Colwyn Bay at the Rhos-on-Sea ground, the result was a win for Llandudno by just 12 runs. This avenged an Oval defeat earlier in the season. Rashid Israr scored 55 runs but John Breeze, always a bottler in derby matches, earned top honours producing a great attacking innings, finding the boundary five times in an invaluable 34 runs.

In a close tussle the following week with a nail biting finish against Wrexham at the Oval it was John Breeze again who won the match for Llandudno. The stage was set when the game went to the final over and to the final ball with two runs to win when the number 11 batsman, John Breeze, took his turn and was watched in nervous anticipation by all those present. He walked briskly and confidently onto the field to take his place at the wicket. After taking his guard, he faced a determined and aggressive, 'charging like a bull' Wrexham bowler. When the time arrived (he kept his eyes open, he said afterwards) he calmly and gently stroked the ball to the boundary to complete the winning runs, rendering the ecstatic delights of the supporters and his team colleagues.

Duck: out for nought, the zero resembling a duck's egg.

Pair: dismissed for a duck in both innings. It's so called because of the supposed resemblance of the two noughts in a scorebook to a pair of spectacles.

Golden duck: out first ball.

Diamond duck: a dismissal without facing a delivery, or a dismissal (for zero) off the first ball of a team's innings. It's also sometimes known as a 'platinum duck'.

King pair: out first ball in both innings.

Emperor pair: a 'pair' by an opening batsman who is dismissed without scoring to the first ball of both innings.

North Wales cricket swung into action with drastic changes ready for the start of the 1981 season. A breakaway competition league was formed comprising the heavyweights of the North Wales League. They were drawn together by a feeling of frustration because the founders of the league, some eight years previously, were dragging their heels not investing in ground improvements and failing to elevate standards. The rebels were Colwyn Bay, St Asaph, Prestatyn, Ruthin, Northop Hall, Mold, Brymbo, Marchwiel and Wrexham.

Because of the action taken the newly-formed North Wales Cricket League Division One comprised the following teams:

Llandudno, Chirk, Bethesda, Shotton, Pontblyddyn, Gwersyllt, Mochdre, Connahs Quay, Llay and Hawarden Park.

Llandudno had no professional player for the 1981 season.

Llandudno 1st XI opened their programme with a win against Gwersyllt.

Dave Robertson claimed a hat-trick finishing with 3/30 in a match Llandudno lost against Hawarden Park on 16th May.

A Trios Competition for the Eric Barker Trophy, after an absence of over 15 years, was held at the Oval on 23rd August 1981. Brymbo beat Prestatyn in the final. As well as the trophy they won £100. The beaten finalists received £30.

Tributes were made in the cricket columns of two local newspapers in 1981 to the club's very popular and welcomed visitor and scorer. Alan Fielding, a visitor to Llandudno for the previous 18 years, would spend two fortnight-holidays every year during the summer months with his mother and father. Their home was in Longton, a village in the borough of South Ribble, Lancashire. The family stayed in a 'bed and breakfast' close to the Oval so that Alan, who had a learning disability, could spend his time there when there was a match or join the members for a few hours on a club night. Alan was recognised as the 'unofficial' scorer who would be found sitting in the Score Box with the official scorers during play, busy entering details of the progress of the game in his own little red score-book. Sometimes during the week he would travel with the team to away matches and do what he did best and that was 'score'. He loved Llandudno CC and was always a welcomed guest to all the social events held in the pavilion when he was around. He really enjoyed himself, was good company, enjoyed a good laugh and mixed well with players and members alike and as a result made lots of friends. He was considered not only the best and neatest scorer members had ever come across but he had an impressive record of Llandudno's matches spanning the whole of the 18 years he had been coming to the Oval. During his time at the club he would collect for his church charity and every year his church would write to the club thanking everyone for making a donation. Alan was often thanked for his fine support and dedication to the club. No doubt if he was about today Alan would be a worthy Life-Member. He has been sadly missed by all that knew him.

Young Howie Thomas displayed his undoubted talents with a superb half-century against Continental CC, a team of West Indies cricketers from the Midlands. An official from the visiting side commented that if Howie Thomas was playing in the standard of cricket prevalent in the Birmingham League he would almost certainly make County grade.

Without a professional groundsman during the 1981 season there was instead a Ground Staff committee led by Graham Gibbons. John and Valerie Gallagher managed the bar.

The treasurer reported that the '250' club had made a healthy profit.

At the Annual Awards Presentation Night the Junior Cricketer of the Year 1981 was awarded to Stephen Nicholls. President Mr J.G.Gibbons, in presenting the award, said, "Llandudno will be expecting a lot from this young man in the future." His father, Jeff Nicholls, was presented with the 2nd XI batting award.

North Wales Cricket League – Division 1

Final Table 1981

	P	W	L	ND	Pts
Chirk	18	12	2	4	121
Bethesda	18	11	4	3	111
Shotton	18	10	4	4	103
Pontblyddyn	18	7	8	3	97
Gwersyllt	18	9	6	3	83
Connahs Quay	18	7	8	3	73
Mochdre	18	6	11	1	69
Llandudno	18	5	10	3	65
Llay	18	6	10	2	65
Hawarden Park	18	3	13	2	55

Divison 3	P	W	L	ND	Pts
Halkyn	18	14	2	2	126
Llanrwst	18	12	4	2	116
Corwen	18	12	4	2	114
Shotton II	18	10	7	1	90
Gresford II	18	8	9	1	90
Hawarden Park II	18	8	9	1	89
Pontblyddyn II	18	6	11	1	86
Dolgellau	18	7	10	1	76
Denbigh II	18	6	10	2	75
Llandudno	18	0	17	1	10

Young Graham Boase, playing in a Sunday match against Bodedern on 25th July 1982, took eight wickets for 25 runs which included a hat-trick.

The 1982 Trios Competition was held up for four hours because of the bad weather. The final between Brymbo and Continental A was not played because of the bad light so officials decided that the Eric Barker trophy that year be shared.

At the 1982 Annual General Meeting held in November at the Sandringham Hotel the chairman, Andrew Roberts, said that the Sports Association saga was still an ongoing topic with the Aberconwy Council. He said that there had been a recent meeting of representatives from the three clubs (hockey, cricket and football) with three Aberconwy councillors. It had been stated that due to financial restraints Aberconwy Council had to reduce their expenditure in some way and so were prepared to lease out the pavilion on, initially, a three-year lease. The clubs were asked to consider this.

Graham Gibbons said he would prefer to go for a 20-year lease so enabling the clubs to apply for a Welsh Sports Association grant for improvements. He also felt that the pavilion was badly sited for visitors who would have to make the long trek across the Oval in winter in muddy conditions. It was after a lot of thought and lengthy discussion that the lease was voted on by the members and it was decided to obtain, initially, a three-year lease.

The David Roberts Memorial Trophy for 1982 for batting went to Dave Robertson and the bowling to Richard Williams. The Junior Cricketer of the Year went to Mark Herbert. The Senior Cricketer of the Year award went to Phil Warburton, who was elected first team captain for 1983. He said, *"I will be spending much of my time being involved with the youth side. I would like to see the junior side of the game improved a lot more. Cricket in Ysgol John Bright has practically gone so I think the youth policy at the club must continue and improve."*

Llandudno had a good eight wickets win over Bangor on 4th June 1983. They scuttled the home team out on their wicket for 39 runs thanks to the fine bowling of Ray Williams (5/20) and Clive Stock (4/1).

On Sunday 19th June 1983 Colwyn Bay entertained Llandudno and the result ended in a draw. Ron Beswick (5/27) was Llandudno's most successful bowler. Phil Warburton (49 not out) was top scorer for the visitors. Colwyn Bay batted first and scored 189/9 dec. Llandudno never looked like getting the runs and finished on 85/7.

There were congratulations all round for junior player Stephen Nicholls on his selection to play for North Wales in a two-day match to be played against South Wales at Brecon to be held on 11/12 July 1983.

Cricket enthusiasts have long argued for the game to be included in the Olympics. It was part of the Commonwealth Games in 1998 but few realise that it was once an Olympic sport. In the 1900 Summer Games a team from Great Britain played a team from France (mainly composed of English ex-pats working in Paris) – but they were the only two competitors. Great Britain won the game, and the gold medal. Cricket has never been included as an Olympic discipline since then because the Olympic authorities argue that there are too few nations in the world that play the game to a professional standard and as such it is a 'minority' sport – try telling that to a billion fans in India and Pakistan. The advent of Twenty20 may at least provide a glimmer of hope for the future as it is felt the format would fit easily into an Olympic schedule.

In fact the latest news is that the MCC World Cricket Committee is backing the inclusion of Twenty20 at the 2024 Olympic Games.

Some very promising junior players were given an opportunity to prove themselves in a 2nd XI match against Mochdre at the Oval on 9th July 1983. In a very close finish they only lost by eight runs but the youngsters all played very well for the team. Stephen Nicholls, the youngest player on the field, bowled really well and had excellent figures of three for 37. Ian Jones, an up-and-coming all-rounder, took 2/28. Young Gary Talbot was the highlight of the Llandudno batting – he could hit the ball with tremendous power for a 16 year old. His knock of 61 was an almost chanceless innings.

Members of the club always looked forward to the annual visit of the Oaklands CC of Birmingham. In those days they brought two coachloads of spectators from the Midlands which included wives and children who loved to spend the day in Llandudno. Sunday 30th July 1983 was no different. At the end of the match there was plenty of music and dancing with a touch of West Indies reggae music enjoyed by all, before they were ready to return home. On that occasion an evening barbecue was provided by the club chairman, Andy Roberts, which went down well.

Llandudno's emphatic win against Llay on 13th August 1983 was indebted to the batting of Dave Robertson who hit a brilliant 93 out of his team's total of 209. He then went on to take five wickets for 51 as Llay were halted on 150. This win for Llandudno kept them in second place in the league behind Bethesda.

Llandudno travelled to Pontblyddyn on the Bank Holiday Monday and were shocked to see the great former West Indies all-rounder Collis King playing for the home team. So Pontblyddyn, or rather Collis King, beat Llandudno almost single-handed. He took 5/25 off 19 overs and then an unbeaten 93 runs. He clobbered Neil Gallagher for 4 sixes in one over after already hitting sixes in previous overs off Dave Robertson, John Breeze and Peter Williams. With Pontblyddyn needing only two runs for victory Collis King rounded things off with another six struck firmly out of the ground. Result: Collis King (Pontblyddyn) 10 points, Llandudno nil.

Collis King

He was a former West Indies cricketer who played nine Tests and 18 one-day Internationals for the West Indies.

Born in Christ Church, Barbados, King played as an all-rounder, but had more success with the bat than ball, especially in Test cricket, where he scored one century and two fifties but only took three wickets – in three different innings. In ODI cricket, his highest – and swiftest – score came in the 1979 World Cup final, when he came in at 99 for four to hit 86 off 66 deliveries, and adding 149 with Viv Richards. King also held a catch and bowled three overs for 13 runs in the match, and the West Indies won by 92 runs.

King went on both the 1982/3 and 1983/4 West Indies' Rebel Tours to South Africa.

In a varied first class career, he played for his native country Barbados in the West Indies domestic competition, but also played for Glamorgan and Worcestershire in English county cricket and Natal in South Africa. In scoring 123 on his Worcestershire debut in 1983, he became the first player in more than 50 years to score a hundred in his first match for the county.

North Wales Cricket League Division 1

Final League Table 1983

	P	W	L	ND	Pts
Bethesda	22	12	2	8	137
Llandudno	22	11	4	7	111
Chirk	22	11	2	9	108
Gresford	22	9	5	7	104
Shotton	22	8	7	7	102
Llay	22	9	7	6	102
Buckley	22	8	8	6	101
Mochdre	22	6	8	8	89
Connahs Quay	22	5	10	7	85
Gwersyllt	22	6	11	5	79
Pontblyddyn	22	3	13	6	73
Bala	22	0	11	11	46

Dave Robinson topped the North Wales League Division 1 bowling averages taking 58 wickets for under 10 runs a wicket.

At the 1983 Annual General Meeting at the Sandringham Hotel it was reported that moves to form a Sports Association had appeared to have come to 'a dead end'. Aberconwy Council had tried to bring it about but the situation had reached stalemate. The President, J.G.Gibbons, in his address said that he had hoped for an improvement in the Oval facilities but it seemed that these had worsened. Andy Roberts, the club chairman, said a representative from a firm that specialised in the maintenance of sports grounds had inspected the field and it was hoped his recommendations would be acted on with help to be given to the Aberconwy Parks Department.

Dave Robertson collected honours galore at the Annual Presentation Dinner on 16th March 1984. The all-rounder won awards for the best 1st XI averages in both batting and bowling in the 1983 season. He won the 'most sixes award'. He also picked up the Senior Cricketer of the Year award. Before he could sit down again he collected the David Roberts Memorial Trophy for batting (93 against Llay) and the David Roberts Memorial Trophy award for bowling (eight for 33 against Gwersyllt). Mark Hughes took the Junior Cricketer of the Year award.

In a 2nd XI match against Mochdre seconds at the Oval on 7th July 1984 the home team welcomed a 6-4 win. The name on everyone's lips at the time was 19 year old Gary Talbot who took nine wickets for 46 runs in a spell of hostile bowling. Fifteen year old Stephen Nicholls picked up the other Mochdre wicket.

In an amazing 2nd XI match against Gwersyllt seconds on 1st September at the Oval the game was tied. Both teams were all out for a low scoring 93 runs.

A crisis at the Oval was highlighted at the 1984 Annual General Meeting held on 6th December when John Breeze stood down as chairman. His action had been due to the apathy of certain members over their lack of support to the club. The meeting was so poorly attended that the club failed to reach a quorum of members to decide some important issues. In resigning as Chairman John Breeze said that due to the apathy the burden being put on his shoulders had been too great. He also admitted that the 1st XI team had had a poor 1984 season following a good 1983 season and that more effort was needed by players both on and off the field to bring the club back to shape.

The club treasurer, Roger Latham, reported a profit for the year. He said that the accounts showed that income from vice-presidents and sponsored balls had increased three-fold due to the enormous effort and hard work by John Breeze and Dave Robertson.

Sunday captain Joe Lambe commented on the team's performance during the season. He was pleased with the standard of bowling and fielding and singled out Andy Davies and Stephen Nicholls as players to watch for the future.

Llandudno 1st XI suffered some major blows at the start of the 1985 season. Unfortunately they lost some key players, who were also hard working club members, a very big loss to the club. Dave Robertson and John Breeze left to join Mochdre CC. Last season's club captain, Phil Warburton, moved to Conwy CC. This unrest had an effect on the first team's performance in the league. They suffered a third defeat in their first five games against Mochdre on 2nd June 1985.

North Wales Cricket League Division 1

Final Table 1985

	P	W	L	T	ND	Pts
Gresford	22	17	3	0	2	145
Buckley	22	14	4	2	2	142
Gwersyllt	22	11	11	0	0	118
Shotton	22	11	9	1	1	116
Mochdre	22	12	9	1	0	114
Chirk	22	10	10	0	2	113
Bethesda	22	10	9	0	3	113
Hawarden Park	22	10	10	0	2	106
Connahs Quay	22	10	11	0	1	97
Northop Hall	22	6	13	0	3	89
Abergele	22	6	16	0	0	71
Llandudno	22	6	16	0	0	59

Division 4

	P	W	L	T	ND	Pts
Pilkingtons	20	19	0	0	1	174
Mochdre II	20	15	5	0	0	143
Denbigh II	20	14	5	0	1	134
Gwersyllt II	20	10	9	0	1	111
Conwy II	20	10	9	0	1	99
Pontblyddyn II	20	11	7	0	2	98
Bersham II	20	9	9	0	2	94
Carmel II	20	9	10	0	1	78
Abergele II	20	1	19	0	0	49
Llandudno II	20	3	13	0	4	36
Llanrwst II	20	3	13	0	4	34

After a dismal 1985 season with Llandudno finishing bottom of the first division the club made its first move towards getting back to the former glory days of the sixties. Clive Stock was elected the new chairman at the AGM. He had been a regular 1st XI player in the sixties and had made many appearances in the Caernarvonshire side. Prior to joining the club he played cricket in his early days in Middlesex and Australia. Llandudno had a 'star studded' team in that glorious period in the sixties and only Ron Beswick was still playing in 1985. There were club stalwarts, Alan Gibbons, Graham Gibbons and Roger Latham who came along in the latter half of the sixties and were also still playing in 1985. The names in that great side just roll off the tongue: Tony Neville, Mike Manson, Doug Rossington, Rene Clayton, Geoff Ellis, Ray Williams, Max Shone, Stan Kidd, Roger Bower, Keith Jones, John Hall, Stan Pounder, Joe Cosgrove and John Collier. Besides the talent on the field the club also had two of the best ever umpires on the North Wales coast in Eric Johnson and Elias Thomas. They were halcyon days at the Oval and it was hoped Clive

Stock would bring back the determination required to help re-build for the future.

Graham Gibbons continued as vice-chairman and would once again be in charge of the ground, preparing the wicket etc. Andrew Roberts was re-appointed President.

The Legendary W.G.Grace was the national 440-yard hurdles champion and also represented England at bowls.

England Test Bowler Geoff Miller, between 1976 and 1984, represented Derbyshire at table tennis as well as cricket.

Llandudno got the result they were looking for in their opening fixture in Division 2 by defeating Dolgellau at the Oval in a low scoring match. The 'Man of the Match' on that occasion was Graham Gibbons. He claimed seven wickets for 16 runs in 14.3 overs. In the following week it was the turn of Ron Beswick who took seven Bala wickets for 31 to help Llandudno gain a second win.

It was a different story half-way through the season because by the time they lost to Dolgellau in the return match there were fears of relegation. They had slumped to bottom place after winning only once in their last nine matches.

While the first team were showing their inconsistency losing heavily in their next game to Bala the young 2nd XI players where putting up a spirited performance going down by only 23 runs against league favourites Carmel seconds. Stephen Nicholls, having taken 13 wickets in his last two games, finished with 5/30. Stephen Williams also bowled well for 4/68. Tony Davies (42) and Richard Stock (36) led the Llandudno reply just short of Carmel's total of 170.

In the final match of the season Llandudno did lose to champions Conwy but Llandudno's consolation was that other results at the bottom of Division 2 went their way and in so doing they avoided relegation by the narrowest of margins.

Richard Stock, who had captained the club's Sunday XI to a championship success in the Gwynedd Sunday League, was named as the new 1st XI captain for the 1987 season. His proud father, Clive Stock, had been captain in 1972 and was now the club chairman. Looking after the youngsters were John Edwards, Nick Davies and Mathew Neale.

Joe Lambe, the 1st XI captain, was commended for steering the side clear of relegation. Alan Gibbons topped the batting averages and Graham Boase took the bowling honours. Other noticeable bowling performances were from Mark Hughes, Graham Gibbons and Ron Beswick.

Richard Stock praised many of the youngsters stating that several were knocking on the first team door. Stephen Williams had already made the breakthrough. Other names mentioned were Stephen Nicholls, Carl Wedge, Phil Williams, Nick Davies, Tim Winnett and Ian Davies. Tony Davies had topped the 2nd XI batting averages and Stephen Nicholls the bowling.

The 1st XI, without eight of last season's regulars, put up a spirited fight in their opening league match of the season at the Oval on 25th April 1987. They narrowly lost to Mynydd Isa by only seven runs. New captain Richard Stock won the toss and invited the visitors to bat first. There was early success when young Stephen Nicholls opened the bowling and quickly got rid of their top batsman for nought. Llandudno needed to beat the visitor's score of 150. While stalwart Alan Gibbons was at the crease Llandudno were in with a chance. The best stand of the innings was when the stubborn batting pair of juniors Phil Williams and Timmy Winnett kept some very aggressive bowling at bay. Unfortunately, when just seven runs off the target, young Timmy Winnett was given out lbw when he was on 16.

Before the start of the match against Rhewl on 25th July 1987, players and spectators observed 'a one minute silence' in respect over the loss of prominent vice-president and local impresario Robinson Cleaver.

Llandudno's cricket, hockey and soccer clubs were facing a financial crisis over the Council plans for the Oval. A combined management committee was considered to take over the running of the sportsground. The Council wanted the three clubs to pay the maintenance costs for the pavilion such as heating, lighting and water sewerage in addition to pitch maintenance. This would put up their financial commitment by an estimated £300 to £700 each year.

The clubs met representatives of the Council and the idea was for the three clubs to form a management committee which would be in charge of renting the facilities out to other local organisations in order to raise money.

Llandudno's hockey club official, Tim Baker, commented: *"We had very fruitful talks last week and we do recognise the financial side is a concern for all sports clubs but hopefully we have found a possible solution."*

Football club chairman Paul Lane added: *"It will be very hard finding the extra cash but we are willing to give it a go and have asked the council to make certain undertakings to help us."*

Llandudno Cricket Club's financial problems had reached a crisis point by the early part of 1988 and it was felt necessary to launch a serious fundraising programme in an attempt to try and secure the future of the club. Fund Raising Secretary, Joe Lambe commented: *"We have been living on a shoestring budget for the last few years and are now in a desperate need for funds. We badly need the support of our members."*

Amongst many other important issues, the club wanted to raise cash to provide urgently needed new nets at the Oval and to stimulate more interest in encouraging youngsters to join the club coaching scheme organised by John Edwards.

In a friendly match against Colwyn Bay which ended in a draw on 26th June 1988, Neil Gallagher scored his maiden century (113 not out) which included 17 boundaries. He followed this up with a fine 50 the next week against Ince Blundell in another friendly.

Llandudno and Caernarvonshire County player Mark Hughes took five wickets for four runs in a tremendous spell of bowling against BSC Shotton on 2nd July 1988.

Llandudno's troubles were not only off-field but were causing concern on-field. With just three games left it seemed inevitable that Llandudno was for the big drop to the 3rd Division.

August 1988

	P	W	Pts
Denbigh	18	13	123
Halkyn	19	13	117
Bala	17	7	92
Menai Bridge	18	8	90
Gwersyllt	18	7	87
Pilkingtons	18	7	86
BSC Shotton	18	7	75
Rhewl	19	5	73
Mynydd Isa	18	5	70
Dolgellau	18	4	67
Pontblyddyn	18	5	66
Llandudno	18	4	64

Final Table

	P	W	Pts
Denbigh	21	16	146
Halkyn	21	13	124
Gwersyllt	21	10	111
Bala	21	8	106
Menai Bridge	21	10	105
Pilkingtons	21	9	93
Mynydd Isa	21	7	89
BSC Shotton	21	8	87
Llandudno	21	6	87
Rhewl	21	5	74
Pontblyddyn	21	5	73
Dolgellau	21	4	73

In a nail-biting finish Llandudno finally ended all threats of relegation as shown in the tables.

At the Annual General Meeting held in October 1988 it was reported that after some years of financial distress the club had made a healthy profit for the year. The Treasurer, Roger Latham, gave the news and added that it was through the excellent fund-raising efforts of Joe Lambe, who had made a tremendous contribution to the upturn of the club's financial position.

The 1st XI captain, Richard Stock, was pleased to report that the side's good form under a lot of pressure in the latter part of the season meant that they had avoided relegation. He even went on to say that in his opinion the team showed signs of a promotion push in the forthcoming 1989 season. Mark Hughes's batting was an inspiration and he was given good support by Alan Gibbons, Joe Lambe and Roger Latham. Neil Gallagher headed the bowling averages supported by the evergreen Graham Gibbons. There was also promising performances from youngsters Carl Wedge and Nick Davies.

Mark Lambe was top of the 2nd XI batting averages.

Thanks were given to the junior coach, John Edwards; Joe Lambe for his back-breaking work on the square and preparing the wickets; John Gallagher, who had worked hard behind the bar; and also umpire Spencer Zeller.

The 1st XI was really showing their class mid-way through the 1989 season. By July they had gone top of the Greenalls North Wales Cricket League Division 2 for the first time. In getting there they had given their best performance of the season by beating Pontblyddyn on 22nd July. Joe Lambe topped the batting with a fine 69 runs.

The champagne corks were popping in the Llandudno dressing room after a narrow win against Menai Bridge on 2nd September 1989. Llandudno 1st XI had clinched the Division 2 championship.

Llandudno made their welcome return to the first division with a win against Bersham on 28th April 1990. In that match, Alan Gibbons opened the batting and finished the team's innings on 96 not out. They also celebrated a new sponsorship deal with the Risboro and Gogarth Abbey hotels, owned by the Maddocks family.

Not to be left out of the celebrations the 2nd XI also had a good win against Shotton. Club Chairman Tony Davies scored a memorable century (102).

Tony was among the players who received special Fosters/Sunday Express Cricketing Awards for his century during May. He received a special tie commemorating his feat.

Club President Clive Stock played his final game for the club in the annual President's XI v Chairman's XI on 4th August 1990. Clive was presented with a trophy to mark the occasion. In this game it is worth mentioning young Mark Lambe's career best 82 and the maturing David Noakes who scored an unbeaten 75 for the President's XI. The match ended in a draw.

Wisden Cricketers' Almanac

John Wisden was born in 1826, the son of a Brighton builder. His father died when he was still a boy and young John went to live, as a pot-boy, with Tim Box who taught him the game of cricket. Wisden was described in chronicles of the time as 'a hungry-looking lad of one's sixpence for his trouble', but by 1845 he had been chosen to play for Sussex. Although only five feet four inches tall and weighing seven stone, he became a feared fast bowler known as the 'Little Wonder' and averaged 225 wickets a season for 12 years. In 1850, he clean bowled all ten wickets in the second innings of a North v South match. He went on to own a tobacconist and sports equipment store in London's Leicester Square, a business in which his chief rival was Lilywhites Brothers & Co. of Islington who, since 1849, had issued the young Cricketer's Guide at 18d a copy. Seeing the value of such a publication for advertising purposes, Wisden decided to produce his own and in 1864 launched the Wisden Cricketers' Almanac. The first issue contained 112 pages and sold for 1s. It has been published every year for almost 150 years, making it the oldest sports annual in the world. Wisden contains a mixture of obituaries, comment, records and awards, including the well-known Wisden Cricketers of the Year awards, which date back as far as 1889. As well as sections on the English domestic and international scene, there are sections on cricket throughout the world. A copy of the first edition of Wisden will cost you around £20,000 to buy today. The first hardback edition of the book, introduced in 1896, will cost anything up to £30,000.

The major sponsor for the 1991 season was the town's Cottage Loaf Pub. On behalf of the club, Mark Lambe presented the Manager, Kevin Chin, with an autographed bat.

Work had started on the building of a new pavilion in January 1991. The council had accepted that the original building had not been fit for its purpose and that the structure of the building had deteriorated to such an extent it had been regarded as unsafe. Club chairman Joe Lambe reported that the Council had agreed to an offer by the cricket club to manage the new building when complete.

Councillors shocked at cost of new cricket Pavilion

The rising cost of a new cricket pavilion for Llandudno shocked councillors who were committed to a new building because the old one had been demolished. The original estimate for the pavilion had been £100,000 but the Community Services Committee was horrified in December 1991 when told that this had risen to £157,790. This was the lowest of six tenders for the contract and some councillors feared that if accepted it could mean other projects within the borough would miss out through lack of funds.

Councillor Brian Bertola said: *"I cannot accept, under any circumstances, a cricket pavilion on the Oval at this price – this is far too expensive."*

Council Officers explained that much of the extra cost had come about because the pavilion was planned for a new location on the Oval and £30,000 would have to be spent on car park facilities.

Councillor Graham Rees said: *"I'm absolutely amazed that somebody somewhere is going to lose out if we go ahead."*

But Councillor Christine Jones said a delay would cost money: *"We have got a good scheme going. I know we have had a bit of a shock but I think we should go for it now."* She went on to say: *"I propose we accept or by the time we get back to the drawing board we will find we get less for the £157,000."*

Councillor Bob Parry added: *"If we cancel it now the next time we go ahead it will be £200,000."*

Councillors voted to accept the tender provided the Policy and Resources Committee approved the extra expenditure.

The committee did.

The go-ahead had been given but there continued some opposition from other councillors who argued that when the budget was just

£100,000, they wanted to know why the cheapest tender for the new pavilion did cost £57,000 more.

Councillor R.I.Thomas told the Policy and Finance Committee: *"It seems we have got our sums wrong here and we should refer back."* In reply, the Finance Director, Ken Finch, said the cost had gone up because various features had been added to the original plan including a £30,000 car park and a bar.

Councillor Christine Jones said: *"We went into this with our eyes open and we're at last getting what we wanted. We should find the extra £57,000."*

Councillor Margaret Lyon said: *"We're doing this because the original building was a pig's ear. We saw sense and pulled it down rather than do it up. It's important after all this time to have a decent building. We can do without the car park for the time being."*

But Councillor Edward Woodward said: *"Is there never any provision for the Conwy valley? I'm worried that this £57,000 must be taken from the valley."*

Councillor Brian Bertola said: *"We can do without the car park, and we have no responsibility to the cricket club – it's up to them to provide a bar."*

Meanwhile, Ian Jones produced his best ever bowling figures against Gwersyllt taking eight wickets for 28 runs on 18th May 1991 which earned him The Cottage Loaf 'Man of the Match' award. Llandudno won by 78 runs. Mark Hughes (75) had batted well in his contribution towards a fine win.

Llandudno youngster Scott Macdonald did the club proud when he played for Caernarvonshire Colts in their win against Denbighshire Colts at Bethesda on 22nd July 1991. He took seven wickets for 36 runs in 14 overs. He followed this up on 17th August for the 1st XI when he produced his best ever bowling figures for Llandudno at the time. He took seven wickets for 21 in what was described as 13 hostile overs in their win against Mynydd Isa.

Neil Gallagher was named Cricketer of the Year for 1991 at the club's presentation night after topping the 1st XI batting and 2nd XI bowling averages. Young fast bowler Scott Macdonald was named Junior Cricketer of the Year. The David Roberts Memorial Trophy went to Richard Pike (batting) and Phil Williams (bowling). An award for Friendly Cricketer went to Carl Wedge.

During 1991 the cricket club's sponsors were as follows:

Cottage Loaf Pub (Kevin Chin), Mrs L.Pike, Mr I.Pennington, James Payne, St George's Hotel, Royal Bank of Scotland, Charles Price and Sons Builders, Horesh, David Roberts Shoes, Mr I.N.Fifield, Dunoon Hotel, Kensington Hotel, Parade Hotel, Trustee Savings Bank, Mr David Hanson, Mr J.J.Breeze, Chamberlain, Johnson and Parke Solicitors, Westbourne Hotel, Risboro Hotel, Gogarth Abbey Hotel, Thorndike, Tierney and Co. Accountants, St Winifred's Hotel, Bengal Dynasty Restaurant, Mr Donald Ball, Allports Opticians, Watkin Jones and Son, Barclays Bank, John Ewston, Speechleys, Gott and Wynne, Lloyds Bank, Jenivore Hotel, Leyland Paints, J.G.Gibbons and Sons, North Wales Joinery, Baxters Bon, Wales Gas, Rhoslan Hotel, Churchill's, Tom Barlow (The Sewing Machine), Pickerings, Simon Baker Shoes, Woolwich Building Society, West Shore Newsagents, Jubilee Video, Pinnock Windows and Doors Ltd., A.G.Davies and Co., Dingle Garage, Penrhyn Old Hall, Waterloo Hotel, H.Neville Chemist, North Wales Video Services, The Ham Bone, A.J.Gibbons, Lord Mostyn, Ellis Newton Investments and Angelo's Restaurant.

The club started a new youth policy in January 1992 with the commencement of winter junior nets at the Ysgol John Bright Sports Hall.

Some of the Llandudno players appeared on television in February 1992 after taking part in a scene featuring star comedian Charlie Drake which was filmed in Llandudno for Granada. The scene was a cricket match with Charlie Drake as an umpire and the Llandudno players took the positions of fielders, bowlers and wicket-keeper.

The club boosted their hopes of promotion in the Greenalls North Wales Cricket League in 1992 by signing Caernarvonshire county pace bowler Matt Fogg from Conwy. Matt Fogg helped Caernarvonshire win the North Wales County Championship in 1991.

Llandudno hoped to complete the signing of Indian professional batsman and wicket-keeper Bhupi Mandrana who had previously been playing for Worthing. He had been offered a job and accommodation in a local Indian restaurant.

The signing of Bhupi Mandrana was completed in time for him to make his league debut against Shotton on 16th May 1992. He opened the batting with an impressive and classy 44 runs. The other new signing, Matt Fogg, scored 42. Llandudno won by 56 runs.

In what was described at the time as a "brilliant innings", Captain Mark Hughes scored 124 to lead the way for Llandudno and help to hoist them into second place in the league. He had completed a good job in guiding the team to an excellent win against Menai Bridge on 23rd May, which rightfully earned him the 'Man of the Match' Award.

1st XI bowler Richard Pike made a piece of cricketing history when he took all ten wickets in his side's win over Llanrwst at the Oval on 6th June 1992. His remarkable figures of 10 for 36 off 20.3 overs represented a club league record. After the game he was presented with the match ball which was mounted and eventually put on show in the new pavilion.

Bhupi Mandrana hit his first century (129) against Bangor in a friendly match at the Oval on 28th June 1992.

In the same weekend the 2nd XI were top of Division 5 after a 7pts – 3 win over Carmel seconds. The 1st XI was lying second in Division 2.

In the Under 16 Junior League there were wins for Dyffryn Road over Craig y Don and Nant y Coed against Blessed William Davies.

In the semi-finals of the Under 11s League Nant y Coed beat Dyffryn Road and Maelgwyn beat Wyddfyd and in a close fought final Maelgwyn beat Nant y Coed to lift the trophy. The League was the brainchild of Assistant Development Officer for the Welsh Sports Council of Wales, Ron Ayabaya, and on a special presentation evening he presented the winning trophy to Maelgwyn captain Gavin Williams.

The Headmasters of all the schools that had entered presented club chairman Joe Lambe with two match balls as a means of saying 'thank you' for running the competition.

It was reported in the North Wales Weekly on 3rd September 1992 the sad news that Huw Tudno Williams had died after a long illness. Huw had been a member and a great servant of the club for over 45 years and had been honoured with a Life-Membership in recognition of the exceptional and outstanding work over the many years he had done for the benefit and prosperity of the club. Huw was very well known throughout the whole of the North Wales cricket circles. He has been sadly missed by everyone who knew him and a great loss to the club.

Matt Fogg produced his best ever bowling figures of eight wickets for 21 to help Llandudno clinch promotion to Division One of the North Wales Cricket League. He accomplished that in Llandudno's final game of the season against Llangefni on 5th September 1992.

Final Table

	P	W	Pts
Bersham	22	14	139
Llandudno	22	13	125
Bala	22	11	119
Abergele	22	9	100
Llanrwst	22	5	91
Connahs Quay	22	8	89
Menai Bridge	22	9	85
Conwy	22	5	85
Northop	22	5	83
British Steel	22	5	81
Llangefni	22	4	78

Llandudno 2nd XI also won promotion by finishing top of Division 5.

At the Greenalls North Wales Cricket League AGM held at Halkyn in December of that year, 1st XI captain Mark Hughes picked up the Vivian Evans Trophy for the best batting performance in any one of the five divisions for his 124 against Menai Bridge. 2nd XI player Richard Protheroe won the 5th Division bowling averages award. These were the first individual awards the club had won since Dave Robertson in 1983.

2nd XI skipper Ian Jones collected the Division Five trophy while Mark Hughes was runner-up in the Division 2 batting averages. Richard Price was runner-up in the bowling averages.

The club also received a 'much improved report' on the state of the wicket at the Oval.

Three club awards which deserve merit in 1992 were:

Richard Pike – Senior Cricketer of the Year and the David Roberts Memorial

Trophy (10 wickets for 36 against Llanrwst)

David Noakes – Tom Barlow Award for much improved fielder.

A new guest player for the 1993 season, announced in March, was to be 21 year old Aaron Barnes, from New Zealand. He had played for Auckland. The club paid half his airfare and fixed him up with accommodation and a job.

In his league debut he produced his career best against Llay taking 8/38. However he couldn't save his team mates from a disappointing defeat at the Oval on 24th April 1993.

By early June, half way through the season, Llandudno were struggling – winning only two matches from 10 in the league and were just three places above the bottom.

It took another spell of fine bowling by Aaron Barnes against Shotton away from home on 26th June 1993 to register another victory. His figures of 7/11 helped the side to a well-earned win.

The Llandudno & District U11s Knock Out Semi-final matches between Dyffryn Road and Maelgwyn followed by Nant y Coed and Ysgol y Wyddfyd ended with Maelgwyn beating Nant y Coed in the final at the Oval on 16th July 1993.

Aaron Barnes scored two centuries in eight days. His first of the season was for Llandudno against the Birmingham side Maple Leaf, when he hit a brilliant 150 to secure a win on the 1st August 1993. The previous Saturday he scored 173 not out for Caernarvonshire. His third century was when Llandudno beat Bethesda at the Oval on 28th August. He blasted the bowling, scoring 112 off only 115 balls which helped end the team's relegation fears. In his final game for the club before returning to New Zealand he scored 147 in a friendly against New Brighton.

He had scored over 1,500 runs for Llandudno and had taken 64 wickets and almost single-handedly saved the club from relegation.

Aaron Barnes became the first player in North Wales Cricket League history to win both the annual Division 1 batting and bowling awards. The club named him Senior Cricketer of the Year.

Some other awards that year went to Daniel Owen, named as Junior Cricketer of the Year, and a new award for the Huw Tudno Williams Memorial Trophy for Clubman of the Year which went to Mark Hughes. Commendation was made to the lady helpers during the season for their support – Pauline and Jane Berrington, Kath Hughes and Debbie Lambe.

It was not the only time the club held what became a regular event in the club's calendar, hosting a video Horse Racing Night in the pavilion in aid of the Children's Variety Club of Great Britain Appeal in December 1993.

Llandudno's new overseas guest player for the 1994 season was Michael Lamont who was also from New Zealand. He made his debut in a pre-season friendly game against Bangor on 16th April hitting a magnificent 136 not out.

The club signed Gary Hughes from Conwy. All-rounder Dave Robertson returned from Mochdre to make a welcome comeback. John Breeze and Huw Edwards had also made themselves available to play for the club.

An outstanding innings of 192 not out by Michael Lamont and an opening stand of 236 with Tony Spencer steered Llandudno to their first win of the season against Pilkingtons on 5th May 1994.

The headlines that captured the sports pages concerned Llandudno's win against neighbours Colwyn Bay on 21st May for a place in the semi-final of the Welsh Cup. Colwyn Bay at one stage needed just 37 to win with eight wickets in hand but lost seven wickets for 27 runs in a dramatic late collapse. Heroes of the day were Dave Robertson (72) and Graham Boase with bowling figures 3/23. There was a magnificent spell of bowling from Matt Fogg who conceded just 13 runs in nine overs which helped to tie the Colwyn Bay batsmen down.

President Graham Gibbons scored his first century, 107 not out, against Conwy Seconds on the 10th June steering his team to a massive total of 256 for four dec. Conwy fought back and made a spirited reply. But the day belonged to Graham and also to the bowlers John Breeze and Gary Talbot who took two wickets each.

Graham S. Gibbons has been a popular, reliable and hard-working member of the Llandudno CC for over 54 years. Initially his talent was recognised very early on in his career as an all-rounder, noted primarily as a fast medium pace bowler and a very handy middle order batsman as well as a keen fielder. On record, he is the longest serving committee member the club has had and after 44 years' service he stepped down in 2011. Graham held many posts during his time with the club – President, Chairman and Treasurer. For a few years he took on the responsibility as groundsman preparing wickets etc., and gave many hours of his time over the years coaching junior members. He also found time to organise special events, raffles, tours etc. He was often seen helping out behind the bar. Father Gordon Gibbons was President for 16 years. His brothers Glyn and Alan had been club members for many years and members of the 1st XI and both were selected to play for Caernarvonshire. Glyn went on to play for Glamorgan. Graham has two sons, Steve and Andy, who both played for the 2nd XI. Wife Pam has been a distinguished local badminton player but found time over the years to help out with the teas in the pavilion during matches. A local Colwyn Bay business man, Graham owns a retail television outlet in the West End and over the years has given thousands of pounds to the club in sponsorships. If there ever was a title for a 'Mr Llandudno

Cricket Club' there is no doubt he would be up there amongst the nominations in recognition for his unselfish and active continuous support of the club.

It was the turn again for New Zealander Mike Lamont to steal the honours scoring another unbeaten century (131 n.o.) in a massive 219 run victory over Mochdre seconds in the Bass North Wales Cricket League. Sharing the honours was Joe Lambe, wicket-keeper, who held three catches and a stumping.

Mike Lamont's 125 not out against top of the table Llay on 23rd July 1994 was his fifth century of the season. He had already topped 1,200 runs.

Graham Boase took seven wickets for 19 runs in a 13 over spell for Llandudno beating promotion rivals Abergele by 10 wickets on 6th August.

Mike Lamont scored his sixth century (148) in a 162 run victory over Bala. Mike and Joe Lambe (43) put on 161 for the first wicket.

Llandudno clinched promotion to Division 1 of the Bass North Wales Cricket League. Neil Gallagher's century (100 not out) was the highlight of Llandudno's innings and maximum points victory over Marchwiel II on 27th August 1994. Carl Wedge bowled exceptionally well with figures of 5/29. Mike Lamont finished the season having scored over 1,400 runs in league games alone.

At the club's AGM Graham Boase was named Senior Cricketer of the Year and he also won the 1st XI bowling award.

Another highlight of the season was the side's fine run in the Welsh Cup before losing in the Northern zone final to Brymbo.

Andrew Roberts was elected President for the 1995 season.

The new committee decided that their priority was to get permission to fence and enclose the playing area on the Oval.

There was disappointment in the winter of 1995 at the poor response to the new indoor junior coaching sessions at John Bright Sports Centre. All the Primary schools in the locality had been advised when the coaching would start. Only four youngsters turned up. This was after the cricket club had paid to get some of the senior members onto a coaching course to get them up to the standard necessary.

"It was a very poor response," said a disappointed Joe Lambe. *"We're only charging 50p for the hour for each child but if only four kids turn up we are subsidising it."* Mr Lambe said that the club had decided to set up the Sunday indoor coaching scheme because schools no longer offered cricket and because the game in the area had declined. *"We want to get the 7 to 11 year olds, boys and girls, in the area interested,"* he said.

In March 1995 club chairman Joe Lambe volunteered to have his head shaved in aid of comic relief.

The club held a successful General Knowledge Quiz Night at the Pavilion on 23rd March to raise more funds in aid of the Primary School League to be held that summer.

Llandudno's annual season tour, organised by Graham Boase, was to Chelmsford in Essex that year to play Willgate CC a Herts/Essex XI, and finishing off the week with a game against Bentley CC. James Allan, New Zealand guest player for the season, scored two unbeaten centuries. The first against Willgate CC 109 not out and 122 not out against Bentley CC.

Llandudno chairman Joe Lambe scored his first century for the club after 18 years of trying when he hit an unbeaten 109 against a Welsh Select XI at the Oval on 16th July 1995. This was a special match arranged by Llandudno Town Council as part of the VE day celebrations. Joe Lambe was named 'Man of the Match' after batting throughout the 50 overs in an opening stand with James Allan (88) in a total 227 for six. The Welsh Select XI was limited to 151 for eight. The players were introduced to the town mayor and Mr Bryn Walker of the sponsors, NatWest Bank.

Graham Boase, playing for Caernarvonshire against Montgomeryshire in the North Wales County Championships on 16th July 1995, took 7/40 to earn the 'Man of the Match' Award helping his side to win the game.

James Allan scored 126 in Llandudno's relegation battle beating Pontblyddyn on 22nd July. He smashed 13 fours and 4 sixes.

Llandudno Taverners lost to Bangor Taverners at the Oval on 13th August 1995 despite a hat-trick from Captain Richard Protheroe and 33 not out by Daniel Owen.

Llandudno 2nds gained a 6-4 win over Northop 2nds in a Division 5 match on 12th August 1995. Llandudno 199 for 7 (Tony Spencer 59, Graham Gibbons 48, Graham Hubbard 30 not out, Ian Jones 20, Alan Gibbons 20). Northop 191/8 (Ian Jones 3/65; Ron Beswick and Graham Gibbons took two wickets each).

Veteran bowler John Breeze, who had been playing local cricket for over 40 years, took his first ever hat-trick in his 5/19 against Lancashire side, Bretherton, on 20th August 1995. Unfortunately, he was unable to save the home side from defeat.

Llandudno finished just four places from the bottom in Division 1 but expected to keep their first division status despite talk that Buckley, Mold, Prestatyn, St Asaph and Wrexham might apply to join the league in the 1996 season. It was thought they might demand places in the top two divisions.

Llandudno Chairman Joe Lambe said, "We stepped down a division when the league was first restructured and having fought our way back to the top division there is no way we would agree to drop out again to accommodate these five clubs. They refused to join us two years ago and if they have to come back now I think they should have to fight their way up through the divisions like everybody else."

Junior indoor winter coaching sessions commenced from Sunday 28th January at the John Bright Sports Centre. Under the watchful eye of senior coach Joe Lambe with the help of qualified coach Mark Hughes there was a good response. Sessions included 7-11 year old boys and girls from 11am to 12 noon and over 11s from 12 noon to 1pm.

Another young New Zealander, 18 year old Mark Tullock from Auckland, was signed up as guest player for the 1996 season. A left handed batsman and left arm spin bowler, in his first match against Mochdre in the Triangular Barker Trophy on 7th April 1996 he scored an unbeaten 86 runs which helped his side to an exciting seven runs win.

The Lord Mostyn Mid-Week Primary Schools League commenced on 16th May 1996.

During 1996 the club continued to run Quiz Nights and hosted Horse Racing Nights at the Oval in aid of club funds and charities.

Llandudno lost to Bethesda by 70 runs on 15th June 1996 in a North Wales Cricket League match. They had only won two out of their first eight games and were second from bottom, just above Shotton.

New Zealander Mark Tulloch hit his first century (110 n.o.) against Mochdre in a high scoring clash at the Oval on 22nd June. Llandudno scored 240 for three (Richard Pike 71 not out). Mochdre just fell short on 234 for seven. They needed just 12 runs off the last three overs and failed.

Llandudno reported the bad state of the wicket at Connahs Quay in a league match on 20th July 1996. This was after two of their batsmen were hit around the face caused by an uneven bounce. Fortunately, Joe Lambe was wearing a helmet when a ball reared up and hit the grill but New Zealander Bruce Tulloch suffered a nasty cut just above the lip.

Joe Lambe said:

> *"The problem was a patch of three to four yards at one end which gradually broke up as the game progressed so by the time we batted it had become very dangerous with the ball rearing up off a length. Bruce was playing a forward defensive shot when the ball just shot up into his face. The same happened to me and the ball struck the grill in front of my jaw. A couple of other players almost got hit, but just managed to duck out of the way."*

Connahs Quay won by 58 runs.

The area of the ground which requires the greatest level of preparation is the wicket. Before a game is played it will be regularly mowed, watered, rolled and kept protected from the weather. Although it is technically a grassed area, it is often clay brown and spongy in texture, more like compacted mud than the lush green outfield. In general terms there are three main types of wicket preparation:

'Green' wickets – Wickets that are under-prepared are sometimes known as green. This is often regarded as an aid to fast bowlers as it makes bounce from the wicket quite unpredictable.

'True' wickets – A wicket that has an even covering of grass that has been prepared under normal conditions will play in a predictable manner. This is good news for the batsmen who will be able to choose their shots with a greater degree of certainty.

'Dry' or 'cracked' wickets – These are wickets that are already beginning to lose the flatness of the surface before the game has begun. This type of wicket will be very good news for spin bowlers who can use the cracks in the wicket to make the ball deviate.

Llandudno signed South African Francois van der Merwe from North Transvaal for the 1997 season. He was a qualified coach and in his first game in a friendly against Menai Bridge he hit a six off his first ball and took a wicket with the first ball he bowled.

The commitment to a Primary School League

The South African toured the primary schools during the 1997 season and helped with coaching the youngsters.

In the Mostyn Estate sponsored mid-week Primary School League there were wins for Ysgol Craig y Don and Ysgol Maelgwyn at the Oval.

In June 1997 Llandudno's U13s side beat Prestatyn in the 1st Round of the Welsh Cup U13s competition under the guidance of coach Gareth Lloyd.

The U15s lost to Prestatyn in the 2nd Round of the Welsh Cup.

Llandudno U11s won the Pwllheli Junior Tournament on 29th June 1997.

Llandudno, in their first fixture in the Gilbert Emery Mid-Week League beat Ysgol Dyffryn Conwy by six wickets on 30th April 1997.

Llandudno CC held a Fun Day at the Oval on 29th June 1997. Ysgol Maelgwyn won the Junior Cricket Competition. Llandudno Swifts 'A' won the under 11s Football Competition and the Llandudno Rugby Club won the 'tug of war'.

Ysgol Nant y Coed (from Llandudno Junction) won the Primary School League knock-out Competition beating Ysgol Craig y Don in the final at the Oval on 11th July 1997.

The club started reaping dividends from the Youth Development Programme as a result of the visits to the local schools introducing and promoting the game. It was not long before attendances at the coaching sessions at the Oval increased dramatically by almost threefold. The U11s won the Eryri County Championship with the second team finishing third. Three members of the junior section (under 14s) – Richard Gere, Daniel Gore and James Wooderson – had been selected to play for the county (U14s).

With so much time and effort been spent by senior club members in taking an interest in coaching juniors it was not long before recognition was realised and support given by the Conwy County Sports and Development Programme and the Sports Council of Wales.

*

Joe Lambe scored his second century (101) for Llandudno in a friendly match against Menai Bridge on 1st September 1996.

South African Francois van der Merwe smashed 15 sixes in scoring his first century (165 n.o.) in a friendly match at Appleton near Warrington on 27th July 1997.

Carl Wilarton scored a half-century helping Caernarvonshire beat Anglesey in the North Wales County Cricket Championship at the Oval on 17th August 1997. He was aided by four of his club mates (Graham Boase, Joe Lambe, Andy Christian and Paul Whitfield) in their 80 run victory.

Llandudno 2nd XI helped their promotion challenge in Division 5 of the North Wales Cricket League by beating Amlwch on 25th August 1997 by 115 runs (Huw Edwards 66, Andy Christian 5/20). They were lying second in a league consisting of a record number of 17 teams.

Llandudno 1st XI was just six points above the relegation zone at the time.

Neil Gallagher scored his third century (102) for the club in the last game of the 1997 season. This was in a close fought match against touring side Appleton by 12 runs. Andy Christian took four wickets for 42 runs.

The 1st XI avoided relegation by just one point above Gresford, Ruthin and Connahs Quay.

Llandudno signed 26 year old New Zealand batsman Jamie Lee for the 1998 season. He was a senior qualified coach and as well as playing cricket for the club would be joining junior club coach Gareth Lloyd to continue the successful link-up with the local primary schools.

During 1997 Llandudno attracted nearly 50 youngsters to join the coaching programme.

Club chairman Joe Lambe said:

> *"The North Wales League at their AGM only narrowly defeated a bid to stop overseas professionals playing in the league. I think it's important that clubs use these players to serve the community by coaching at schools and helping to promote the game to local youngsters."*

Llandudno's youth policy was reflected when a young 2nd XI captain, Martin Bean, was elected for the 1998 season.

An unbeaten century (102) by Jamie Lee steered the 1st XI to an 85 run victory in a league match against Hawarden Park on 2nd May 1998. He followed this up on the 17th May when he hammered his second century (107 not out) when they beat Llanrwst.

Llanrwst witnessed an amazing record-shattering performance by Australian cricketer Neil Schlittler in a Welsh Cup match at Gwydyr Park, Llanrwst on 17th May 1998 for St Asaph.

Schlittler smashed an astonishing 310 not out as St Asaph rattled up 429 for 0 in just 45 overs. His innings included 13 sixes and 39 fours and beat the Welsh Cup record set 15 years previously by former Test star Collis King when he was playing for Pontblyddyn.

St Asaph stalwart and former captain of St Asaph, Ken Hodkinson said, "I have never seen an innings like it in 50 years of watching and playing cricket at the club."

Llandudno's under 11s, recent Eryri champions, pleased the crowds at the Glamorgan v Lancashire match at the Rhos-on-Sea ground on 24th July 1998. They gave an exhibition of mini-cricket during the lunch interval to everyone's delight.

Llandudno finished runners-up in Division 3 of the Gilbert Emery Evening League in 1998. In doing so they were promoted to Division 2 for the 1999 season.

Jamie Lee smashed 133 not out against Mochdre at the Oval on 31st August 1998. That had followed an unbeaten 93 at Gresford two days before. Llandudno did win both these games but unfortunately it was not enough to avoid relegation from Division 1. Hopes had been relying on the last game of the season but it was rained off. Both teams had to settle with three points. It was not enough. Llandudno were three points adrift of Llay which meant they went down with Bersham to Division 2 that season.

Chairman Peter Kearney announced that the club had received a draft lease on the Oval pavilion and ground from the Council starting from 1st April 1999. This was good news for the club as it would mean the committee could go ahead in the future and apply for Sportlot grants.

New committee members for the 1999 season included Joe Evans and Colin Stanley. The Secretary elect was Mark Hughes and Joe Lambe was voted club Chairman.

Llandudno signed up South African all-rounder Craig Wilson. After the disappointment of relegation from the first division it was hoped the Springbok could help the club spring back into the top flight at the first attempt. The arrival of Craig Wilson never happened. Another overseas player Tarique Khan from Udaipur in India stepped in as a last minute replacement because Wilson became unavailable due to "personal problems".

Mark Hughes, who hadn't bowled regularly for over two years, produced remarkable figures of 7/24 to earn Llandudno a surprise win against Denbigh on 1st May 1999 by just 31 runs. This was followed up a week later by 17 year old Dave Edwards who took five wickets for four runs in an astonishing 15 overs. The win that day against Marchwiel meant Llandudno had made a great start to the season completing a hat-trick of wins in Division 2 of the Readers Romida North Wales Cricket League.

A century stand between Dave Owen (59 n.o.) and K.Hitchen (45 n.o.) helped Llandudno Colts to a third successive victory in Division 3 of the Gilbert Emery Evening Cricket League. They put on 103 together to sweep Llandudno to a five wicket victory over Rhos Fynach Taverners after being set a target of 115 runs on 21st May 1999.

Conwy Borough Council was doing their bit to help to promote junior cricket in the Llandudno area by donating new equipment to local clubs. John Huband, Development Officer, presented some very useful equipment for the benefit of the U11s.

The new overseas player, Tarique Khan, played his first match on 28th April 1999 against Bersham for Llandudno but it was not until the game against Bangor seconds on 12th June did he show his class taking six wickets for 18 runs which helped his team to a well-deserved victory.

Llandudno reached the final of the Caernarfonshire Knock-out Competition thanks to a century (104) from Tarique Khan in their mid-week semi-final win over Conwy on 21st July 1999.

Neil Gallagher scored 112 not out for Llandudno 2nd XI which gained a welcome win over Brymbo seconds on 24th July 1999 in Division 4 of the North Wales Cricket League. Dave Robertson scored 52.

Llandudno pulled off a major surprise by beating high-flying Bangor by seven wickets on 4th August 1999 in the Caernarfonshire Knock-out Final at the Oval.

Tarique Khan struck his first league century (100) against Bangor 2nd XI to help his side to a 9pts – 1 win and maintain a promotion challenge.

Llandudno and Abergele fought out a thrilling tie in the final fixture in Division 2 of the North Wales Cricket League. The result meant Llandudno, having been one of the favourites for most of the season, missed out on promotion finishing eight points behind second placed Connahs Quay.

Llandudno 2nd XI finished in bottom place in Division 4 and was relegated.

Better known as the hero of England's 1966 World Cup-winning soccer team, Geoff Hurst had previously played one first-class cricket match for Essex against Lancashire at Liverpool in 1962. He made 0 not out in his first innings and followed that up with a duck in his second innings. But he did contribute to a 28-run victory for Essex by taking two catches for his side. Bobby Moore was also a promising schoolboy cricketer and indeed the first time Hurst and Moore played on the same side at any sport was for the Essex schools cricket team.

Joe Lambe was elected 1st XI captain for the 2000 season although Mark Hughes remained as club captain.

Other captains included 2ⁿᵈ XI Neil Gallagher, Sunday Carl Wedge and Mid-Week Andrew Foster.

There were new rules that came into place for the coming North Wales League season. All bowlers were restricted to 12 overs each and all games had to start at 1.30pm.

The club held a charity general knowledge quiz on 25th February 2000 in aid of the 'Holly Roberts Trust'.

Llandudno CC received a £500 grant from Pearl Assurance towards the installation of an all-weather surface wicket at the Oval ground. Vice-Chairman Martin Bean, who was Pearl's District Manager based at Bangor, successfully applied for the grant under Pearl's Employee Community Support Programme in which employees who spend more than 80 hours a year helping local groups or charities can apply for grants. At a special ceremony, Martin Bean presented a £500 cheque to club Chairman Graham Boase watched by the 1999 Player of the Year Andrew Christian, 2ⁿᵈ XI captain and junior coach Neil Gallagher and some of the club's junior squad.

Llandudno signed Australian left-handed batsman Steve Smith from Adelaide as their guest overseas player for the new North Wales Cricket League season. The 25 year old was the club's first Australian guest player since the very successful Tasmanian Robert Knight in 1976. He was a qualified coach and would be able to assist both senior and junior players.

The club continued to run Under 11s, Under 13s and Under 15s junior sides plus the Primary School Outreach Programme under the guidance of Youth Development Coach Gareth Lloyd.

Australian Steve Smith made an early impact for promotion hopefuls Llandudno taking five wickets for 17 runs on his debut in the win over Menai Bridge at the Oval on 6th May 2000. He was supported by Carl Wedge who also bowled well with figures of 4/34.

Llandudno junior Elgan Williams was selected to join the newly formed Wales U11s squad after going through numerous trials and a tough selection programme.

Chairman Graham Boase commented:

> *"Elgan's selection for Wales is an honour for both him and the club and is a reflection of the strong junior section we have here at the club."*

The club received a £1,000 grant from the Sports Council of Wales towards its junior cricket programme and the Primary Schools Outreach initiative. The award which was administered by the Tourism and Leisure Department of Conwy County Borough Council was used to finance the efforts in introducing as many primary school children as possible to the game and providing them with new equipment.

In the Gilbert Emery Evening Cricket League Llandudno gained their sixth win in succession by beating Lex by four wickets on 7th June 2000. They were riding high at the time as Division 3 leaders.

Colwyn Bay (80 for seven) beat Llandudno (64 for nine) in an under 13s Welsh Cup match on 14th June. In the following week Llandudno beat Colwyn Bay in an under 11s match.

Llandudno snatched a dramatic victory over Bethesda on 24th June 2000 with Australian all-rounder Steve Smith undoubtedly crowned 'Man of the Match'. After top scoring with 65 in a Llandudno total of 175 for nine, he took five wickets for 52 runs. Bethesda was all out for 158.

The 2nd XI had a good day beating Castell Ason by eight wickets. It was three youngsters who shared the honours that day. John Gallagher and Craig Lloyd both took three wickets each. Aled Williams scored a fine half-century with the bat.

The Colwyn Bay & District Cricket League was founded in 1965 for local players to participate in a game of cricket on a summer's evening. Until 2008 the League was sponsored by local sports store Gilbert Emery of Colwyn Bay.

Ysgol Maelgwyn won the Mostyn Estates sponsored Primary Schools Cricket U11s League on 23rd July 2000 beating Blessed William Davies School by 67 runs. Ysgol Maelgwyn scored 187 and restricted their opponents to 120 in reply. Peter Caldwell of Mostyn Estates presented the trophies.

Llandudno easily won both their games on their annual tour in 2000. It was Nottingham they visited first and beat a combined Papplewick and Linby side on 12 July. Steve Smith scored 80 and Joe Lambe 67 in a total of 161 for two. The hosts were bowled out for 94. In the second match they beat Thursby village near Carlisle by seven wickets; Steve Smith (48), Graham Boase (44 not out).

Carl Wedge scored his maiden century after 20 years with the club as he captained the Sunday XI to victory over Sneyd CC from Stoke. Not forgetting Joe Lambe on the day. Together they produced a magnificent unbeaten opening stand of 249 with both players carrying their bats to score undefeated centuries. In reply Sneyd could only manage 110/9.

Llandudno openers Kevin James and Tim George both scored 30 not out to steer their side to a 10 wickets victory over Llanrwst in the Gilbert Emery Evening Cricket League's Tom Barlow Cup Final. Llandudno just missed out winning Division 3, losing to new champions, Caerhun, by three runs. Caerhun pipped Llandudno by just two points.

Llandudno's Tim George, playing for Caernarfonshire, was one of the top scorers for his side with 25 runs but unfortunately not enough to beat Denbighshire at Bangor on 30 July 2000. They lost by 88 runs.

The Eryri under 14s cricket select side, made up mainly from Llandudno and Colwyn Bay players, performed superbly to finish runners-up to Cardiff and the Vale in the National under 14s Inter-Counties Competition. This was held in North East Wales on 13th August 2000. They did win the prestigious Fair Play Award selected by the umpires and the county managers. The Llandudno players in the squad were: Jonathon Gallagher, Adam Blakeway, Naveed Ahmed, Craig Lloyd and Aled Williams.

Steve Smith was introduced to Calypso cricket when Llandudno hosted the Continental CC once again and on this occasion for his Benefit match. This West Indies team from Birmingham had been coming to Llandudno regularly for a number of years and always had a big West Indian following helping to provide a real calypso party atmosphere every time they came. The pavilion after the match on 27th August, which incidentally Llandudno won, was full of Afro-Caribbean music and dancing.

Chairman Graham Boase who was full of praise for Steve Smith commented:

> *"Steve has proved to be an excellent overseas guest player especially with his approach to the coaching of our youngsters and has been very popular around the club."*

Llandudno 1st XI finished fourth in Division 2 – won 12, lost six.

Llandudno 2nd XI finished third in Division 5 – won 11, lost five missing out on promotion by just nine points.

An expectant father rang the hospital to see how his wife was getting on. By mistake he dialled the number for Lord's.

"How's it going?" he asked.

"Fine," was the answer. "We've got two out already and hope to have the rest out before lunch. The last one was a duck."

1st wife: "Did you manage to get away from cricket at your wedding?"

2nd wife: "Don't talk to me about it. I thought it was a bad sign when we had to enter under an arch of cricket bats, but it got worse."

1st wife: "What happened?"

2nd wife: "The choir sang The Bails of St Mary's!"

It was the after-lunch session and the batsman had been drinking too heavily during the break. He staggered up to the captain and confessed that he could see three of everything.

"Well," said the captain, "when you get out there and the three balls come towards you, just hit the middle one."

The batsman weaved his way to the crease and was bowled first ball. He made his way back.

"What happened?" demanded the captain. "Didn't you hit the middle ball?"

"Yesh," replied the batsman, "but I used the outside bat!"

North Wales Cricket League – Premier Division 2001

The North Wales Cricket League decided on a newly formed Premier Division for the 2001 season. The new elite division consisted of 12 clubs and games were restricted to 110 overs with the team batting first restricted to a maximum of 60 overs. A 'winning draw' was introduced if the team batting second didn't reach the target but were not bowled out. This restructuring of the league meant that Llandudno were promoted to the premier division.

First team captain Joe Lambe commented:

> "It's great news for the club and a big honour to be involved in the inaugural season of the new North Wales Premier Division. But we all know it is going to be very tough. We'll be up against some very good teams and we have got to adapt to a new playing format of 110 overs per match. But our promotion means we may now be able to attract one or two new quality players keen to play at the higher level and we'll certainly be giving it our best shot."

The club welcomed Australian overseas player Steve Smith back for the new season. He was sponsored by the Broadway Boulevard of Llandudno.

Following the success in obtaining a Sportlot grant, work on the artificial pitch and the new practice nets were completed in time for the 2001 season. There had been some real concern for some time at the lack of facilities on the ground. A great deal was owed by the club to Graham Boase for the work he had put in to secure the grant. The players were now able to benefit from superb facilities not experienced before at the Oval.

Llandudno lost their first four matches into the new season so it was a welcome eight-wicket victory against Pontblyddyn on 26th May. This was worth 20pts - 0 in the new scoring system in the league. Young seam bowler Jonathon Gallagher returned match winning figures of five for 13. The 15 year old Ysgol y Creuddyn schoolboy had just that week been chosen to play for Wales under 15s for matches against Derbyshire and Worcestershire.

Llandudno U15s beat Chirk U15s by eight wickets in the North Wales zone final of the Wales U15s cup at Newtown. They lost to St Fagans of Cardiff and the Mid-Wales qualifiers Llanrhian.

Llandudno U13s beat Colwyn Bay in their Northern zone semi-final on 27th June and then went on to beat Chirk in the zone final. They also finished third in the Welsh Cup losing to Porthcawl and St Fagans.

The U13s finished that year runners-up to Pentraeth in the Eryri Junior league.

At senior level, Llandudno's Martin Roberts played for Caernarfonshire against Flintshire at the Oval on 22nd July 2001. Caernarfonshire was dismissed for 116. Flintshire cruised to victory finishing on 119 for two.

Fifteen year old Aled Williams played a match saving innings against Pontblyddyn securing Llandudno's place in the Premier Division for the next year on 10th August 2001. The youngster, who was a product of the club's youth scheme, and who had captained the U15s side to the finals of the Welsh Cup, scored 30 not out. He shared an unbeaten eighth wicket stand with Graham Boase to hold out for a draw and nine precious points.

An unbeaten century (112 n.o.) from 19 year old Martin Roberts helped Llandudno to a crucial last over 'derby' victory over Mochdre on 27th August.

Llandudno 2nd XI also won their 'derby' match against Mochdre by seven wickets on the same day (Dave Roberts 32, Andrew Christian 4/18).

Australian Steve Smith scored 79 not out in a drawn match against Bethesda on 20th September 2001. His innings helped Llandudno to secure their place in the Premier Division in 2002.

Llandudno finished eighth in the league.

Played 22, won four, drawn 10, lost six, points 211

An unbeaten century (100 n.o.) from Dave Robertson helped Llandudno 2nd XI end their campaign in Division 3 in emphatic style with a 10pts-0 win over Denbigh 2nds on 15th September 2001.

Llandudno 2nd XI finished a respectable 3rd in Division 3.

Played 20, won 12, lost five, points 123.

All-rounder Martin Roberts scooped three awards at the club's Annual Presentation Dinner at the Evans Hotel on 21 December 2001.

He was named Senior Player of the Year and won awards for the best batting average and best batting performance in a match.

Elgan Williams was named Junior Player of the Year.

Some junior members of the club travelled to Lancashire's Old Trafford ground in April 2002 for special coaching.

A local businessman, Mike Battersby, ran in the London Marathon to help raise money for the club's junior section.

Keith Paddington scored what was described as a magnificent 101 not out as Llandudno seconds maintained their lead at the top of Division 3 of the North Wales Cricket League with a maximum points 10-0 win over Pontblyddyn seconds.

Overseas player Tarique Khan's home club, the Rajput Warriors from India, played against a Llandudno XI at the Oval on 4th June 2002.

The game ended in a draw. The visitors scored 175 for seven declared with Welsh U16s Jonathon Gallagher taking four wickets. Llandudno replied ending up playing for a draw on 130 for eight (Steve Smith 63).

Llandudno U13s beat Colwyn Bay U13s by eight wickets at the Oval on 14th June. Sam Rimmington was top scorer with 21 runs and took two wickets for six runs.

Steve Smith scored his third half-century of the season in the winning draw against third-placed Brymbo on 29th June. Tarique Khan bowled well taking five wickets for 13 runs.

The unbeaten 2nd XI was 21 points clear at the top of Division 3 after an eight-wickets victory at Flint.

Llandudno's Aled Williams scored an unbeaten 75 to take the newly-formed Gwynedd Colts U19s side to within 21 runs of beating Denbighshire Colts in the North Wales Inter-County Colts Championship on 30th June at Llay.

Llandudno 2nd XI suffered their first defeat of the season after nine straight wins on 28th June against St Asaph 2nd XI. They still head Division 3 by 20 points.

Martin Roberts (4/50) and Graham Boase (2/46) both bowled well for Caernarfonshire against Denbighshire on 7th July 2002. However, it wasn't good enough to stop Denbighshire winning the match by 37 runs in the North Wales County Championship.

Two good wins against Bangor and Mochdre moved Llandudno into second place in the North Wales Cricket League Premier Division. They beat Bangor by 47 runs on 20th June (Tarique Khan 5/18) and the following week beat Mochdre by five wickets (Tarique Khan 74 not out and 4/15).

Skipper Bryn Hughes took 5/9 for Llandudno U15s in their win by seven wickets against Bangor in the Eryri junior cricket league on 24th July 2002. He carried his bat with 48 not out.

The Eryri U15s Select XI lost by just 16 runs to Oldham. Colwyn Bay's Andy Pitman had his season's best bowling figures of five for 13. Llandudno players Andrew Boyd, Jack Rimmington, Huw Williams and Mark Williams also took wickets.

Llandudno's Sunday XI smashed a record breaking 364 for five wickets in 40 overs on 4th August 2002 to win a top of the table grudge match with Llwyngwril-Tywyn to clinch the Division 2 title in the Gwynedd Cricket League. Australian Steve Smith led the way with 26 fours and 2 sixes in scoring a magnificent 152 not out. Martin Roberts supported him with a gallant 73. The following week James Edwards took eight for 22 in six overs helping his side to a further win when they beat Menai Bridge.

On 31 August 1968, Garfield Sobers became the first batsman ever to hit six sixes in a single over off six consecutive balls in first-class cricket. The feat consisted of five clean hits for six and one six where the ball was caught but carried over the boundary. Sobers was playing as captain of Nottinghamshire against Glamorgan in Swansea. The unfortunate bowler was Malcolm Nash who on 28th September 1975 played for Glamorgan at the Oval against a Llandudno XI. This tally of 36 runs in an over broke a 57-year-old record of 34 runs, held by Ted Alletson. The ball was collected from a garden by 11-year-old Richard Lewis who later gave the ball to Sobers. In 1984–85, Indian batsman Ravi Shastri equalled the record by scoring six sixes in an over while playing for Bombay versus Baroda.

2002-2014

Llandudno Cricket Club's 'Golden Years'

Llandudno 2nd XI was confirmed Division 3 champions after a 9pts-1 win over Flint at the Oval on 21st August 2002. Proud captain Mark Lambe commented:

> *"To win the championship with two games still to go is one of the proudest moments of my cricketing career. We have a good blend of youth and experience and every member has contributed to the success."*

Played 22, won 20, lost 1, drawn 1, Points 168.

Championship honours again to Llandudno U11s side in the Eryri Junior Cricket League. They were also runners-up in the prestigious Welsh Cup.

Llandudno won the U13s North Wales Police Challenge Trophy beating Brymbo U13s in the final (Sam Rimmington 23, Owen Jones 26 not out, Luke Taylor 23, Elgan Williams 2/6, Darren Nuttall 2/19).

The 1st XI finished 3rd in the Premier Division of the North Wales Cricket League behind Brymbo and winners Bangor.

Played 22, won 11, drawn 6, lost 3, Points 314.

Llandudno were Division 2 champions in the Gwynedd Sunday Cricket League at their first attempt in 2002. Captain Joe Lambe said:

> *"We entered the league to give more experience at senior level to the youth of the club and it has proved an immediate success. Experienced senior players Steve Smith, Carl Wedge and Tarique Khan scored centuries during the campaign but it was also the young players that shone which included James Edwards, David Barlow, Scott Jones, Bryn Hughes, Owen Jones,*

Elgan Williams, Sam Rimmington, Mattie Lambe, Jordan Kane and Ajay Dhawan."

Tarique Khan returned from India to help Llandudno once again in their bid for further honours for the 2003 season.

Club captain Mark Hughes commented:

"Last season Tarique played consistently well both with bat and ball which greatly helped Llandudno finish in the top three of the Premier Division. Everybody at the club is looking forward to seeing him here again. He had said he would like to come back to Llandudno in 2003 where he has made numerous friends both at the club and in the local community. His commitment to the game has rubbed off on both senior and junior players alike."

Andrew Christian returned his best bowling figures (7/27) helping Llandudno 2nd XI to a 34 win against Hawarden Park 2nd XI on 19th April 2003. That win opened their campaign in the higher Division 2 of the North Wales Cricket League.

The 1st XI opened their season with a flying start annihilating Halkyn on 26th April gaining a 20pts - 0 win. A six wicket haul by Martin Roberts and an unbeaten 73 by skipper Steve Smith led the way.

Llandudno 2nd XI picked up maximum points (10-0) in their win on 3rd May against Brymbo seconds. Young Mark Bithell (5/6) took his first four wickets without conceding a run.

Sixteen year old Aled Williams scored 89 in Llandudno's 1st XI win against St Asaph on 9th May. At that stage of the season Llandudno had moved into 2nd place in the league.

Three junior members achieved recognition by being chosen to play for Wales during 2003 in their respective age groups. They were Jack Rimmington for the U15s against Cheshire and Yorkshire and Elgan Williams and Owen Jones for the U14s against Essex.

Llandudno routed leaders Hawarden Park in the Premier Division on 21st June. Tarique Khan did the damage with bowling figures 7/14.

An unbeaten century (102 n.o.) by Jonathon Gallagher helped Llandudno to a comprehensive 10-0 point victory against Bethesda on 22nd June. This was a Division 1 match in the Gwynedd Sunday Cricket League.

The U15s did themselves proud by beating Bangor by 76 runs in a Welsh Cup match on 25th June 2003. (Owen Jones 30, Elgan Williams 16, Jack Rimmington 18, Mattie Lambe 16.)

The U11s in the same week maintained their unbeaten record with victory over Menai Bridge. (Jordan Kane 32 not out.)

Llandudno held a car boot sale at the Oval on 6th July 2003 as part of a Fun Day to raise funds for the club. It also included a children's Fun Fair, tombola, donkey rides, coconut shy, bouncy castle and a barbecue. There were also displays by the Ambulance Fire Service, police and a rescue dog team from Penmaenmawr.

Llandudno U11s finished unbeaten in the Eryri league and were able to claim the crown after their victory against Anglesey Aluminium at the Oval on 4th July 2003.

A century (115 not out) by Kevin James in a big victory over Claverham was the highlight of Llandudno's tour in the Bristol area (July 14-17).

The Lady Taverners of North West Wales donated a kit bag containing cricket equipment worth £500 to the club for their junior section.

The U13s beat Colwyn Bay U13s by six wickets at the Oval on 2nd August 2003 (Sam Rimmington 46).

Llandudno lost against Dolgellau in the final of the Pike Trophy of the Gwynedd Sunday League on 4th August 2003.

Father and son Neil and Jonathon Gallagher took eight wickets between them in a 25 – 6 points win against Mold. This was a Premier League match on the 9th August at Llandudno. That win moved Llandudno back up to third place in the league.

Llandudno Juniors won all their matches on their first tour and on this occasion North Yorkshire. They beat Stamford Bridge, Malton and Acomb.

A century (100 not out) by Sam Rimmington led the way for Llandudno juniors beating Anglesey Aluminium. This was an end of season friendly on 1st September 2003. Owen Jones scored 51.

The 1st XI finished 6th in the Premier Division of the North Wales Cricket League.

Llandudno Cricket Club's long-serving umpire Elias Thomas retired after 50 years' service with the club and the North Wales League. He started umpiring at Llandudno in the 1952 season and went on to officiate at the top level in North Wales during which time he umpired games at the Glamorgan festivals where players like Tony Lewis, Don Shepherd, Peter Walker and Malcolm Nash took part. As a token of the club's appreciation a special presentation to him was made by the club President, Graham Gibbons. Elias was regarded as the best umpire at county and club level locally in his day and was known and respected by clubs all along the North Wales coast. He was an inspiration to many 'budding' umpires. Jeff Nicholls, in particular, who did umpire for the club for a while at Premier Division level in the 1980s, looked upon Elias as a role model for his honesty and decency and the knowledge and respect he had towards the laws of the game.

1st XI captain and club coach Steve Smith tipped 15 year old Elgan Williams to go all the way to the top level in cricket. This was after the teenager took five wickets in one over including a hat trick with his first three balls against Northop in a Premier League match on 2nd May 2004. Llandudno won that game by eight wickets.

Steve Smith said:

"I have never seen anything like it before. He is the best young player I have ever coached either here or in Australia. He has got a fantastic cricket talent and if he continues to work hard he can go as far as he wants to in the game."

Elgan was already playing for the Wales U16s.

Llandudno U13s lost to Bangor by nine wickets in their opening game of the season on 6th May 2004.

Jordan Kane scored an unbeaten 106 in Llandudno's U13s win against Mochdre on 24th May in the Eryri Junior Cricket League.

In the Colwyn Bay and District Evening League Llandudno led the Division 2 table with five wins from five games.

In a Wales U15s match against Gloucestershire on 17th June 2004 Elgan Williams took three wickets in four balls. Wales won by four wickets.

Llandudno went top of the Premier Division with a win against Llanrwst on 26th June at the Oval. Indian all-rounder Tarique Khan led the way scoring 59 with the bat and taking four wickets for 31 with the ball.

The 2nd XI beat Corwen on 3rd July at the Oval. The visitors set a big total of 218 for six declared. Llandudno accepted the challenge and in great style and team effort finished with a better score of 220 for four. Martin Roberts scored 95 not out.

In the Colwyn Bay and District Evening League, Llandudno continued to do well and were clear favourites to win the title after beating top-of-the-table rivals Bryn y Neaudd on 1st July. Llandudno did finish champions and completed the double that year by winning the Tom Barlow Cup on 2nd July 2004.

Llandudno Team Manager Mo Owens said:

"Tom Barlow who passed away recently was a long-time player, supporter and a very popular figure at the Llandudno Cricket Club and it was fitting for us to win the cup this year."

In a high scoring match against Marchweil/Wrexham Llandudno were set a target of 241 runs. In reply Tarique Khan (90) and Steve Smith (58) put on 130 in a second wicket stand which set up a victory charge. It was Dean Morrison and his unbeaten 153 which sealed the win.

Captain Steve Smith said:

"We didn't bowl or field very well as we can but to win the game after being set such a big target was very pleasing."

Elgan Williams took 4/11 and Jack Rimmington 2/25 for Gwynedd in their 51-run victory against Flintshire in the North Wales Colts County Championship at the Oval on 15th August 2004.

A hat trick by Tarique Khan helped Llandudno back to the top of the Premier Division. He finished with 5/17. He also scored a half-century to lead Llandudno to a 55-runs win.

A man was in a pub, describing his first cricket match to his mates.

"Well," he said, "these two old men in white coats come out, followed by eleven more, also in white. Then a couple of fellows with small planks of wood come out, one of the other lot threw a ball at him, he took a swipe at it, and if I 'adn't pushed the wife in the way, it would have smashed me right in the face!"

Llandudno were crowned North Wales Cricket League Premier Division champions for 2004. This was the first time in the club's history and they achieved it on 11th September. With their own game against Brymbo abandoned at 4pm because of rain when they looked all set for victory, they had to wait until 7pm before the title was confirmed.

Captain Steve Smith said:

> "It was very tense in the dressing room while we were waiting for the news from Hawarden Park but I think we deserve to be champions. We won more games than Hawarden Park and had a win and a 'winning draw' in the two games against them. I am sure we would have gone on to beat Brymbo today but for the weather. We bowled very well and had Brymbo struggling (121 for six) and it would have been hard to swallow if Hawarden Park had won and nicked the title off us while we were stuck in the Pavilion. This is a reward for a lot of people who have put in a lot of hard work both on and off the field. Four years ago we were a mid-table team in the second division and now the sky's the limit. We started the season with six teenagers in the side and they have been incredible. They not only have a lot of ability but they worked hard to improve their game and listen to the advice we gave them. We have had a great blend of youth and experience this year and it has been a real team effort."

Llandudno finished just six points clear at the top of the division:

	Pl	W	D	L	ND	pts
Llandudno	22	13	3	4	2	357
Hawarden Park	22	11	4	5	2	351

Llandudno 2nd XI finished 8th in Division 2:

	Pl	W	D	L	ND	pts
	22	8	-	3	3	92

Owen Jones and Elgan Williams, both contributors to the 1st team's success, were also members of the Wales U15s team. Wales shared the 2004 ECB/Lord Taverners U15s competition with Yorkshire and Surrey. The pair were also in the Eryri County U15s squad which reached the Welsh County Final. Both players received an Excellence Fund Grant from Conwy County Borough Council in 2003 which assisted in improving their sporting ability.

Llandudno CC was featured in the finals of the 2004 Conwy County Borough Sports Awards night celebrating the sporting achievements of the year held at Venue Cymru, Llandudno on 19th November.

Finalists in the 'Senior Team of the Year', Joe Lambe for 'Services to Sport', Elgan Williams 'Junior Sportsman of the Year' and Owen Jones 'Most Improved Sportsperson'.

Young schoolteacher Laura Hume became the first female cricket coach for Llandudno after passing the 'Level 1 Coaching Award'. The 25 year old, who was teaching Geography at Eirias High School, Colwyn Bay, was helping to coach the U11s as they prepared for the new season. During the 2004 season she joined the Conwy Celts Ladies Team who played in the evening cricket league. *"I really enjoyed it and thought I would like to get involved in the coaching side,"* she said.

During the winter months the club was holding indoor nets at the John Bright Sports Centre in Llandudno.

At the start of the 2005 season, Captain Steve Smith was in a confident mood. He let it be known that he was pleased with the quality of the pre-season work and said:

> *"Being such a young squad we just continue to improve and the ability and attitude of the group of players are exceptional. All the lads look sharp and are confident and hungry for more success this season. I know we will be pretty hard to beat. The club has really turned itself around over the last five or six years and I believe we now lead the way in terms of our preparation and professionalism. In terms of the quality of our cricket, our training and the number of talented young cricketers we are producing, we have to be the*

strongest club in North Wales and I include Colwyn Bay and Northop Hall when I say that."

The junior cricket got underway in May 2005. The U9s team (252 for seven) lost to Mochdre U9s (260 for five) while the U13s (45 for one) beat Mochdre U13s (43 all out). (Jordan Kane 22 not out and two wickets for five runs.)

Mixed fortunes for the league champions at the start of the season. They lost their first four matches in the Premier Division and were in a disappointing fourth from the bottom of the table without a win. However, some welcome success in the Welsh Cup beating Mochdre in the 1st round by six wickets. They followed this up in the 2nd round beating Halkyn with a superb spell of bowling from Jonathon Gallagher who took six wickets for 14 runs.

Llandudno CC reached the semi-final of the Welsh Cup for the first time in their history after a dramatic victory over Pontblyddyn in the Northern Zone final at the Oval on 10th July 2005. Fifteen year old Sam Rimmington was the hero, hitting the last ball of the game for six to clinch a nail-biting three wicket win.

"To reach the last four in Wales is a magnificent achievement for a small club like Llandudno and it shows the strength in depth we have at the club now," said skipper Steve Smith.

The elation of the epic last ball win against Pontblyddyn was replaced by the anti-climax of defeat in the Semi-Final to the eventual winners – Usk.

In the Premier Division a last ball run out rescued Llandudno from a damaging defeat in a dramatic finish at Bangor on 23rd July. Llandudno got a 'winning draw' rather than a tie because Bangor still had two wickets in hand. The game had finished with both teams on 226/8. Llandudno earned 19 points and kept their third spot in the league table. The highlight of the match was Tarique Khan's century (102) and an opening stand of 157 with Captain Steve Smith (86).

The 2ⁿᵈ XI just managed to hold their own in Division 2 after a mid-season wobble and they climbed away from the relegation zone.

Llandudno completed a league and cup double in the Colwyn Bay and District Evening League on 26ᵗʰ July. They added the Robertson Cup to their Division 1 championship triumph.

A century (107) off just 77 balls by Kevin James helped Llandudno move to within two points of leaders Brymbo. Llandudno scored 266/8 declared against St Asaph and bowled them out for 166 clinching a massive 30 points.

Llandudno ended the season runners up in the premier division to Mold finishing an agonising six points short of retaining the championship. A maximum 30 points win in their final match against Mochdre was not enough to retain the league title.

	Pl	W	D	L	ND	pts
Mold	22	12	4	4	2	384
Llandudno	22	10	6	4	2	378

Llandudno won the inaugural North Wales Cricket League's Development Cup with a 10 run victory over Bersham in the final. After receiving the shield, Captain Dave Barlow said:

"This was a good first season in the Development League and we would encourage other clubs to enter. A good mix of young and experienced players had led to some demanding games."

During 2005 the club's younger players dominated the Gwynedd Colts side, and the U11s, U12s, and U13s were the backbone of the Eryri teams. The U15s made it to the finals of the Welsh Cup in Newtown.

The success in delivering cricket for all age groups and abilities was very satisfying and spoke volumes for the enthusiasm of the coaches, players, supporters and workers at the club. The Junior Committee had worked hard raising funds to support the costs of Junior Cricket which was entirely paid for from these funds. This meant that in 2005 a record number of young cricketers representing their club at county level and playing for their country was achieved. The committee also funded the course costs for the club's first lady coach, Laura Hume, and contributed towards the cost of new wicket covers and Water Hog.

The Mostyn Estates sponsored the Primary School Cricket League which was again successful. Joe Lambe and his helpers coached the U11s to success winning their league. He was involved in coaching the County U11s and also followed up a disabled coaching venture by organising a triangular competition between the club's Taverners side, a Conwy Ladies side and the North Wales Multi-disability Cricket side over the Bank Holiday weekend.

During 2005 the club was being well supported on the social side by over 400 members. The Social Committee continued to strive to arrange events for members to boost revenues in the winter and their good work was appreciated. It was accepted that the darts teams, playing in the local league, were an important part of the club and that dominoes on Monday evenings filled the pavilion and added to the bar takings.

The trading figures for 2005 were down on the previous year. The turnover was much the same but the payroll of staff had increased. The main factors were the rise in the National Minimum Wage and some late costs for 2004 in the current 2005 year. Expenditure was higher as well, the costs of decorating the pavilion being a notable one off. The replacement of the boiler led to kitchen improvements to improve storage and serviceability and new floor covering. Ground expenses included extra work on the wicket at the end of the season and repairs to the artificial wicket and net carpets that give vital service during the season. Insurance costs were increasing at an alarming rate. The situation had been noted by the committee and for 2006 extra effort was promised on raffles and draws, sponsorship and timely collection of membership subscriptions were intended. Colin Edwards had taken over the role of sponsorship drives and had successfully kept the level received up to previous years. A well-attended sponsors' night had been held at the beginning of the season with comedian John Martin, Llandudno Town Council representatives and the Mayor Cllr Ann Parry graciously in attendance supporting the event.

Llandudno CC signed 19 year old Alistair Fraser from Adelaide, Australia for their 2006 season. He was a highly-rated fast bowler who had played for South Australia under19s. Llandudno had also bolstered their squad by signing all-rounder Duncan Midgley who had had trials with Glamorgan.

Llandudno 1ˢᵗ XI opened the 2006 season with two good wins and a draw. They had also beaten Dolgellau in the 1ˢᵗ round of the Welsh Cup with a convincing nine wickets win. Captain Steve Smith top scored with 40 runs.

A brilliant unbeaten century (134 n.o.) by Aled Williams helped Llandudno into the 3ʳᵈ round of the Welsh Cup beating Llanrwst by 140 runs on 5ᵗʰ June.

In the Premier Division the day before, Aled Williams (66) and Duncan Midgley (63) in a second wicket stand of 102, set up a seven-wicket victory against Pontblyddyn which moved Llandudno into the top three of the table.

An unbeaten 85 by 14 year old Jordan Kane helped Llandudno 2ⁿᵈ XI to an 8-2 points victory over Dolgellau on 11ᵗʰ June 2006. Sam Rimmington took four wickets for only seven runs in just six overs.

Centuries by Joe Lambe (102 not out) and 14 year old Jordan Kane (100) created history for Llandudno 2ⁿᵈ XI when they produced an unbeaten second wicket stand of 179 against Abergele. This was in a Division Two match in the North Wales Cricket League on 8th July 2006. The stand was a league record for the team and the first time two individual centuries had been scored in the same innings for the club in the league. But the achievement was in vain as rain washed out any chance of a result. After the match Joe Lambe said:

"Jordan is an immense prospect. Technically he is so gifted that, to be honest, the world is his oyster. We are expecting big things from him."

Llandudno cricketers felt that they could reach the final of the Welsh Cup after a fine victory over Colwyn Bay on 23rd July 2006. A century partnership between Australians Alistair Fraser (114 not out) and Steve Smith (58) powered the side to a memorable win. Skipper Steve Smith described this performance as Llandudno's best result in his time at the club.

Young Jordan Kane produced another stunning all-round performance to lift Llandudno 2nd XI into the top four in Division 2. He scored his second century (134) in three weeks and then took 4/14 in a 52 run victory over Halkyn on 23rd July 2006. Andy Christian took 3/26.

Former Llandudno player Geoff Ellis, who made 75 first-class appearances for Glamorgan, was backing Llandudno to lift the Welsh Cup after their semi-final win against the South Wales side Mumbles at the Oval on 30th July. It was 26 years since Ellis had played for Llandudno at the Oval but although he had little joy on the pitch playing for Mumbles (six runs with the bat and bowling figures of 0/30) it was a memorable occasion for him when he was made a life member of the Llandudno club after the game, in recognition of his achievements with Glamorgan. Geoff Ellis had played for Llandudno for seven years from the age of 12 before being signed by Glamorgan and playing for them between 1970 and 1976.

Llandudno batted first and set a competitive total of 256/7. A superb century by Aled Williams (129) and a 150 run stand with Alistair Fraser (52) for the third wicket was the highlight of the Llandudno innings. When Mumbles replied, for a while they looked a serious threat when they put on 85 for the third wicket. The turning point came when Graham Boase broke the partnership with a glorious diving catch at mid-on. That did it because the last seven wickets fell adding only 45 runs giving a well-earned victory to Llandudno.

Club Chairman John Rimmington commented:

> *"It is tremendous for the club and the town to be in the final for the first time after the disappointment of losing the semi-final last year. I hope we can take good support down to Cardiff to cheer the boys on."*

By early August of that year, and well into the second half of the season, Llandudno were joint-leaders of the Premier Division. On 4th August they had a dominant 203-run victory over Menai Bridge. Alistair Fraser scored a mighty 98 and young Jack Rimmington took four wickets for just 10 runs.

Llandudno were crowned champions of Division 1 of the Colwyn Bay and District Evening League despite losing their last match to Abergele on 2nd August 2006. They went on to do a second league and cup double when they won the Robertson Cup beating Bryn y Neaudd in the final.

Llandudno became the first North Wales club for nine years to win the Welsh Cup when they beat Gowerton by four wickets at Sophia Gardens, Cardiff on 13th August 2006. Llandudno's triumphant cricketers were to be honoured by the town council. The town mayor, Cllr Phillip Evans, made a point of wishing the team well before they set off for Cardiff on the eve of the match. He said on their return:

> *"They are a real credit to the town. The result in Cardiff reflects the ability of the team and the hard work they have put in."*

Skipper Steve Smith paid tribute to the side which included eight teenagers:

"They are just fantastic. Playing on a big stage like Sophia Gardens didn't overawe them at all; they just take everything in their stride."

He went on to say:

"We bowled and fielded well to set up what was a thoroughly deserved win. Winning the Welsh Cup for the first time shows just how far this club has come in a very short time."

Jonathon Gallagher won the 'Man of the Match' award after taking five wickets for 23 runs. Gowerton was bowled out for 138. Llandudno reached 139 for six with seven overs to spare.

In a 2nd XI match, youngster Jordan Kane hit 99 not out in an 85-run victory over Conwy on 28th August. This win maintained Llandudno's 2nd XI's promotion challenge. Neil Gallagher 5/52.

Llandudno celebrated in style after their Premier League win against Northop on 9th September 2006. They had become Premier League champions and in doing so completed a fantastic league and Welsh Cup double.

John Rimmington, club chairman, said:

"Everyone at the club is thrilled. After last year's disappointment this is just fantastic."

Captain Steve Smith added:

"This is a magnificent achievement for the Llandudno Cricket Club. It reflects the hard work and commitment given by all team members and proves the club's youth policy of bringing forward our youngsters works."

Final Premier League table (top two)

	Pl	W	D	L	ND	pts
Llandudno	22	13	4	2	3	398
Pontblyddyn	22	11	1	5	5	347

Llandudno 2nd XI finished 3rd in Division 2 behind Rhewl and champions Brymbo 2nd XI.

Chairman John Rimmington at the Annual General Meeting on 17th November 2006 summed up the season as follows:

"Cricket 2006 saw a remarkable year for the club with the triumph in the Welsh Cup replacing the disappointment of last season. Many shared in that and wide acclamation was gained for the club. To then finish as clear winners of the Premier League again banished the disappointments of 2005. The achievement was recognised regionally by the Scottish Power/Trinity Mirror awards at the end of October as the 'sporting team of the year'. Steve Smith is standing down as first team captain and what a year to finish on. We know that Steve will continue to make a big contribution and is nominated for the post of Club Captain. Duncan Midgley made a great contribution and was named as Welsh Player of the Year by Wisden Cricket magazine in its review of Premier Leagues across the UK. Ali Fraser was a good playing asset as overseas guest player and very popular with the members. The 2nd XI finished tantalisingly short of a promotion position in Division 2. The Development side had a good season under the captaincy of Ajay Dhawan. They won the Development League Cup Final beating Halkyn at the Oval in September. The mid-week side in the Colwyn Bay and District League achieved a second successive double in winning both Division One and the Robertson's Cup. The Junior Committee continued to raise funds with a Boxing Day Dip, bag packing at a local store and numerous raffles. Joe Lambe continued his good work coaching our youngsters and keeping the Llandudno Primary School League going with tremendous success. Trading during 2006 was a much improved year for the club financially. We have re-established the profit margin on the bar sales through a combination of

price adjustments and more business in the club. There has been investment in shutters to secure the front of the pavilion after attempted break-ins and also a new television in time for the Football World Cup. These items have been refinanced through our brewery loan facility. Sky TV costs continue to rise as Sky increase their charges for 'Pay per View' football and we have to look at this for next year as the coverage of games is split between different satellite broadcasters for the first time. In 2007 we will have to implement the new law prohibiting smoking in clubs introduced by the Welsh Assembly Government. We will keep members informed about the requirements of this legislation and what facilities we will be able to provide.

We had some valuable support from sponsors again this year. On the social front the Taverners had another good year of fixtures. The highlight was winning the inaugural 'Tashes' trophy against the Maesdu Golf Club. The Australian Night was a success which also raised funds for Ali Fraser's Benefit. A sponsored walk to raise funds for 'Tyddyn Bach' respite hostel was also a credit. The Social Committee continue to arrange events for members to boost revenues. The success of the Fun Day, organised by the club and with support from sponsors, allowed us to make donations to the 'Save Llandudno Hospital Appeal' and to the funds of 'Disability Cricket'.

The year 2006 was a momentous season for the club; let's hope for more success in 2007."

Election of Officers:

President: Graham Gibbons, Chairman: John Rimmington, Secretary: Colin Edwards, Treasurer: Hawley and Co., Fixture Secretary: Kevin James, Club Captain: Steve Smith.

Committee: M.Burroughs, G.Hawley, C.Shanley, M.Hughes, S.Jones, L.Owen, D.Robertson, D.Roberts.

"The word 'cricket' has become a synonym for all that is true and honest. To say 'that is not cricket' implies something underhand, something not in keeping with the best ideals." – Sir Pelham Warner

In February 2007 a 10-week cricket course for juniors commenced at the indoor nets at John Bright Sports Centre. Mark Hughes was appointed the new Junior Manager. Fifteen qualified coaches had committed themselves to maintaining the standard of young players the club had developed in recent years which had played a major part in the club's success at senior level. The course was followed by outdoor nets from April at the Oval.

The club had secured 29 year old opening bowler Steve Green from Sydney, Australia to be the overseas player for the 2007 season. Steve Smith said:

"He is top of the bowling averages at the moment in Sydney at First Grade cricket level which is an amazing standard and is probably the strongest club cricket in the world. We are very lucky to get him because he could easily have gone to one of the top leagues in England."

An exciting challenge was bestowed on Aled Williams who, at 20 years of age, was then the youngest ever 1st XI captain appointed by the club.

"I am really looking forward to the challenge and can't wait to get started," he said.

Jordan Kane, as well as proving to be a very gifted cricketer, was also getting noticed as a talented footballer at 14 years of age, with a future. The Wrexham Football Club had thought so and had recently put him on their 'books'. Playing for Llandudno in the North Wales

Coast Football Association U15s he scored a hat-trick of goals helping his side to a commanding 6-0 victory over an Anglesey Select XI at Maesdu Park, Llandudno on 17th March. He was chosen to play for the North Wales U15s side to play against Shrewsbury on 22nd April.

An unbeaten knock of 82 off 62 balls by Owen Jones spearheaded another strong 1st XI team effort opening the defence of their Premier League title with a comprehensive 30-points victory over Mold on 30th April 2007.

The 2nd XI also had a good opening victory against Shotton.

In the following week the Welsh Cup holders opened their defence of the trophy with a seven-wicket win at Corwen.

It was a fine five-wickets haul by Australian Steve Green for Llandudno to claim a third successive win in the league at the expense of Menai Bridge on 12th May.

An unbeaten century (106 not out) by Neil Gallagher couldn't save Llandudno 2nds from a four-wicket defeat at home to Carmel on 12th May in Division 2.

A century (110) by Joe Lambe and an opening stand of 154 with Neil Gallagher (71) helped Llandudno 2nds gain a 116 runs win over Mynydd Isa on 26th May 2007.

Llandudno suffered their first defeat of the season against Connahs Quay. A brilliant century by Martin Burger blasted Connahs Quay to a seven-wicket victory on 9th June. Llandudno still topped the Premier Division but by only one point.

Jack Rimmington of Llandudno top scored for Gwynedd Colts with 62 but it wasn't good enough to prevent an eight-wicket defeat to Denbighshire in the North Wales County Colts Championship match at Corwen on 8th June 2007. Brother Sam added 25 not out in a Gwynedd total of 196/7 dec. Denbighshire reached that total in the thirty-eighth over with a century from James Hughes of the Marchweil and Wrexham club.

Llandudno reached the fourth round of the Welsh Cup on 17th June with a comfortable nine-wicket win over Halkyn.

In the Eryri Junior Cricket League young Philip Wilson did the hat-trick with three wickets (all bowled) as Llandudno U11s beat Llanrwst by 73 runs on 1st July 2009.

Australian Steve Green produced a man of the match performance as Llandudno went 43 points clear at the top of the Premier Division. He took 5/5 as Llandudno dismissed Mold for 84 and then scored 12 not out including the winning runs to help Llandudno scramble to victory by just one wicket at 86/9 in the twenty-seventh over on 14th July 2007.

Llandudno lost their Welsh Cup Quarter Final match against Usk in a very close nail-biting finish. Usk batted first and scored 187/9. Llandudno replied and in a gripping finish needed eight to win with two overs to go but failed by one run finishing on 186/7.

Mark Hughes hit a brilliant 95 to steer Llandudno 2nds to a nine-wicket win over Conwy on 25th August and go four points clear at the top of Division 2.

Two boys were playing cricket in the street. This always annoyed the man outside whose house they were playing and he ran out and accosted the one who was bowling.

"How many times do I have to tell you? I don't want you playing cricket outside my house! Do you understand?"

The boy said nothing.

"I said do you understand?"

The boy remained silent and walked away.

The irate householder turned to the other boy. "He's not much of a talker, is he?"

"He's not much of a bowler either. He just put the ball through your window!"

Llandudno captain Aled Williams believes the club are set for still more success in the coming years after being crowned North Wales Premier League champions for the third time in four years. They swept aside Brymbo with a 10-wicket victory to retain their title with two games still to play.

"It's been fantastic to retain the championship in my first season as captain and all the lads have been superb. We have been outstanding in the field which is the main reason for our success this year and Jack Rimmington and Australian Steve Green have proved a tremendous opening bowling attack."

An unbeaten century by Jonathon Gallagher (146 not out) left the club's 2nd XI on course for a championship double as they went six points clear at the top of Division 2. He helped the team to a 116 run victory over Abergele seconds on 2 September 2007. Llandudno's Development League team failed to win the Development League Cup which would have been for the third time losing to Hawarden Park in the Final on 9th September at St Asaph.

Jordan Kane struck a match winning half-century as Llandudno 2nds became Division 2 champions which secured the club's first title double in the North Wales Cricket League. They beat rivals Corwen by three wickets to finish seven points ahead of them at the top of the table.

Top of the League tables – Club's first title double.

Premier League

	Pl	W	D	L	pts
Llandudno	22	15	3	1	398
Hawarden Park	22	9	4	7	317

Division 2

	Pl	W	D	L	ND	pts
Llandudno 2nds	22	16	-	5	1	136
Corwen	22	12	-	6	4	129

Club awards 2007:

Senior club Player of the Year: Elgan Williams

Junior club Player of the Year: Luke Regan

U9s Player of the Year: Isaac Williams

U11s Player of the Year: John Beattie

U13s Player of the Year: Hayden Bellinger

Development Player of the Year: Joe Lloyd

Two other players – Sean Kitchen (U11s) and Jordan Kane (U15s) were selected to play for Wales.

At the Club's Annual General Meeting held on 3rd November 2007 the Chairman, John Rimmington, in his report remarked that the 2007 season had been another very successful one for the club. The

1st XI's triumph in winning the North Wales Premier League was near flawless and a great year for Aled Williams in his first year as captain. The 2nd XI had also done well in their major achievement of winning Division 2 with notable contributions from Skipper Andrew Christian with the ball and Joe Lambe and Neil Gallagher with the bat. He congratulated Neil Gallagher on being named by the Wisden Cricket magazine as cricketer of the year in Wales. He thanked the overseas player for the year, Steve Green, who had worked tirelessly every week with the junior coaching sessions supporting the age group coaches.

Chairman John Rimmington received a letter dated 21st September 2007 from Bob Sugden, on behalf of the Mochdre Cricket Club as follows:

"Dear John,

Yet again we wish to congratulate Llandudno CC on their outstanding successful season. This is getting monotonous!!

The points' difference between yourselves and second place is virtually the same as the difference between second place and Mochdre at 3rd from bottom which just shows how far ahead you are of the rest of the league. We lived with you for the first month then fell away badly. On top of this your 2nd XI have won the Second Division which puts your club in the ideal position of having your teams now in the top 2 divisions – that's a real show of strength. No doubt if and when you have a 3rd XI they will also march up the divisions.

You have a strong club and the rest of us will have to work hard to catch you up. Well done Llandudno.

Yours sincerely,

Bob Sugden

Chairman, Mochdre Cricket Club"

John Rimmington

Born in the West Riding of Yorkshire and moving to North Wales with his career in Public Transport in 1989, a resident within 400 yards of the Oval for 25 years.

Two young sons were a motive to get involved in Junior Cricket in the Club from 1998 with like-minded parents to ensure that the coaches got the support and help they needed.

In November 2001 he was elected to be Chairman of the Club.

During that time the Club has won the North Wales Premier League eight times and the Welsh Cup once, but also the Junior sides have prospered and developed winning both Eryri Leagues and Junior Welsh Cups over the years.

John's eldest son Jack is the present First Team Captain and his younger son Sam is a committed coach and all-rounder.

Bob Woolmer (14 May 1948-18 March 2007) was an international cricketer, professional cricket coach and also a professional commentator. He played in 19 Test matches and six One Day Internationals for England and later coached South Africa, Warwickshire and Pakistan. He was appointed coach of the Pakistan team in 2004.

Like a classic whodunit, the case of Pakistan's murdered cricket coach Bob Woolmer remains unsolved. On 18 March 2007, Woolmer died suddenly in Jamaica, just a few hours after the Pakistan team's unexpected elimination at the hands of Ireland in the 2007 Cricket World Cup. Shortly afterwards, Jamaican police announced that they were opening a murder investigation into Woolmer's death.

Like the best novels in the murder-mystery genre, the Woolmer case is less compelling for the banal details of the evil act than for what it reveals about the cricket playing world.

The known facts of the case are relatively simple: Woolmer was found naked and dead in his hotel room in Jamaica, and it was reported at the time the cause of his death was strangulation, although police were investigating whether he may have been poisoned as well.

Even before police announced that Woolmer's death had been the result of foul play, former Pakistan bowler Sarfraz Nawaz publicly proclaimed not only that Woolmer had been murdered, but also charged that he had been killed in order to protect the ongoing scourge of match-fixing. Sarfraz accused a number of Pakistan players of being involved in betting, and suggested that the team's lacklustre performances against the West Indies and Ireland had been more sinister than simply a failure of technique on match day. Pakistani cricket officials angrily rejected such allegations.

Once the cause of death was confirmed, allegations of match-fixing filled the media throughout much of the cricket world as a number of insiders — former players and coaches — added their voices to suggestions that Woolmer's death was a symptom of corruption at the heart of the game. To be sure, hundreds of millions of dollars were reportedly wagered on cricket matches in South Asia, creating a huge incentive for gambling syndicates to find ways of manipulating outcomes. Although Pakistan's team spokesman Pervez Mir denounced the match-fixing allegations as a distraction from the murder investigation, it's a line of inquiry the Jamaican police were certainly taking seriously, as demonstrated by the fact that the murder investigation was working with the Anti-Corruption and Security Unit of the International Cricket Council.

A major international match-fixing scandal exposed in 2000 had lifted the lid on the seamy underside of a game on which betting syndicates linked to organized crime in South Asia made millions of dollars. And in the wake of Woolmer's death, a number of former players alleged that the 2000 inquiry had merely scratched the surface, and left the game still in the clutches of the betting mafias. Former South Africa captain and Woolmer associate Clive Rice said Woolmer had previously shared with him extensive information about players and officials involved in match-fixing. Rice had "absolutely no doubt" that the Pakistan coach was killed because he knew too much.

In November 2007, a jury in Jamaica recorded an open verdict on Woolmer's death, after deciding that there was insufficient evidence of either a criminal act or natural causes.

On 3rd November 2011, three Pakistan cricketers and an agent were sent to prison in Britain for their involvement in one of the biggest fixing scandals to tarnish the sport.

Former captain Salman Butt received 2½ years, the longest term of the three players. Mohammad Asif was sentenced to one year, while 19-year-old Mohammad Amir served six months.

Agent Mazhar Majeed was sentenced to two years, eight months.

The players were found guilty of conspiring with Majeed to bowl deliberate no-balls as part of a betting scam during the test match against England at Lord's in August 2010.

Llandudno had an application to run a third team in the North Wales Cricket League in 2008 accepted. They started the season in Division 6.

The club had a new overseas player for the 2008 season. He was 18 year old Australian seam bowler Romain Grenville from Victoria.

Llandudno started the 2008 season with three straight wins and were just behind Connahs Quay by just two points who had also won their first three games and were leading the table.

Llandudno 2nds lost to Gresford in Division 1 on 10th May. A superb century by Mark Hughes failed to save them. He scored 117 but nobody could provide the necessary support at the other end. They lost by just 14 runs.

Llandudno stayed top of the Premier Division despite suffering their first defeat of the season by 113 runs against Pontblyddyn on 24th May.

Llandudno thirds claimed an 8-2 points win over Llangollen and moved up to second place in Division 6 just behind Rhewl. Joe Lambe top scored with 84. Laura Lambe was the pick of the Llandudno bowlers with two wickets for 10 runs.

Llandudno had their hopes of reaching the Welsh Cup Quarter Finals dashed when they were heavily defeated by over 200 runs in their tie at Northop Hall. The victors were at the time top of Division One of the Liverpool and District Cricket Competition league.

"We are all disappointed with our performance; we didn't give Northop Hall much of a game," admitted skipper Aled Williams.

Mark Bithell returned outstanding bowling figures of eight wickets for just seven runs as Llandudno 3rds gained a maximum points 10-wicket victory over Rhewl on 6th June 2008. They remained 2nd in the league just three points behind Halkyn 2nds.

Jordan Kane won his first football cap for Wales U17s when he played against Norway at Vineberg on 17th July 2008. Jordan was playing for the Llandudno club's junior sides before taken on by Wrexham. This was a bit of a blow for the cricket club as he had been told by Wrexham that his cricketing had to stop once full football training started. The 16 year old was on a two-year YTS Course with Wrexham and it was while playing for that club's youth team he was spotted by Wales coach Brian Flynn.

Sean Kitchen was in the Eryri U12s cricket team that finished fourth out of eight competing regions in the Welsh Championships in Swansea in July.

Llandudno 3rds won the Division 6 in their first season. Skipper Joe Lambe said:

> "To win the league at our first attempt is an excellent result and it is a great start for the up and coming young players in the squad. I am happy with the performance of all who played in the team and we are working forward to the challenge of playing in Division 5 next year."

Some 3rd XI players to mention included in the squad were: Stephen Gibbons, George Thomas, Mark Bithell, Lewis Pike, Colin Edwards, Laura Lambe, Laurence Clair, Simon Beards, Joe Lambe (captain), Neil Gallagher, and Paul Thornton.

The disgruntled batsman stormed into the pavilion and flung down his bat.

"Terrible," he shouted. "I've never played so badly before"

"The captain looked up. "Oh, you've played before, have you?"

Llandudno won the Premier Division and for the second year running the club celebrated a championship double.

At the 2008 AGM chairman John Rimmington was full of praise again after seeing another great year for the club. The 1st XI had become champions of the North Wales Premier Division for the third year in a row. He expressed how pleased he was that the 2nd XI had done well in being the highest placed 2nd XI team in the North Wales cricket leagues. The 3rd XI in their first season were proud winners of Division 6 and the wisdom of having such a side by the mixture of youth and experience had paid off handsomely. He thanked the sponsors for their support again and commented on the highlight of the year which was the new electronic scorebox gratefully presented through the generosity of club President Anthony Neville and to John Breeze for his ongoing support towards the project.

Llandudno Mayor Cllr Billy Evans officially opened the cricket club's new electric scoreboard on 6th September 2008. Both Anthony Neville and John Breeze were present at the ceremony.

Club cricketer Ian Jones was in the Welsh darts team that retained the Celtic Cup in an International Round Robin event in Ireland on 9th October 2008. He won all his three matches as Wales beat the Isle of Man, Republic of Ireland and Northern Ireland in the competition.

Overseas professional Keegan Nagan recorded a half-century on his debut as the Premier Division champions earned a 9-8 points draw at Brymbo on 3rd May 2009.

A fourth wicket stand of 145 between veterans Joe Lambe (74 n.o.) and Martin Bean (70 n.o.) helped Llandudno 2nds to a 12-4 points winning draw against Brymbo 2nds in Division 1.

South African Keegan Nagan cracked a stunning century and Jack Rimmington grabbed six wickets in a seven-wicket win at Mochdre on 3rd May 2009. After two winning draws they claimed a first win to move up to fourth place in the Premier Division.

Mark Bithell took a hat-trick of wickets as Llandudno 3rds picked up a first away win of the season against Pwllheli 2nds in Division 5 on 3rd May. Opener Joe Lambe topped the batting with 89 and Mark Bithell added 41 not out. He finished with 5/15. He had claimed his first hat-trick in 26 years of playing senior cricket. The team gained maximum points in that match.

Llandudno 1ˢᵗ XI had to settle for an 8-6 points winning draw at Bangor on 16ᵗʰ May when several rain stoppages ensured there would be no finish in the match. On a blustery showery afternoon at Ty Newydd, the Llandudno players all wore black armbands as a mark of respect for Keegan Nagan, who had had to return to South Africa due to the sudden death of his father.

Ajay Dhawan hit his maiden century (101 not out) for Llandudno in the Development side's 10-0 points win over St Asaph.

An unbeaten century from Jordan Kane (101 n.o.) saw Llandudno 2nds claim a six-wicket victory over Pwllheli on 20ᵗʰ June, despite being set a high target by Pwllheli who declared on 209/3. Llandudno finished on 210/4 to claim the win. Jordan was well supported by Alex Owen who scored 44.

Young Jordan Kane did it again the following week but this time for the 1ˢᵗ XI when they thrashed Mold on 27ᵗʰ June scoring 247/2 and dismissing Mold for 84. Playing his first game for the 1ˢᵗ XI that season Jordan and Keegan Nagan both finished scoring 101 not out and together blasted an excellent 189 partnership.

Opener Duncan Midgley produced the innings of a lifetime as his unbeaten 160 earned Llandudno a crushing nine-wicket victory against Pontblyddyn on 7ᵗʰ August 2009. The defending champions after that game were enjoying a 23 point lead at the top of the Premier League table.

Fifteen year old Lewis Jones was in scintillating form for the 3rds when he recorded his maiden century (132) against Mochdre 3rds on 8ᵗʰ August 2009. Llandudno gained a maximum 10-0 points victory in this Division 5 encounter.

An unbeaten 103 by Captain Joe Lambe paved the way for another fine victory on 16ᵗʰ August for the 3rds against Chirk 2nds at the newly enclosed Oval cricket ground.

A nail-biting climax to the North Wales Premier Division League 2009 season saw Llandudno claim the championship for a fourth successive year. Runners-up Mochdre finished just one point behind.

Triumphant captain Aled Williams said after their last match against Menai Bridge:

"I am delighted to win the league again and for a fourth successive year. This achievement shows the strength in depth that Llandudno Cricket Club has. It has been an excellent effort by all the players."

The 2nd XI finished in a mid-table position in Division 1. The 3rd XI consolidated their position in Division 5 after promotion the previous year and were placed third in the table at the end of the season.

Llandudno CC achieved the Club Mark Accreditation of ECB in 2009, a requirement of the North Wales Cricket League's Premier Division which provides a structure and support in the development of North Wales clubs in the future.

Club Mark – Quality Club Accreditation

This is the ECB's nationally recognised standard which ensures a safe, effective and child friendly environment in cricket clubs.

It shows that a club provides the right environment to ensure the welfare of members and encourages everyone to enjoy sport and stay involved throughout their lives.

There were celebrations in the air when the champion club held their end of season presentation evening on 3rd October 2009. Amongst the many awards presented that night, Sam Rimmington received the Player of the Year accolade. Junior Player of the Year went to Tom Bleasdale and the Youth Player of the Year to Luke Regan.

The club's U11s team won both Eryri and the North Wales titles.

A major development on ground improvement was the installation of a boundary fence line and hedging which had been given approval by the two Councils and Mostyn Estate. (In reply to one complainant and an objection from a member of the public received by the Council's Planning Enforcement Team, the person was advised that the fence constructed around the cricket ground did not require formal planning permission as it was less than one metre high. Therefore it was what is termed 'permitted development'. The reply went on to say that although it made no difference to the Planning Enforcement team's assessment of whether planning permission was required the club was advised that they should leave gaps within the fence, as it stood, to allow public access.) Support from sponsors helped fund this which greatly improved the appearance of the ground. The new scorebox was used for the first full season and the overall effect was of the Oval regaining the presence it had before the 1960s as a cricket ground worthy of the Champions of North Wales.

Llandudno's overseas player for the 2010 season was Gordon Kerr from Hobart, Tasmania. He was a right arm medium fast bowler and a middle order batsman.

Sam Rimmington was the 'star of the show' when he cracked a century (124) and took 3/28 in Llandudno's crushing eight-wicket win at Pontblyddyn on 22nd May 2010.

Youngster Sean Kitchen was selected for the Welsh National Junior team in 2010. He was a pupil at Rydal and an automatic selection for all junior level matches, and the 2nd XI and 3rd XI sides. He had already been chosen to play for the Wales U14s. He played his first game that season against Gloucestershire on 31st May 2010.

Jack Sissons, also a Rydal School pupil and skipper of Llandudno's U11s, had been picked for Wales in his age group. He played his first Welsh game against Gloucestershire in June. Young left arm paceman Jack Sissons, who was regarded as one of the country's brightest cricketing prospects in his U11s age group, shone on his International debut against Gloucestershire at Pontypridd. He dismissed both openers and finished with 4/12 helping Wales to a six-wicket victory over previously unbeaten rivals.

The selection process for getting into any of the boys' Wales cricket teams is long and arduous, beginning in October and only ending in early May, just in time for the outdoor season. This was the second year Jack Sissons from Rydal Penrhos Prep School had tried to go the distance and this time, in his own age group, he finally made the team. Jack's speciality is left-arm fast bowling and his great gift is a consistency of line and length that many of his peers struggle to maintain. His first appearance for Wales U11s was on Tuesday 15th June at Pontypridd, when the opposition was Gloucestershire, who were already undefeated in their first five matches. Jack had the honour of opening the bowling on a scorching hot day that surely favoured the batsmen rather than the bowlers, with a firm crosswind that didn't make accuracy easy at all. Yet it only took two balls before Gloucestershire's most dangerous opener was trudging disconsolately back to the pavilion, the bails on the floor. Jack had thoroughly beaten him for pace and swing. In Jack's second over the other opening batsman was also taking the long walk back to the early bath after a caught and bowled that was quite magnificent, being low down and firmly struck. In the U11s age group, bowlers are only allowed a maximum of two spells of four overs. Having taken two wickets in his opening spell Jack returned later in the game to dismiss two more Gloucestershire players, one bowled and one caught. Jack nearly ended with the coveted 'fiver' in his very first game for his country. As it was, figures of four overs, two maidens, four wickets for 12 runs could hardly disappoint. Gloucestershire made 112 all out in 36 overs out of a possible 40, and Wales reached the total comfortably with six wickets and as many overs to spare: an impressive beginning for the team and especially for Jack. His father, Nick Sissons concluded:

"Whilst praising Jack's achievement, the contribution to it made by the early encouragement and coaching skill of Mr Jamie McLeod at the Prep School and of Mr Joe Lambe at Llandudno Cricket Club should not be underestimated. They have taken a raw talent and shaped and cajoled it into something quite wonderful. We should also acknowledge the support given by Conwy County Borough Council, whose Excellence Fund Committee awarded Jack a considerable sum of money towards the even more considerable cost to us, his parents, of allowing him to pursue this career in this most beautiful of sports."

Llandudno cruised into the semi-finals of the North Wales section of the Twenty 20 Cockspur Cup with a 10-wicket thrashing of Brymbo on 30th May 2010.

Multi-talented Jordan Kane scored 145 off 111 balls as Llandudno 2nds held second placed Denbigh to a draw in Division 1. Jordan, who had also played football for Wrexham and for Wales U17s side, was then showing his cricketing skills at the Oval on 5th June 2010.

Llandudno 3rds took top spot in Division 5 with a comprehensive 130 run win over Menai Bridge 3rds at the Oval on 14th June. Openers Alex Owen (90) and Joe Lambe (71 n.o.) had a perfect start with a 155 stand for the first wicket. Llandudno 202/2, Menai Bridge 72 all out. At the same time the 1st XI had a 31 point lead in the Premier Division.

Jack Sissons was in fine form with the bat in Llandudno U11s' 65-run victory over their Bangor counterparts. He scored 30 not out.

Eighteen year old Jordan Kane hit a senior best 176 not out and passed 2,000 runs for the club as Llandudno 2nds dished out a ruthless hammering to high flying Conwy in Division 1 on 19th June 2010. Llandudno declared on 265/3. Conwy was all out for 153. The following week he played for the 1st XI and scored a cracking 70 which included 11 fours and a six against second placed Mold. Llandudno's 32 run victory gave them a huge 73 point lead at the top of the league. Skipper Duncan Midgley scored 37.

The day after the game against Mold they were beaten by Mochdre, the 2009 Twenty 20 champions, missing out making the final of the North Wales Cockspur Cup which was again won by Mochdre.

The 1st XI increased their lead at the top of the Premier Division by beating Llanrwst on 19th June. The visitors declared on 207/9. Llanrwst was all out for 152.

Llandudno crashed out of the Welsh Cup after a surprise home defeat to Hawarden Park on 11th July 2010.

Llandudno 3rds secured the North Wales League Division 5 title with a maximum points win against Mochdre 3rds on 22nd August 2010.

Ajay Dhawan's remarkable bowling figures of 5/7 inspired yet another Llandudno victory against Hawarden Park giving them an almost unassailable 113 point lead in the Premier Division on 21 August 2010. The team that knocked them out of the Welsh Cup, five weeks before, could only score 71 in reply to Llandudno's 158/8 dec.

In a tense game, a batsman was given run out, a decision with which he obviously disagreed. He paced up and down outside the pavilion until the umpires came in.

"I wasn't out, you know," he said to the umpire.

"Oh no? Look in the paper tomorrow!" said the umpire.

Llandudno was crowned champions of the North Wales Cricket League Premier Division in 2010 for the fifth successive season on 28th August when they thrashed Chirk by nine wickets at their Holyhead Road ground.

Llandudno was Division 2 champions for 2010 in the Colwyn Bay and District Evening Cricket League, played for the first time under the new 20/20 rules.

At the Club's AGM on 26th November 2010 Chairman John Rimmington's review of the season included the following comments:

"Winning the North Wales Premier League for the fifth year in a row was remarkable and by a record margin as well. Under the captaincy of Duncan Midgley they set a break neck pace and were almost out of sight by the middle of the season. Our overseas player Gordon Kerr and Jack Rimmington each took over 50 Premier League wickets. Jack Rimmington has won the Premier League bowling award and Duncan Midgley the batting award. A good season for the 2nd XI saw them climb up the table in the second half of the season and had influence on the eventual promotion places. Mattie Lambe through periods of injury led the seconds to a good sixth place with up and coming youngsters and also some rejuvenated veterans. Andrew Christian took 46 wickets. The 3rd XI had another great season and won the 5th Division. Joe Lambe led the 3rd XI winning Division 5, and again young players were coming of age. Joe Lambe won the league's batting award and Neil Gallagher bowling, both setting an example of commitment to their teammates. Junior cricket saw many youngsters work hard at improving their game with the guidance and commitment of our strong coaching team. Sean Kitchen and Jack Sissons represented Wales and many of our young players represented Eryri at different age levels. Hannah Thornton played for North Wales girls in a tournament."

Junior indoor net sessions at Ysgol y Creuddyn Sports Hall in Penrhyn Bay commenced on 9th February 2011. Joe Lambe, Mark Hughes and Jack Rimmington (all Level 2 qualified coaches) headed the sessions at U11s, U13s and U15s age levels. Assistant coaches (Level 1) Howie Thomas, Steve Cheung, Luke Regan and overseas player Gordon Kerr supported.

Llandudno's 1st XI, 2nd XI and 3rd XI all lost their opening games in the 2011 season in the North Wales League.

The 1st XI hit back after their defeat with an eight wicket victory at Bangor on 1st May 2011. Skipper Steve Smith produced a true captain's innings of 89 not out and commented after the game:

> *"I was very pleased with the team's performance. After last Saturday's disappointing start all the players responded well to get a good victory at Bangor."*

Captain Steve Smith (107) and Jordan Kane (112 not out) put on 166 for the second wicket against Brymbo on 14th May 2011. Llandudno amassed 265/2 dec. In reply Brymbo batted doggedly ending short on 215/7 to claim a draw.

Steve Smith (120) and Jordan Kane (110) repeated their run feast together, this time against Menai Bridge on 11th June 2011. Llandudno rattled up a winning 295/5 dec. Menai Bridge fought back well scoring 264 and just hung on with nine wickets down at the end of play. Llandudno collected 21 points, Menai Bridge 11.

Llandudno's bid for a 6th successive league title was given a boost by the return of former skipper Duncan Midgley who had been playing for Bangor.

Llandudno's young cricket prospect Hannah Thornton continued to make good progress on the International scene. She played for Wales U15s against Staffordshire at St Fagans Cardiff opening the bowling; she took a wicket with her first ball. Staffordshire won that game. In the return match on 1st July 2011 she bowled well returning an analysis of six overs, three maidens and two wickets for five runs. Staffordshire won that game too but by only 10 runs. Hannah was playing regularly for Llandudno 3rds.

Captain Steve Smith added another ton to his collection with a stunning century (119) against Bangor at the Oval on 16th July. This was his 3rd century of the season and put him on 814 league runs at an average of 90.44. Bangor had set 202 as the target to beat. Llandudno finished with 203/3 wrapping up a 28-0 points win.

Llandudno CC held a past and present players night on 29th July in the Pavilion. The evening was well attended.

Llandudno reached the Welsh Cup Semi-Finals beating the Swansea area club Mumbles by 71 runs on the 24th July 2011.

Also in July the U11s won the Eryri League by winning eight of their nine matches. One had been rained off.

The U13s beat Colwyn Bay by nine wickets in the League Cup Semi-Final. Hannah Thornton, Jack Williams and Jamie Grimshaw each grabbed two wickets. Colwyn Bay scored 73. Llandudno replied with 74/1. Dan Evans scored 39 not out and was well supported by Ryan Bean who scored 31.

In another local derby match, Llandudno U11s defeated Conwy by 40 runs.

Daniel Evans took 3/36 for Wales U13s against Staffordshire. Wales on that occasion were beaten by 20 runs. Against Hampshire, Daniel contributed in a Wales win by taking 2/13. Against Gloucestershire he took 1/33 in a game Wales also won by eight wickets.

In a match for Wales U15s Hannah Thornton scored nine runs against Cheshire before being brilliantly caught and bowled. Wales scored 128. Cheshire won with six balls to spare.

Skipper Steve Smith passed 1,000 runs for Llandudno in all competitive games in 2011 with a knock of 81 in an emphatic win at Brymbo on 30 July. Llandudno moved to within five points of leaders Menai Bridge in the Premier League.

Llandudno booked a place in the Final of the Welsh Cup against Swansea after pulling off a thrilling 18-run victory over Ammanford at the Oval on 14th August 2011. Duncan Midgley was Llandudno's batting hero hitting a master-class 72. Graham Boase's, with his

3/14, was Llandudno's best bowler. Llandudno scored 135 all out and in reply Ammanford scored 117 all out.

Llandudno 3rds beat Abergele 2nds in a Division 4 clash on 14th August. Joe Lambe hit a tidy 70 not out in Llandudno's total of 163/7. In reply Abergele fell short of the target managing only 116. Derek McFee's five wickets for only 13 runs did the damage.

Young Daniel Evans was captain of the Wales U13s team throughout the 2011 season. His team was unbeaten in all 11 matches Daniel played in. He took 12 wickets in total with his best figures of 2/23.

Captain Steve Smith expressed his disappointment after an emphatic Welsh Cup Final defeat against a formidable Swansea side on 29th August 2011. Llandudno lost by eight wickets at Cardiff's Swalec Stadium.

> *"We are disappointed that we didn't perform better but we were beaten by a stronger side on the day. It was a great experience for our lads to play at the Swalec Stadium and we would have liked to have given Swansea a better game but there's always another year."*

Llandudno scored 178 all out. Swansea took the challenge in their stride as their two key batsmen both scoring half-centuries steered them to a winning 172/2 with six overs to spare.

Llandudno finished runners-up to Connahs Quay in the Premier League in 2011. In their last game they beat Mold by 143 runs on 11th September.

Steve Smith scooped the North Wales League Batting Award for scoring the highest number of league runs (1,115) in the season at the league's Annual Meeting in December 2011. His runs came from only 20 matches at an average of 79.64 and included four centuries.

League Chairman Dilwyn Hughes urged member clubs that they needed to bring enjoyment back in the game. His plea at the meeting in Halkyn was the result of what he described as a "difficult year" for the Management Committee which found they had to deal with several disciplinary matters during the season. Mr Hughes said:

> "The North Wales Cricket League is held in high standing and we need to maintain those very high standards. My hope is we try and improve the standards of play facilities and behaviour and I would urge all clubs to help us to bring back the enjoyment of cricket again."

One time title contenders Menai Bridge, one of six clubs in the 12 member Premier Division that transgressed, were penalised 20 points for fielding an ineligible player during the run-in.

At the AGM on 25th November 2011 the Chairman, John Rimmington, gave a detailed report containing the performances and league placing of the cricket teams over the past season. He congratulated Connah's Quay CC in winning the North Wales Premier Division. He thanked the Llandudno Taverners for their substantial fund raising activities over the years and their invaluable support for the club and various charities during the past year. He thanked the steward and bar staff for their efforts in a year of financial instability for all. He also thanked the Management Committee for their unpaid support and hours given to the club in the past year. He gave his views on the financial position of the club and asked the members to achieve as much sponsorship as possible in the coming year. He thanked Kevin James, in particular, for all his hard work and achievements in getting so much sponsorship from so many different quarters during the year.

The membership subscription was increased to:

Senior cricket player £50

Junior cricket player £25

Social membership £15

Social couple members £25

Senior citizen member £10

Junior member £8

Llandudno suffered a shock defeat in their first match of the 2012 season against St Asaph at home on 28th April. Put into bat Llandudno were bowled out for just 84 runs. St Asaph responded ending on 88/5.

Llandudno seconds fared much better beating Marchweil and Wrexham by 154 runs in Division 1. (Jordan Kane 76, Ajay Dhawan 4/14.)

Conwy 2nds romped to a 9-1 points win over Llandudno 3rds in Division 4.

Llandudno 2nds celebrated after defeating local rivals Conwy by six wickets on 9th May. Conwy batted first and chalked up a useful 187/6 dec. In reply Jordan Kane then took centre stage with his bat and with an unbeaten 101 led the hosts to 190/4 off 48.2 overs.

Llandudno 2nds continued to lead Division 1 after a thumping win at home to Gresford on 12th May 2012.

Llandudno moved to the top of the Premier Division after a nine-wicket win over Pontblyddyn. Gordon Kerr was in superb form for Llandudno finishing with figures 7/36.

The last man in for Glamorgan against the Indian tourists at Cardiff, Peter Judge was bowled first ball by Sarwate. To save time when Glamorgan followed on, Judge kept his pads on and opened the batting. Once again, he was clean bowled by Sarwate first ball for the quickest pair in history.

A mammoth opening partnership of 226 between Aled Williams and Duncan Midgley laid the foundation for a big victory in the Premier Division for the leaders at Northop on 2nd June 2012.

Aled Williams hit 124 off 158 balls including 19 fours and a six. Duncan Midgley made his 120 off just 87 deliveries and slammed 11 fours and 2 sixes. Llandudno declared on 284/2. Captain Jack Rimmington took 6/54 and his brother Sam Rimmington 2/26, demolishing the opposition for just 123.

On the 20th June Llandudno U13s were in tremendous form recording a nine-wicket victory over Llanrwst. Matthew Jones (26), Jack Sissons (14) and Adam Sabri (14) showed their skills with the bat. Llandudno U11s defeated Mochdre by 60 runs, made possible by Will Sissons (30 n.o.), Matthew Jones (17 n.o.) and the bowling of Matthew who grabbed 2/5. There was a wicket each from the bowling of Leigh Bradley, Will Sissons and Refeez Mortaza.

An U9s soft ball match was played in July 2012 between Llandudno and Colwyn Bay. This contest ended with a win for Llandudno by just 10 runs. Top scorers for Llandudno were Oliver Hughes and Jamie Jeffrey (captain). Other team members who contributed to this fine win were Tom Hocking, Savanna Dickens, Dan Jones, Lucas Hughes, William McKinley, Daniel James, Charley Jones, Miles Jones and Sam Thompson.

Llandudno U11s defeated Llanrwst by 71 runs also in July 2012. Will Sissons and Ethan Hill were the two top scorers for Llandudno with Marcus Chalk the best of the bowlers. The team followed that win up by beating Colwyn Bay by just nine runs in a thrilling encounter at the Rhos-on-Sea ground. Luke Russell and Jack Rhodes produced some fine batting strokes as top scorers for Llandudno. Leigh Bradley and Matthew Jones were the top wicket-takers. In an U10s friendly contest Colwyn Bay beat Llandudno by 27 runs. Oliver Hughes batted well for Llandudno.

Llandudno's senior side sealed a place in the Welsh Cup Semi-Final with a two-wicket win over South Walian side Ynystawe on July 22nd 2012. Mochdre thrashed another South Walian side, Usk, setting up an all North Wales confrontation in the semi-final. Llandudno's captain, Jack Rimmington, said:

"The best two teams in North Wales will be going at it 'hammer and tongs' that day. One positive about playing Mochdre is at least one of us will make the final which is great for North Walian cricket. Whoever makes the final there will be a fine representation for North Wales with so many good players in each team."

On 26th August 2012 Llandudno and Mochdre did meet in the semi-final of the Welsh Cup and it was the Llandudno cricketers who came off best and won the day. Unfortunately for the spectators who were expecting a show-piece of a match it turned out to be a largely one-sided contest. It was Llandudno's Steve Smith who emerged the hero of the day hitting a superb 79 helping his side reach 195/9 off 45 overs. In reply Mochdre were scuttled for a meagre 57 runs. Jordan Kane took 3/6 off five overs.

On the previous day against Bangor in a Premier league match Llandudno moved 19 points clear at the top of the table after imposing a humiliating nine-wicket defeat against weak opposition. Bangor batted first and could only manage 30 all out. Gordon Kerr 5/7. Llandudno scored 32/1.

"You have to be fit to play cricket, don't you?"

"You certainly do. I get up at five, run for two miles, come back and do four hours of exercises."

"How long have you been doing it?"

"I start tomorrow."

Llandudno lost in the Welsh Cup Final for the second year running. They were only second best to Swansea at the Swalec Stadium, Cardiff on 2nd September 2012. The North Walians batted first and were all out for 155 before the South Walians responded with a winning total of 160/6.

Not all was lost, however, because on the previous day they thrashed Brymbo by 176 runs to move to the brink of the Premier League title. Duncan Midgley slammed 171 and Steve Smith 61 as the seasiders set a massive 304/5 declared. Gordon Kerr claimed 5/46 as the steel men were shot out for a measly 126.

In fact just one week later and after a run of six straight victories Llandudno secured a sixth North Wales League Premier Division title in seven years. It meant the seasiders had been crowned champions every year since 2006 apart from 12 months previously when Connahs Quay ended top of the pile.

Jack Rimmington, who lifted the championship trophy in his first season as captain, could not have been more delighted:

"This has to rank as one of our very best title wins as we had a lot of key players missing in various parts of the season. The young lads who came in early in the season really showed their worth."

The curtain-closer at the Oval saw Llandudno rattle 294/4 against Mold with opener Duncan Midgley hammering 172, beating his 171 he had scored the previous week by one run.

"I couldn't have asked for better," said Jack Rimmington. *"The players have made the job so easy for me."*

Llandudno U13s beat Pwllheli by nine wickets in the Eryri Cup Final.

In the U11s league Cup Final Llandudno also triumphed at the expense of Anglesey Aluminium.

At the end of season Awards Night at the Oval, Jack Rimmington was chosen as Player of the Season. The 2nd team Player of the Season was Ken Jones and for the 3rd team David Barlow.

Senior Player of the Year: *Duncan Midgley*

Youth Player of the Year: *Danny Evans*

Junior Player of the Season: *Will Sissons*

Players' Player of the Season: *Tom Hocking (U9s), Matthew Jones (U11s, Jamie Grimshaw/Adam Sabri (U13s), Jamie Grimshaw (U15s)*

Coach's Player of the Season: *Oliver Hughes (U9s), Rohan Ingleby / Solomon Dickens (U11s), Rhydian Morgan (U13s), Jack Sumblan (U15s)*

U11s Eryri League and Cup Winners

U13s League winners and Cup runners-up

U15s Cup Winners

There were four very proud Llandudno players who represented Wales:

Will Sissons (U11s)

Jack Sissons (U13s)

Dan Evans (U14s)

Hannah Thornton (U16s)

Will Sissons was named Eryri Player of the Season for his performances at County and National Level.

Llandudno extended their lead at the top of the Premier Division with a comfortable 10-wicket win at St Asaph on 18th May 2013. St Asaph batted first and toiled to 129/9 declared off 40 overs. Gordon Duncan 5/42. Llandudno replied with openers Duncan Midgley (63 n.o.) and Jordan Kane (59 n.o.) easing their way to 130/0 in 21 overs banking 26 points in the process. Jordan Kane had amassed 412 league runs in just five innings.

Llandudno took a 21 points lead by maintaining their unbeaten start to the season with a 79 runs win over Brymbo on 25th May 2013.

Llandudno lost both their unbeaten record and the leadership of the Premier Division when Mochdre celebrated a surprise victory at the Oval on 22nd June. The hosts batted first and were bowled out for 178. Jordan Kane scored 75. Mochdre reached the target with the loss of only three wickets picking up a 26-4 points triumph.

The following week against Menai Bridge they had to settle for a 15-4 winning draw. Unstoppable Jordan Kane took centre stage again and scored 102 to record his third century of the summer. Llandudno set a formidable 282/5 dec.

In reply Menai Bridge clung on desperately at 115/9. Jack Rimmington scooped five wickets for 38 runs.

Llandudno 2nd XI lifted themselves off the bottom of Division One with a welcome five-wicket victory over Pontblyddyn seconds.

Llandudno 3rd XI celebrated a narrow win by just six runs against Carmel seconds. Stephen Cheung was the hero with both bat and ball. After scoring 43 with the bat he went on to take four wickets for 24 runs.

Llandudno 1st XI returned to the top of the table after beating Pontblyddyn and establishing a 12-point lead. Pontblyddyn batted first and scored 164 all out. It was a fairly comfortable win for the seasiders finishing the contest on 167/5 in 49.5 overs.

Llandudno U15s took on Conwy and won by 61 runs. Ethan Hill top scored with 34 not out. Jamie Grimshaw finished unbeaten on 25 and Tom Jones added 24. Conwy were restricted to 70/5.

In a close U11s match against Bangor Matthew Jones led the way for Llandudno with some fine scoring batting strokes. Llandudno triumphed over Bangor by 10 runs.

Llandudno U13s defeated Conwy by 33 runs. Luke Summer and Solomon Dickens batted well for Llandudno. Jack Jones was the best of the bowlers with three wickets for three runs.

Llandudno reached the semi-final of the Welsh Cup after defeating Menai Bridge, Prestatyn, Denbigh and Northop on the way.

Llandudno 2nd XI just held on for a losing draw at home to Menai Bridge seconds on 27th July 2013 at the Oval. The visitors amassed 235/4. Llandudno managed to cling on to finish at 189/9. (Michael Kitchen 57, Jordan Kane 42.)

Llandudno reached the final of the Welsh Cup by beating Port Talbot on 4th August 2013. The South Wales visitors were bowled out for 107. Llandudno's innings was cut short due to rain but reaching 76/4 in 21 overs was enough to secure victory on a faster run rate.

Twenty four hours earlier Llandudno had marched on towards a seventh North Wales Premier League title in eight years as they moved 52 points clear after thrashing St Asaph. Llandudno 230/7 declared, St Asaph 178 all out. Number three bat for Llandudno was 15 year old prospect Daniel Evans who was run out just one short of a half century.

Lewis Jones's unbeaten 113 led Llandudno seconds to a priceless maximum points victory over Bodedern which lifted the seasiders out of the relegation zone in Division One. Lewis Jones and Alex Owen (62 n.o.) starred in a third wicket stand of 110 as Llandudno posted a massive 242/2 dec. The Anglesey visitors were dismissed for 161. Chris Hardy took 4/21 and Tom Thornton 4/41 to seal a 30-3 points success.

The show-piece Welsh Cup Final at the Swalec Stadium in Cardiff on 18th August 2013 brought heartbreak for a third year running for Llandudno. The South Walians Panteg dished out a painful defeat on their North Walian opponents.

Panteg won the toss and Llandudno were put into bat and sent packing for a paltry 123 all out. In reply Panteg breezed to 124/1 to seal a nine-wicket triumph.

It was Laurence Claire's 66 not out that helped Llandudno 3rd XI in Division 4 to a 9-1 points success over Castell Alun on 26th August 2013. The home team batted first and were restricted to 133/7 due to tight bowling by Neil Gallagher (4/28) and Daniel Evans (3/24). Llandudno won comfortably, reaching a score of 136/1. The previous day did not go so well losing to Buckley 2nd XI in a low scoring game. Llandudno 55, Buckley 56/2.

In Division 1 Llandudno seconds did their prospects well with a four-wicket triumph over Conwy. Chasing Conwy's total of 160/9 Llandudno reached 162/6 for a 24-5 points win. (Lewis Jones 94 n.o., Peter Tcherewick 4/30.)

For the 8th time in 10 years Llandudno were crowned champions of the North Wales Cricket League Premier Division. They wrapped up the title in some style when they thrashed Llanrwst by 151 runs at the Oval on 31st August 2013. The 30-4 points victory gave Jack Rimmington's side an unassailable 91 point lead with two matches to play.

Llandudno wrapped up their season with a minimum of fuss, putting visitors Llanrwst to the sword with another magnificent batting display at the Oval. Taking first knock, the home side were given a good start by opener Duncan Midgley, who hammered 70 off 64 balls, but his dismissal at 96-2 the first of four Llandudno victims for the addition of only 27 runs. However, that was to be the extent of the visitors' success in the field. Sam Rimmington (103 n.o.) teamed up with Gordon Kerr (66 n.o.) to share a stand of 154 that took the hosts to 277-5 declared off 50 overs. Rimmington's unbeaten 103 from just 86 deliveries included nine fours and four sixes while quick-fire Kerr scored an unbeaten 66 off 40 balls. Overseas professional Matt Redinger proved to be the anchor for the visitors with a knock of 48 from a total of 69 when his was the fifth wicket down and, although Callum Jones added a dogged 38, it was all over in 34 overs with Llanrwst managing just 126.

Eryri League winners, Llandudno U15s were runners-up in the North Wales Regional Finals at the Oval on 22nd September 2013. They lost in the final to Gresford U15s by 20 runs.

Llandudno Junior section awards for 2013:

Coach's Player of the Season: *Harry Cheung (U9s), Ethan Jones (U11s), Ethan Hill (U13s), Ryan Bean (U15s)*

Players' Player of the Season: *Daniel James (U9s), Tom Hocking (U11s), Matthew Jones (U13s), Rhydian Morgan (U15s)*

Junior Player of the Year: *Dan Evans*

Coaches: *Mike Jones (U11s), Colin Hocking (U11s), Joe Lambe (U9s/ U13s), Duncan Midgley (U15s)*

Llandudno youngsters did really well at the Annual Eryri Junior Cricket Awards for 2013:

Six of the ten Welsh Internationals from North Wales were from Llandudno. They were: *Savanna Dickens (U11 girls), Will Sissons (U11 boys), Jack Sissons (U12 boys), Dan Evans (U14 boys), Sean Kitchen (U15 boys), Hannah Thornton (U17 girls)*

Dan Evans scooped the Eryri Player of the Year for 2013 accolade.

If you are choosing a bat for a junior and want to get the size right, follow the rule that bats should come to the top of the thigh when stood against the leg. Don't be tempted to buy a bigger bat for a junior to 'grow into' as this will harm technique.

The champions Llandudno began the quest for an eighth North Wales Premier Division title in nine seasons with a convincing victory over Mold on 26th April 2014. Put into bat Llandudno chalked up 193/7 off 50 overs. Jordan Kane 63, Kevin Jones 59. Mold was dismissed for 98. Skipper Jack Rimmington took five wickets for 35 runs.

In their second game of the season Llandudno lost by 113 runs to St Asaph.

Llandudno 2nd XI in their Division One clash lost to Marchweil and Wrexham by 10 wickets.

The club's juniors were enjoying great success on the International front. Will Sissons was selected as U11s captain, whilst Rhydian Morgan was chosen for the U15s squad. Matthew Jones had made the National U12s team and Hannah Thornton was chosen to be in the team representing Wales U18s in Abu Dhabi in February 2015.

Jordan Kane's second half-century of the season (54 n.o.) led champions Llandudno to a convincing six-wicket home victory over Connahs Quay on 3rd May 2014. Kane, who had amassed over 1,000 league runs in the 2013 season, was on his way to a four figure haul again after emerging as the batting mainstay in his team's win. Connahs Quay chose to bat first and regretted it after they were rolled over for a meagre 99 runs in 43 overs. Llandudno finished the game early when they reached 101 for the loss of four wickets.

On 30th May, four wickets from Ajay Dhawan helped Llandudno to victory against Pontblyddyn. Llandudno batted first and scored 175. Pontblyddyn failed to reach the target and were all out for 113.

Llandudno 2nd XI was also victorious with a win against Llay Welfare at the Oval on the same day. They won by 31 runs.

Llandudno were lying third in the Premier league after their win against visitors Mochdre on 7th June 2014.

Llandudno U13s lost by eight wickets to Northop Hall in their Welsh Cup semi-final game in June. In the Eryri League they lost by 17 runs to Pwllheli. They fared better against Mochdre U13s winning by 60 runs.

The U11s lost to Colwyn Bay U11s.

The U15s had a very good win against Mochdre U15s. Batting first Llandudno scored 141/2 (Jamie Grimshaw 63, Rhydian Morgan 57 not out), Mochdre 81 (Luke Sumner 2/3).

Llandudno U15s were impressive winners over Bangor on 19th June 2014. Rhydian Morgan claimed two victims as Bangor were limited to 65/2 in their innings. Llandudno then reached the winning post at 66/3, Ethan Hall leading the way with a well-earned 23 not out.

Llandudno U9s were beaten by just four runs in their local derby match against Mochdre. The scores were 107 to Mochdre and 103 for Llandudno. That game was followed up a few days later when they were involved in a rare tie with Abergele.

On 21st June Llandudno beat Brymbo and had kept their second place in the Premier Division at that stage behind Menai Bridge. Brymbo batted first and recorded a decent 164 all out. For Llandudno, Jack Rimmington (45) and Jordan Kane (59) set the tone by concocting a 106 run allegiance for the first wicket. Matthew Lambe added an unbeaten 41 as Llandudno coasted to 168/2 off 33 overs.

Eleven year old Savanna Dickens took a hat trick of wickets for Llandudno U13s on 25th June 2014 against Abergele. Llandudno batted first and set a formidable 170/3. Ethan Hill (41), Matthew Jones (38), Keating Hoc Pike (23), Jack Jones (21) and Solomon Dickson (18) had all batted well. Abergele replied and against aggressive bowling could only score 38 runs, young Savanna taking the starring role with the ball.

Llandudno U13s lost by eight wickets against a strong Pwllheli side in the same week. Llandudno did bat well scoring an enterprising 123/2 (Matthew Jones 50, Rhydian Morgan 41 not out), but Pwllheli hit back to score 124/2 to finish the game in their favour.

Llandudno 1st XI lost to front runners Menai Bridge in the Premier League on the 29th June at the Oval by 137 runs.

Conwy easily won the Division 1 derby against Llandudno 2nd XI on 5th July 2014. Lewis Jones did score an unbeaten 103 for Llandudno in their total of 185/8. But it was not enough to stop Conwy responding well finishing on 186/1 in 39.3 overs to win the game.

Llandudno 1st XI lost to Bangor on 5th July. They were limited to 184/8 against Bangor's bowlers. In reply Bangor breezed to 186/3 in 36 overs.

It was a bad day for Llandudno 1st XI whose grip on the title slipped further away after a humiliating defeat against bottom-of-the-table Pwllheli on 9th August 2014. Put into bat first, Llandudno crawled to 156/9. Pwllheli, struggling during the season, needed just 40.3 overs to reach their target at 157/5.

Llandudno 2nd XI was blasted out on the same day for just 80 against Pontblyddyn seconds who had scored 181.

Llandudno's worst season in over a decade suffered a further knock with a two wicket home defeat against Pontblyddyn on 16th August 2014. Llandudno batted first and were dismissed for 174. Pontblyddyn were coasting when their score was 153/3. It was then up to the Captain Jack Rimmington (4/16) who came on to bowl and very quickly Pontblyddyn lost five wickets. Pontblyddyn's Chris Moss (16 n.o.) and Jamie Chambers (11 n.o.) took the crease and steered them over the line finishing on 180/8.

On the same day, Llandudno 2nd XI lost by seven wickets against Llay Welfare. David Barlow did make an impressive 62 in Llandudno's total of 126/9 but it was not enough to stop the opposition winning the match on 127/3. (Andrew Christian 3/58.)

Llandudno 1st XI lost again on 30 August, this time to Llanrwst in a crushing 104 run defeat. South African Matt Redinger cracked an unbeaten 136 for Llanrwst. At the end of the 39th over, when Llandudno were batting, the umpires called a halt to play due to bad light. The match was originally recorded as abandonment but later changed to a 12-3 points win for Llanrwst.

Llandudno 2nd XI, with only nine players, lost heavily to Gresford by 231 runs, on 30th August, who had amassed 281/1 declared. In reply Llandudno could only muster 50 runs.

In the following week, and again with only nine players, Llandudno 2nd XI lost to visitors Bersham. With Llandudno scoring a mere 66/8, Bersham replied scoring 67 without loss in just 10.4 overs.

Menai Bridge finished the 2014 season as champions of the North Wales Premier Division, thus ending Llandudno's domination of North Wales cricket over the previous 10 years.

The Anthony Neville Club Scoreboard

Welsh Cup 2006

Duncan Midgley

The Oval, Llandudno

Llandudno's Cricket Pavilion 2015

Llandudno Cricket Club, Welsh Cup Winners 2006

Llandudno Cricket Club 2005 Midweek Team –Sponsored by Breeze and Co
Winners of the Gilbert Emery Midweek Division 1 Title 2005 and the Robertson's Cup 2005
Standing Left to Right: Trevor Taylor, Mike Atkinson, Carl Wedge, Elgan Williams, Steve Usher, Owen Jones, Paul Thornton, Jonathon Gallagher, Ajay Dhawan, Jack Rimmington, Sam Rimmington, David Barlow, Andy Christian
Front Row Kneeling: Mo Owen (Manager), Kev James (Captain)

Conwy Sports Awards Team Of The Year 2006

LLANDUDNO CRICKET CLUB 2nd. XI. 2010

Back Row:- Lewis Jones. Alex Owen. Chris Hardy. Thomas Bleasdale. Owen Jones. Aled Williams. Thomas Thornton.

Front Row:- Philip Williams. Martin Bean. Mathew Lambe. Graham Boase. Andrew Christian.

The Oval Cricket Nets 2015

Swalec Stadium

Team Picture

Under 11s

Jordan Kane

North Wales Cricket League Awards 1978-2014

Year	Batting Award	Bowling Award	Wicket-Keeping Award
1978	P.EVISON, Bangor	A.MORRIS, Marchwiel	P.LLOYD, Brymbo
1979	J.W.LLOYD, Wrexham	R.CLAYTON, Colwyn Bay	C.WILLIAMS, Mold
1980	J.P.BELL, Marchwiel	A.MORRIS, Marchwiel	P.LLOYD, Brymbo
1981	A.A.LYGHT, Bethesda	K.PHILLIPS, Chirk	S.PARRISH, Chirk
1982	A.A.LYGHT, Bethesda	K.P.ROBERTS, Connah's Quay	G.JONES, Connah's Quay
1983	A.PHILLIPS, Chirk	D.ROBERTSON, Llandudno	B.BRAND, Gwersyllt
1984	S.WILSON, Mochdre	K.PHILLIPS, Chirk	I.GIBSON, Gresford
1985	P.TRICKETT, Buckley	E.MARSHALL, Gresford	No Qualifier
1986	R.MORRIS, Mochdre	J.JONES, Chirk/ D.ROBERTS, Bethesda,	M.STEIN, Mochdre
1987	D.WALLACE, Conwy	A.COPPACK, Hawarden Park	No Qualifier
1988	D.WALLACE, Conwy	G.CHAMBERS, Connah's Quay	M.CHAMBERS, C/Quay
1989	D.WILLIAMS, Gresford	D.WILLIAMS, Gresford	M.CHAMBERS, C/ Quay
1990	M.HUGHES, Pontblyddyn	M.EASTELL, Shotton	M.E.BRISCOE, Halkyn
1991	M.NEEDHAM C, Quay	E.OWEN, Bethesda	M.E.BRISCOE, Halkyn
1992	M.G.THOMAS, Halkyn	J.HENSHAW, Hawarden Pk	M.E.BRISCOE, Halkyn; M.CHAMBERS, C. Quay
1993	A.BARNES, Llandudno	A.BARNES, Llandudno	M.E.BRISCOE, Halkyn
1994	S.WILLIAMS, Brymbo	N.G.ROBERTS, Brymbo	M.E.BRISCOE, Halkyn; M.CHAMBERS, C.Quay
1995	N.G.ROBERTS, Brymbo	A.Jones, Brymbo	M.E.BRISCOE, Halkyn

Year	Batting Award	Bowling Award	Wicket-Keeping Award
1996	N.G.ROBERTS, Brymbo	A.Jones, Brymbo	M.E.BRISCOE, Halkyn
1997	J.PARRY, Llay	No Qualifier	M.E.BRISCOE, Halkyn
1998	S.WILLIAMS, Brymbo	N.ROBERTS, Brymbo	M.E.BRISCOE, Halkyn; R.BLACKWELL, Brymbo
1999	M.JONES, Brymbo	G.W.THOMAS, Halkyn	M.E.BRISCOE, Halkyn
2000	M.PHENNAH, Llay	P.BANHAM, Bangor	B.WILLIAMS, Mold
2001	I.ROWLANDS, Hawarden Pk	C.WILSON, Hawarden Park	B.WILLIAMS, Mold
2002	N.G.ROBERTS, Brymbo	P.BANHAM, Bangor	B.WILLIAMS, Mold
2003	G.CHAMBERS, Pontblyddyn	S.SPEED, Hawarden Park	M.PARTON, Hawarden Pk
2004	D.RHYS, Brymbo	C.MARR, Hawarden Pk	M.PARTON, Hawarden Pk
2005	G.CHAMBERS, Pontblyddyn	G.THOMAS, Northop	G.EVANS, Mold
2006	P.DAVIES, Pontblyddyn	J.RIMMINGTON, Llandudno	O.JONES, Llandudno
2007	E.ROBERTS, Gwersyllt Park	A.WOOD, Menai Bridge	O.JONES, Llandudno
2008	J.GRIFFITHS, Mold	A.WOOD, Menai Bridge	O.JONES, Llandudno
2009	R.JONES, Menai Bridge	T.KHAN, Llanrwst	W.EVANS, Mochdre
2010	D.MIDGLEY, Llandudno	J.RIMMINGTON, Llandudno	D.JONES, Connah's Quay
2011	S.SMITH, Llandudno	G.CHAMBERS, Pontblyddyn	W.EVANS, Mochdre
2012	D.MIDGLEY, Llandudno	A.WOOD, Menai Bridge	G.KING, Brymbo; W.EVANS, Mochdre
2013	J.KANE, Llandudno	G.CHAMBERS, Pontblyddyn	O. JONES, Llandudno

North Wales League

THE VIV. EVANS TROPHY FOR BEST BATTING

Year	Name	Team	Score	versus	Date
1992	M.HUGHES	Llandudno	126	v. Menai Bridge	16.5.92
1993	T.WILLIAMS	Llanrwst	15 3 n.o.	v. Northop	17.7.93
1994	M.LAMONT	Llandudno	192 n.o.	v. Pilkingtons	14.5.94
1995	G.SALAN	Hawarden Park	169	v. Pilkingtons	24.6.95
1996	T.WILLIAMS	Llanrwst	173	v. Brymbo II	17.8.96
1997	J.PARRY	Llay	206	v. Ruthin	16.8.97
1998	I.PEARSON	Gwersyllt II	148 n.o.	v. Rhewl II	25.5.98
1999	C.PARRY	Amlwch	171 n.o.	v. Shotton II	21.8.99
2000	S.ROWLAND	Gresford II	158	v. Hawarden Park II	29.5.00
2001	A.SHILCOCK	Conwy	193	v. Pwllheli	11.8.01
2002	S.WILLIAMS	Bodedern	188 n.o.	v. Denbigh II	27.7.02
2003	J.PARRY	Llay	164*	v. Bethesda	26.04.03
2004	D.BLACKWELL	Brymbo II	149	v. Connah's Quay	11.09.04
2005	N.ALDRIDGE	Corwen	204	v. Bodedern	03.09.05
2006	W.ECCLES	Bodedern	153	v. Bala II	22.07.06
2007	J.PARRY	Llay	186	v. Menai Bridge	15.9.07
2008	J.GRIFFITHS	Mold	162 n.o.	v. Bangor	7.6.08
2009	I.WEAVER	Gresford II	Average	104.29	
2010	W.EVANS	Mochdre	216 n.o.	v Chirk	21.8.10
2011	K.SALISBURY	Llay II	199 n.o.	v Marchwiel and Wrexham II	29.8.11
2012	D.MIDGLEY	Llandudno	173	v Mold	8.9.12
2013	M.HUMPHREYS	Mochdre II	201 n.o.	v Northop III	1.9.13

North Wales League

Year	Batting Award	Bowling Award	Wicket-Keeping Award
1979	R.ISRAR, Llandudno	I.SIKANDER, Llandudno	
1992	R.PROTHEROE, Llandudno II		
1997	A.CHRISTIAN, Llandudno II		
1999	R.A.FOSTER, Llandudno		
2000	M.BITHELL, Llandudno	R.A.FOSTER, Llandudno	
2001	G.GIBBONS, Llandudno II		
2002	K.PADDINGTON, Llandudno II	K.PADDINGTON, Llandudno II	
2006	J.KANE, Llandudno II		
2007	M.HUGHES, Llandudno II		
2008	J.LAMBE, Llandudno III		
2011	J.LAMBE, Llandudno III		

League Champions (Present)

Year	Premier division	Division 2	Division 3
2014	MENAI BRIDGE	BETHESDA	BRYMBO
2013	LLANDUDNO	DOLGELLAU	CARMEL
2012	LLANDUDNO	BUCKLEY	RUTHIN
2011	CONNAH'S QUAY	PONTBLYDDYN II	BODEDERN
2010	LLANDUDNO	MENAI BRIDGE II	BUCKLEY
2009	LLANDUDNO	CONWY	PONTBLYDDYN II
2008	LLANDUDNO	PWLLHELI	ANGLESEY ALUM
2007	LLANDUDNO	LLANDUDNO II	BERSHAM
2006	LLANDUDNO	BRYMBO II	ST. ASAPH II
2005	MOLD	CONNAH'S QUAY	PWLLHELI
2004	LLANDUDNO	MENAI BRIDGE	MOCHDRE II
2003	HAWARDEN PARK	MYNYDD ISA	CORWEN
2002	BANGOR	ABERGELE	LLANDUDNO II
2001	BANGOR	ST. ASAPH	BANGOR II

Division 5

2014	ABERGELE
2013	BODEDERN
2012	PWLLHELI II
2011	MENAI BRIDGE III
2010	LLANDUDNO III
2009	GRESFORD II
2008	LLAY II
2007	CONWY II
2006	MENAI BRIDGE II
2005	PWLLHELI II
2004	LLANRWST II
2003	DENBIGH II
2002	CHIRK II
2001	CONWY II
2000	RHEWL

League Champions (Past)

Division 2	Division 5	Division 6
1989 LLANDUDNO	1992 LLANDUDNO II	2008 LLANDUDNO III
1979 LLANDUDNO		

North Wales League

Year	Batting Award	Bowling Award
1979	R.ISRAR, Llandudno	I.SIKANDER, Llandudno
2000	-------------------------	M.BITHELL, Llandudno
2006	J.KANE, Llandudno II	

North Wales League

Year	Batting Award	Bowling Award	Wicket-Keeping Award
1979	R.ISRAR, Llandudno	I.SIKANDER, Llandudno	
1992	R.PROTHEROE, Llandudno II		
1997	A.CHRISTIAN, Llandudno II		
1999	R.A.FOSTER, Llandudno		
2000	M.BITHELL, Llandudno	R.A.FOSTER, Llandudno	
2001	G.GIBBONS, Llandudno II		
2002	K.PADDINGTON, Llandudno II	K.PADDINGTON, Llandudno II	
2006	J.KANE, Llandudno II		
2007	M.HUGHES, Llandudno II		
2008	J.LAMBE, Llandudno III		
2011	J.LAMBE, Llandudno III		

Index